Power BI for the
Excel Analyst

Your Essential
Guide to
Power BI

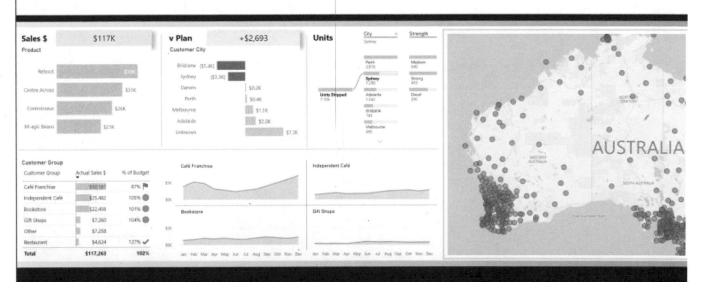

Wyn Hopkins

Power BI for the Excel Analyst

Author: Wyn Hopkins

Layout: Bronkella Publishing

Copyediting: Deanna Puls

Tech Edit: Ken Puls

Proofreader: Bill Jelen

Cover Design: Shannon Travise

Indexing: Nellie Jay

Published by: Holy Macro! Books, PO Box 541731, Merritt Island FL 32953, USA

Distributed by: Independent Publishers Group, Chicago, IL

Printed by Sheridan South, Brimfield Ohio

First Printing: August 2022 E-Book version 20220719c

ISBN: 978-1-61547-076-1 Print, 978-1-61547-164-5 e-Book

Library of Congress Control Number: 2022934210

Table of Contents

Foreword

I'm assuming that due to the title of this book you might be a bit like me, you're that person from department XYZ who's good with Excel and interested in learning Power BI. Welcome to the book.

I'm a massive fan of Power BI and Excel and I've been building solutions for clients using both products for many years. I've also trained a few thousand people in Excel and Power BI so I know the common hurdles and challenges that people face.

My first taste of data was as a fresh-faced intern with Hewlett Packard back in 1995. I was quickly hooked on Lotus123, one of the earliest spreadsheet packages, and within 8 months I had automated away most of my month-end tasks. I clearly had a knack for this stuff. Over the following years, I moved through my career learning more tricks and techniques from colleagues and the occasional training course. I always enjoyed the data part of my job. I liked the puzzles work presented and the workarounds and hacks were challenges that I enjoyed.

In 2007 I moved to Perth, Western Australia, and joined a dedicated Excel consulting and training company, I'm still there now. My timing was perfect as Excel was suddenly on a rapid path of improvement. Excel 2007 and 2010 with a new Ribbon and Tables and then... then came the big one... the functionality known as Power Pivot, closely followed by Power Query. If you haven't heard of these things, then you're not alone.

A silent revolution happened to Excel. In plain sight but under cover of add-ins and understated menus.

Power Pivot and Power Query – the Parents of Power BI

Have you heard of the concept of a "sleeper car"? It's when someone takes a boring-looking beaten-up old car and puts fuel injection and souped-up suspension in it.

Power Pivot and Power Query brought that super-power to Excel. Suddenly you could build highly flexible reports that could be updated with a click of a button. No longer were you limited to 1 million rows of data or chained to the laborious tasks of copy-paste then filtering and writing thousands of VLOOKUPS that you must remember to drag down when new rows of data get added.

I think more people have now heard of Power BI than have heard of Power Pivot or Power Query, but the core concept was born out of making analysis easier for Excel users. The Power BI of today started by taking Power Query, Power Pivot, and a visualisation layer called Power View and wrapping them together into a single package. Have no doubt that Excel and Power BI are still strongly related with a core set of genes that are infused into both.

> ☕ If you'd like to hear more about the history of the product then I'd recommend this interview between Amir Netz (CTO of Microsoft Analytics) and Kasper de Jonge (Principal Program Manager Power BI) url.pbi.guide/kasper. At the 20-minute mark, Amir discusses how he came up with the algorithm for the magic behind the scenes of the Power Pivot / Power BI "engine" while sitting naked in his kitchen!

Why I Wrote this Book

I love helping people and I feel there is space for a book that gives an overall instructional guide on how to get started in Power BI aimed at the Excel Analysts of the world. There are millions of us and Power BI's popularity is continuing to grow.

There are many great books out there that I have learned from, and they tend to have a focus on single elements such as Power Query or DAX or come at Power BI from an IT user perspective.

I wanted to be able to recommend a book to people that covers the whole Power BI process aimed at Excel users transitioning to Power BI. This has been my story and I think I have learned from enough mistakes over the last 7 years and seen enough people struggle with certain elements that I'm well positioned to write a book that helps Excel users make a successful start with Power BI.

The challenge with writing a book on Power BI is how quickly it changes and what to leave out. Since its launch in May 2015 Power BI has developed at an astonishing pace. Every month there are multiple updates, and it has now grown into a fully-fledged Business Intelligence ecosystem. It pulls together the two worlds of the Excel Analysts and the corporate IT departments with a shared product and language.

This book aims to help you learn the core essentials of Power BI from the viewpoint of an Excel user. Excel is the world's most popular programming platform. That's right, if you're writing Excel formulas you ARE a programmer. Put "Functional Language Programmer" on your résumé right now! Many of us push Excel to its limits, creating and copying hundreds of thousands of formulas, VLOOKUPS, and XLOOKUPS everywhere, throwing in some Macros where required. But there is now a new way to build robust refreshable reports without any of that.

Chapter 10 of this book is an "Intermission for Excel fans". This goes a little into the history of Power Pivot and Power Query and shows you how to apply the things you have learned in the book to Excel. One of the main reasons I'm such a fan of Power BI is that it doesn't force you to choose Power BI or Excel, it's about using both with a shared set of techniques.

I hope the book gives you a kick-start on your learning journey.

> ☕ It's virtually guaranteed that the names or positions of certain buttons, labels and other elements will have changed by the time you read this book. However, the core principles you learn here will remain relevant for many years, so I hope you can forgive any user interface discrepancies. It's simply impossible to have a book that is in exact step with a product that is evolving so rapidly.

Acknowledgements

I owe a debt of gratitude to all the Power BI content creators out there. I have learned so much from their books, videos, blogs and presentations that this book simply wouldn't exist without them. Throughout the book I have added links to various additional resources created by many of the people I have learned from. There are also those who have inspired me to push myself past the point of procrastination and into the world of action. Often these people don't realise that they lead by example, that they inspire others, and that they make all our lives that little bit better each day.

I'd also like to thank everyone that's given me positive feedback after a training course, a thumbs up on a social media, or left a kind comment on my YouTube channel. All those moments acknowledging that I have something useful to share, encouraged me to write this book.

Thanks to Microsoft for building an awesome product and for listening to my feedback so willingly.

A massive thanks to Ken and Deanna Puls for helping to make the book far better than I would have managed on my own. And of course, a grateful shout-out to Bill Jelen, MrExcel himself, for publishing this book and patiently answering my questions.

Chapter 1 - Getting Started with Power BI

Power BI allows you to create and share robust, interactive, refreshable reports in a secure environment. It is a platform consisting of several elements that allow report creators to provide information that is easily accessible and easily refreshable.

Power BI was officially launched in July 2015 and is rapidly becoming commonplace in workplaces around the world. You may well have seen it in action already.

The aim of this book will be to teach you how to build a simple interactive report like the image below and for you to understand how to refresh it and share it with others.

Importantly I'll be sharing my best practice tips and advice to give you a solid foundation in building and sharing reports the right way.

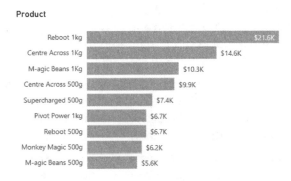

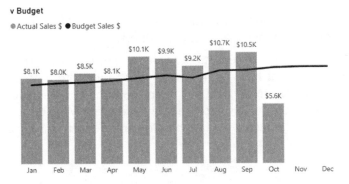

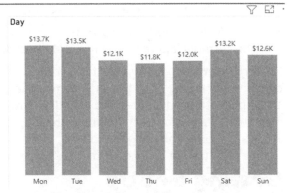

Power BI has brought about a complete change from the old days of Business Intelligence projects. Those solutions required dealing with software salespeople followed by weeks of requirements gathering by business analysts. The requirements were then sent to distant developers creating what they think you said you need, rounded off with "out of scope" re-work. Ultimately the project took 6-12 months, and it was then out of date or not exactly what the business needed.

Power BI enables business users, especially those currently "living" in Excel, to build these fully functional business intelligence solutions themselves in a few weeks. This is not hyperbole; it is a proven fact. The ability for someone who already knows the business to quickly build something useful is what Excel analysts have always done. The difference with Power BI is there's now an entire ecosystem designed to make these reports more robust and easier to scale out and re-use.

Power BI consists of 2 main elements:

1. Power BI Desktop is where you build your reports

2. PowerBI.com (otherwise known as "the service") is where you share your reports

Power BI Desktop			PowerBI.com
Power Query	**Data Model**	**Canvas**	**The Service**

Power BI desktop consists of 3 core areas of functionality.

Power Query is the World's greatest washing machine for dirty data. It allows you to connect to different sources of information and re-organise it to make your report creation easier. If you've ever copied and pasted multiple blocks of data, filtered a column, used Text to Columns, MID, RIGHT, LEFT, CONCATENATE, etc. then Power Query will blow your mind!

The Data Model is the world's greatest data wardrobe. Hang up all your nice clean data (from Power Query) and then organise the related items so that you can easily press a button to see blue clothes or shirts or evening wear. An Excel sheet has about 1 million rows, whereas the Power BI Data Model can technically hold unlimited rows and 1,999,999,997 distinct values per column. Yep, that does say 2 billion!

The Canvas is where you add your visuals using the data from your Data Model. Charts, Tables, Matrix visuals, Slicers, buttons, text boxes all contribute to communicating useful information to the report consumer to assist them in making an informed decision.

This is also where you start to write formulas to enrich your report with ratios, variances, cumulative totals, etc. This formula language is called DAX (Data Analysis eXpressions) and takes your reporting to the next level.

PowerBI.com, also known as "the service", is where you save your reports to share with others. The report consumers can log in to PowerBI.com to view the reports that have been shared with them. Alternatively, the reports that have been published to PowerBI.com can be embedded into Teams, SharePoint, and even websites. There is also the ability to share a report with the entire world for free via a Publish to Web option. The Data Model you build for your report can also then be connected to via other Power BI reports and Excel to create a suite of reports from this "single source of truth".

Getting Set Up

Before you start with Power BI you will need to have Power BI Desktop installed on your machine (Windows machines only, no Mac sorry). Your IT department may be in control of this process and have different methods to the ones I'm about to suggest.

The recommended approach is to install the version from the Microsoft Store as this automatically stays up to date. Make sure it is Power BI Desktop that you download, as there's also a view only application called Power BI. Here's the link to the correct version https://aka.ms/pbidesktopstore

Occasionally this option may be blocked for you, so then you will need to go to https://powerbi.microsoft.com/en-us/desktop/ or use this shorter link url.pbi.guide/Man64 where you will see something like the screenshot below. I'm sure these screens will change by the time you're reading this book, but hopefully, you'll get the idea.

You'll ignore the Download free button (1) as that simply takes you to the Microsoft Store version again. Click "See download or language options" (2). You should pick the 64-bit version. With this method, you will then be prompted each month to download the new updated version.

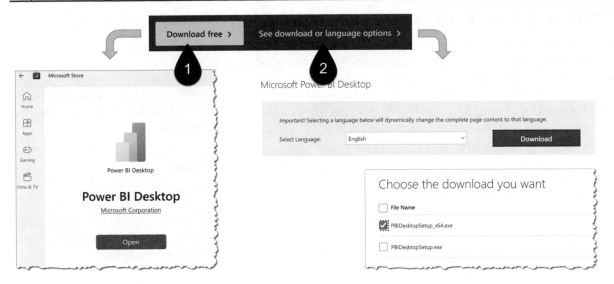

💡 The 64-bit version can utilise more RAM from your machine and is, therefore, a more powerful and less crash-prone option than the alternative 32-bit version. The more RAM you have on your machine the better when it comes to Power BI. It will improve your report development experience as tasks will run quicker. In my view, 16GB RAM is the minimum that you need.

Using this Book and Downloading Sample Files

For the best result, you should follow along with the Power BI software open in front of you, clicking the clicks, and physically replicating the exercises. There is no substitute for hands-on practice to help you remember what you need to do. However, I also wanted people to be able to read this book and follow along even without a copy of Power BI desktop to play with. Hopefully, I've achieved that.

I've added a lot of screenshots marked up with icons that I will reference in the paragraphs before the image such as the black numbered icons like (1) which generally indicate something you should (left) click on. Yellow icons like (2) which mean look but no need to click, and then green icons next to a mouse signifying a right-click (3). There's also the occasional use of orange rectangles and arrows just to highlight elements.

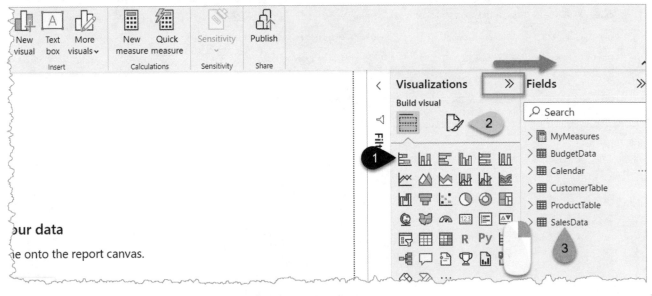

You will notice a few icons have been used in comment boxes

☕ - coffee chat moments, consisting of my thoughts and general comments

💡 - insights and tips that relate to the topic

⚠ - warnings and other very important things to be aware of

Download the Exercises and view the List of URLs

I have created a companion website for this book called <u>PBI.guide</u>, where you can download all the exercies and files used in this book (see 2 in the screenshot below) along with example Power BI files at various stages of completion as the book progresses. For a direct link to the downloads page use this shortened URL <u>url. pbi.guide/PBIXL</u>. After you download the zipped folder, you will need to extract the files or open it and copy and paste the exercises folder into a different location. That page also includes all the links referenced in this book, so if you're reading this in hard copy go to that page and simply click the links there.

If you are going to use the solution files I've created, then I recommend that you open the folder called Solution Files and read the PDF "Changing connections on the solution files to point to your system".

The PBI.guide Website

<u>PBI.guide</u> is a useful resource for continuing your Power BI learning journey beyond the end of this book. I will be adding content, articles, and flagging updates to keep you up to speed with the rapidly evolving world of Power BI. Bookmark the site or add it to your favourites bar for ongoing future reference.

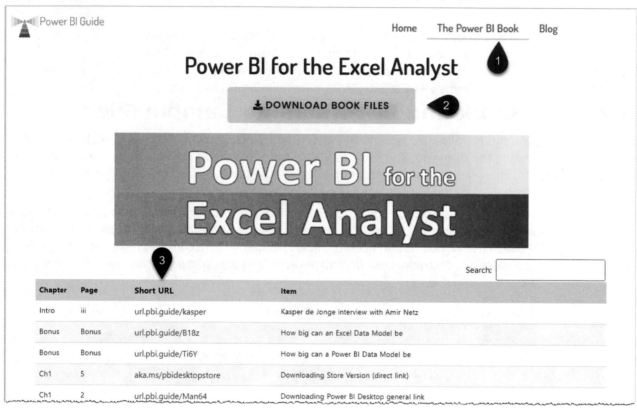

Chapter 2 - First Look – an Introduction to Power BI Desktop

Once you have downloaded the folder as mentioned on the previous page, go into the exercises folder, and double-click on the file called **First Look Demonstration.** This should launch Power BI desktop. For those of you not sitting in front of your laptop don't worry we'll have screenshots for it all.

💡 You can also look at the online version via <u>url.pbi.guide/FirstLook</u>, noting that you don't need to hold Ctrl when clicking buttons with the Web Version

The cover page should appear.

Interacting with a Power BI Report

- Hold the Ctrl key and click on the button labelled First Look (1)

These first few pages are simply a showcase of a few of Power BI's report features. The detailed instructions will come in later chapters, for now just follow along and see what's possible.

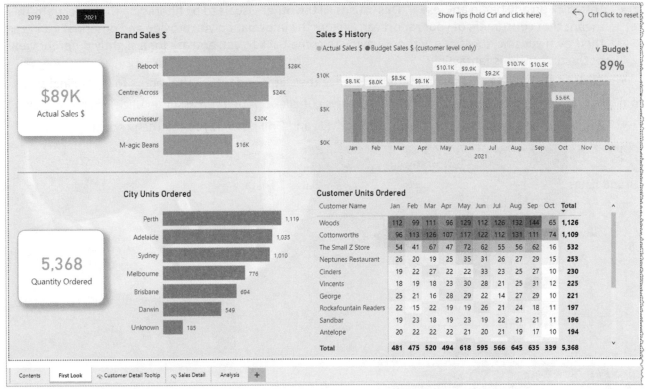

- Hold Ctrl and click on the Show Tips button in the top right corner (1) and multiple text boxes will appear with tips about how you can interact with the report

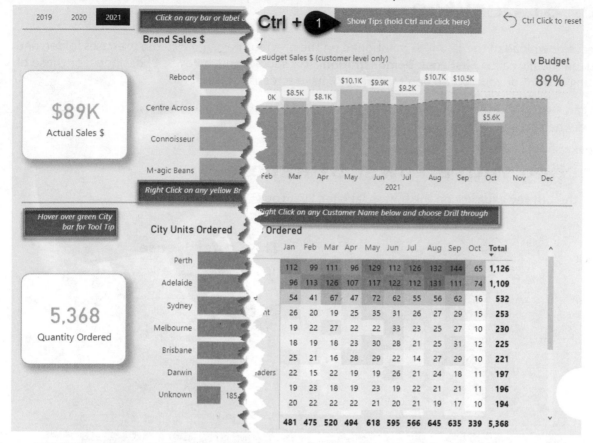

💡 You quickly discover that when building reports in Power BI desktop you must hold the Ctrl key when clicking buttons to trigger their action. The report consumer will not need to hold Ctrl once you share this report with them via Power BI.com. Clicking on bars or values in visuals will magically "filter" the other visuals on the page. This does not require you to hold Ctrl.

- Left-click on any bar in any visual. This causes all the other visuals to be filtered by that selection. This means that consumers of your report can explore the information you provide and potentially answer their own specific questions without having to come back to you and ask for a slightly different view of the data. This is fantastic!

- Click on the same bar a second time to remove that filter and return the report to its original state.

From this point on, unless the book states to use the right-click option then assume "click" means left-click

- Right-click on the bar for the brand "Reboot" (1) and Drill down (2) to see the products

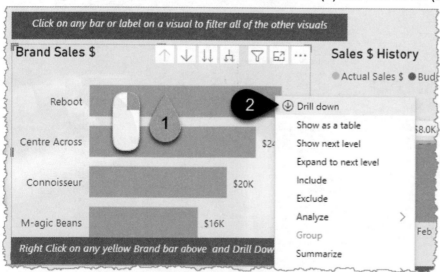

- Right-click on one of the product bars (1) and select drill up (2) to return to the original display

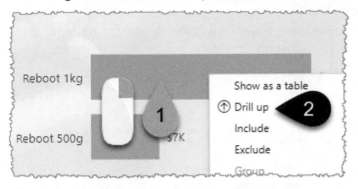

- Hover your mouse over the bar for Brisbane (1). A tooltip will pop up giving more information

- Click on the Reset button in the top right corner to remove any filters you may have applied. Remember that you need to hold the Ctrl key when you click the button
- Right-click on the Neptunes Restaurant February value of 20 (1) and then hover over the Drill through option and click the Sales Detail label (2)
- You will jump to a page showing detailed transactions for that customer. Ctrl-click the "Back Button" (3) to return to the main page

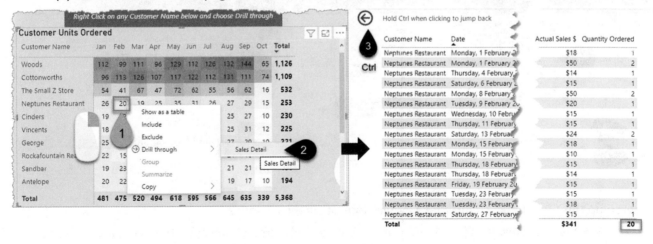

- Click on the Analysis Page. This page contains a visual called the Decomposition Tree which allows you to explore the factors influencing Actual Sales $
- Click on the different branches to explore the data, and hovering will also display the tooltip!

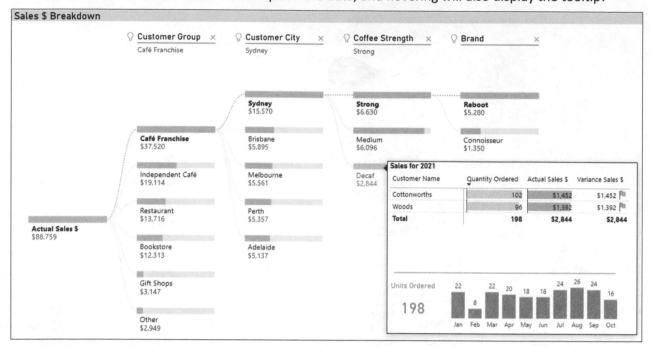

You will explore and understand these features along with many other elements as you progress through the book.

The Four Screens of Power BI Desktop

The Report Canvas (1). It's the one you're already seeing and is where you add your charts and other visual elements that the report consumer will see and interact with.

The Data View (2) where you can see the underlying data.

The Model View (3) where you link tables to each other.

Power Query (4) where you connect to and clean up/reorganise your data into well-structured tables. This is where your Power BI journey will start in the next chapter.

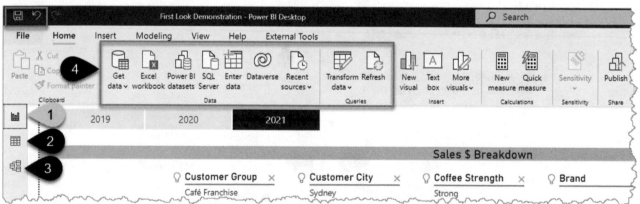

To wrap up this "first look" chapter take a quick look at screens 2 and 3.

- Click the data view icon (see 1 in the image below). This screen is never visible to the report consumer. It is an interface where you, as the report builder, can view and filter and sort the data without impacting the report in any way. There is the ability to add extra calculated columns but more on that later
- Clicking the name of a Table of data on the right (2) changes which data is being displayed

☕ Occasionally I've seen those learning Power BI mix up this screen and the Power Query screen. You'll see next that they do look similar at first glance, but they are very different. The important thing to note for now is that filtering your data here has no impact on your report.

- Click the Model View icon (see 1 in the image below)

This is where much of the real power of Power BI lies. It is here that you relate tables to each other so that data can be sliced and diced a hundred different ways without having to write thousands of different formulas. It's in this screen that a single line between 2 tables can replace millions of lookup type formulas. Whether you use VLOOOKUP, INDEX MATCH or XLOOKUP think about the power that replacing millions of formulas with a few lines can give you.

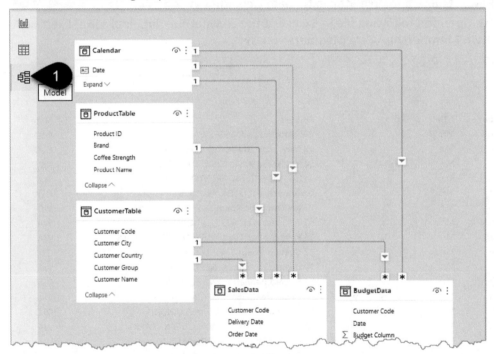

That's the brief introduction and first look at Power BI desktop. I hope that you're interested in learning more about these features and building some beautiful, useful reports that are simple to update.

- Close this demonstration file, there's no need to save any changes

You will now build a report from scratch starting with what I consider to be the greatest ever development for the Excel Analyst... Power Query.

Introducing Power Query

Power Query is the Worlds' greatest washing machine for dirty data.

I've worked with companies of all sizes, and no matter how big the company is there's always a need to clean up the data before you can present or analyse it.

It is truly a revolutionary feature that was originally an add-in for Excel. It's now natively part of Excel, found under the Data tab, and it's the same Power Query that exists in Power BI. The Power Query lessons in this book are therefore also applicable to Excel. As you'll see later you can even easily copy and paste queries between Excel and Power BI.

> ☕ I've seen people's jaws drop when I show them what Power Query can do and then tell them it's been built in since Excel 2016. They feel a combination of excitement that their daily lives are about to get much easier coupled with low-level resentment that no one told them about this earlier!

Importing and Cleaning Data using Power Query

Here are the steps you'll follow to introduce Power Query in the context of Power BI:

1. You will import some data from an Excel file

2. Clean it up and re-organise it

3. Load it into the Power BI file and build a simple chart

4. Then go back into Power Query and do a little extra data clean up

   - Before you start, open the following file in Excel just to see what the data looks like: Exercises\Data Sources\Gym Membership\Gym Membership.xlsx

	A	B	C	D		I	J	
1	Membership Data							
2								
3	Member Number	Last Name	First Name	Title	Birthda		Address	State
4	1	Savage	zachary	Mr:			99 Random Road, 4856, WALTER LEVER ESTATE	QLD
5	2	Owen	Jayden	Mr:			12 May Dupp Street, 4850, HELENS HILL	QLD
6	3	Ferguson	luke	Mr:			54 Holthouse Road, 5232, CUDLEE CREEK	NSW
7	4	Jones	Sian	Ms:			4 Quay Ct, 6020, SORRENTO	WA
8	5	Bull	Sophie	Mrs:		le	5 Norton Street, 2084, AKUNA BAY	NSW
9	6	Barber	Harvey	Mr:			17 Maintongoon Road, 3833, GENTLE ANNIE	VIC
10	7	Lambert	Matilda	Mrs:			53 Atkinson Way, 6725, DJUGUN	WA
11	8	Hutchinson	samuel	Mr:			55 Point Walter Road, 6167, THE SPECTACLES	WA
12	9	Watts	paige	Mrs:		e	22 Goebels Road, 4341, LAIDLEY	QLD
13	10	Upton	brian	Mr:			10 Highmead Avenue, 6025, PADBURY	WA
14	11	Kennedy	Jennifer	Ms:			54 Edward Bennett Drive, 2137, CABARITA	NSW
15	12	Randon	gwen	Ms:		e	9 Taylor Street, 3646, MOUNT MAJOR	VIC
16	13	Bailey	Jake	Mr:			74 Mandible Street, 4825, ALEXANDRIA	QLD
17	14	Stroud	helen	Ms:			23 Chatsworth Drive, 6107, QUEENS PARK	WA
18	15	Randall	Gareth	Mr:			19 Insignia Way, 6429, BOORABBIN	WA
19	16	Austin	Al	Mr:			34 Davis Street, 4069, BROOKFIELD	QLD
20	17	Walton	Emma	Ms:			78 Amiens Road, 2850, CANADIAN LEAD	NSW
21	18	Campbell	Amanda	Mrs:		e	9 Atkinson Way, 6714, GNOOREA	WA
22	19	Thompson	noah	Mr:			87 Ferny Avenue, 4670, NORVILLE	QLD

   - Close the Excel file before proceeding. Power Query sometimes is unable to pull in data from open files. The screenshot above gives you an idea of the contents of the file

   - Start a new Power BI file. If a cover screen appears close it (1)

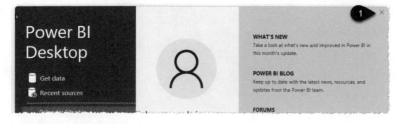

There are 3 different points you can click to import data from Excel. They all do the same thing, which is to allow you to connect to an Excel file and then import the data.

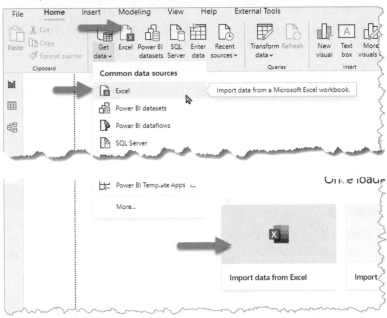

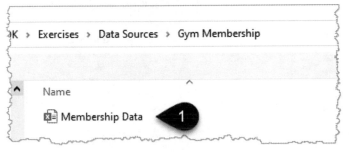

- Click on any of the 3 Excel icons shown above and then navigate to the folder Exercises\Data Sources\ Gym Membership\
- Double-click on the Membership Data Excel file (1)

- This launches the Power Query Navigator window as shown below. The left-hand side lists any sheets, Tables, or range names that exist in the Excel file.
- Click on the word "Members" (1) and a pre-view appears
- Right-click on the word "Members" (2) and 2 options appear
- Click on Transform data (3). 99% of the time you choose Transform data as this then allows you to clean up the data in the "washing machine" before you load it into the Data Model

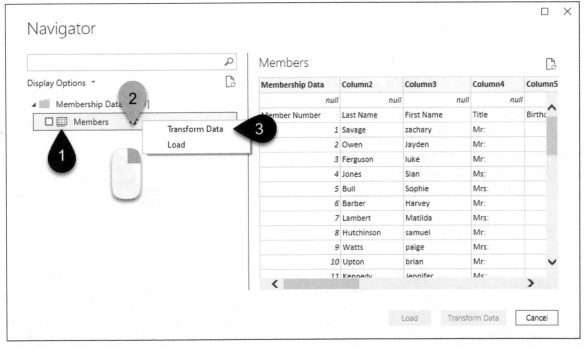

💡 As an alternative to the right-click option, you could instead tick the check-box next to Members and then use one of the buttons in the bottom right corner. The check-box method is useful when there are multiple sheets or tables to transform or load in one go.

You are now in the wonderful world of the Power Query Editor, look at the following items in the screenshot below.

1. The 3 key menus to use when converting data into well-structured tables
2. The list of your Power Query tables and other elements. You normally have more than one table of data in your Power BI data model
3. The data preview area, showing the first 1,000 rows of your data
4. The Formula bar, showing the "M" language formula
5. Just a few of the magical Power Query buttons that help you convert your messy source data. There are more buttons on each of the 3 menus
6. Query Name. Short and meaningful names should be used
7. The Query Steps, where each click of a button is recorded as a single step

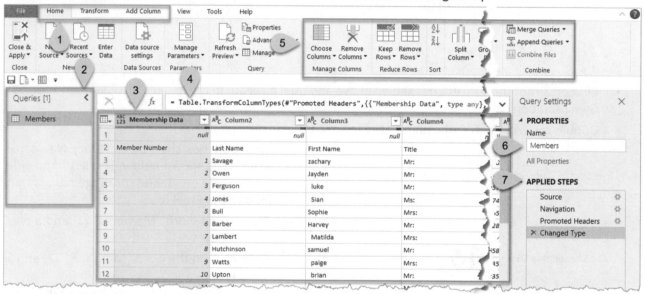

💡 If the formula bar is not visible then click on the View tab and tick the checkbox for the formula bar. You can gradually begin to learn the "M" language by reviewing the formulas that are generated by button clicks. "M" stands for Mashup.

Start by looking at the Applied Steps in the right-hand panel.

•   Click on Source (1) and it shows you the connection to the Excel file in the formula bar. The contents of that Excel Workbook is then shown in the preview area

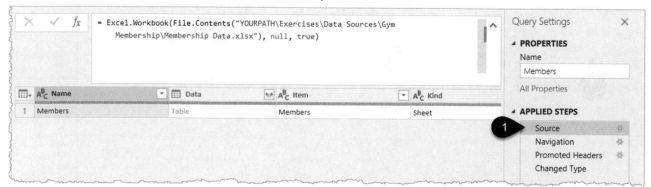

•   Click on the Navigation step. The preview pane then shows the contents of the Members sheet since this is the sheet you selected in the navigation pane at the start of this process

Then Power Query tried to be helpful and added two more steps automatically for you. The Promoted Headers step (2) pushes the first row of your sheet into the column headers. The Changed Type step (1) is created by Power Query scanning the columns to work out if they are filled with dates, numbers, text, etc.

We'll come back to these items later, but for now, you should delete them as you can see the headings are actually in row 2.

- Delete the Changed Type (1) step by clicking the cross next to it
- Delete the Promoted Headers step (2)

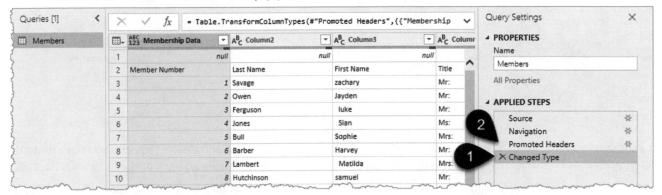

Now that you are back to the navigation step, you will see the heading you need is in row 3. To remove the top 2 rows, there is a helpful button on the Home tab called "Remove Rows" (1).

- Click Remove Rows (1)
- Choose Remove Top Rows (2), then type a 2 in the box that appears followed by OK

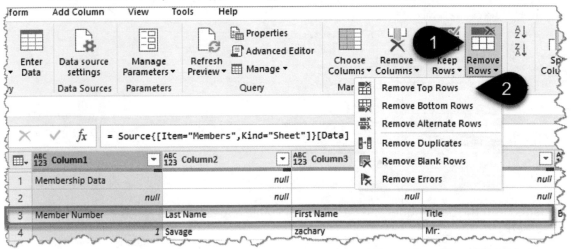

- Click the "Use First Row as Headers" button (1) and the first row will be promoted into the column headings

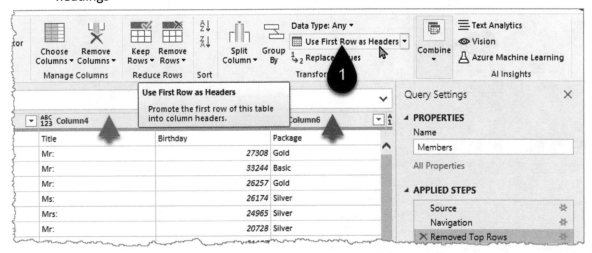

☕ Use First Row as Headers is possibly my favourite named button in all of Power BI. Bravo Power Query team!

Now you can see in the right-side panel that not only has the Promoted Headers step been added, but an extra Changed Type step also appears. Power Query has scanned your columns and added this Changed Type step to set your columns as Whole Number (123), Text (ABC), etc.

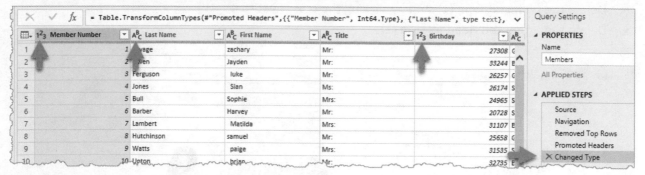

For those of you that have recorded Macros in the past, this is a much simpler and clearer process. You see the steps being added, you can delete the mistakes that you've made, and you can easily go back and edit or insert a step.

The real power of Power Query is that these steps can now be run at any time in the future by clicking a refresh button, or even by scheduling it to run at certain times of the day.

Before you do any further clean up to this data you probably want to know where this is leading, so load the data as it is then you can come back later to finish cleaning it up.

- On the Home tab click Close and Apply, there's no need to click the drop-down, just click the big button (1)

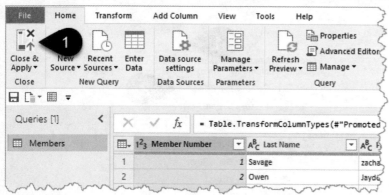

The data is now loaded into the data model and the Members table appears in the Fields Panel on the right-hand side of the screen.

- Click the expand icon (1) to open up the table and display all the columns in the table

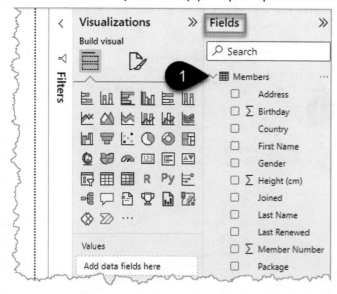

Create Your First Power BI Visual

- Tick Package (1) followed by Member Number (2) and a table of results should appear. But Member Numbers are being summed up, which is not what you want
- Click on the small V arrow next to Member Number (3) and choose Count (4)

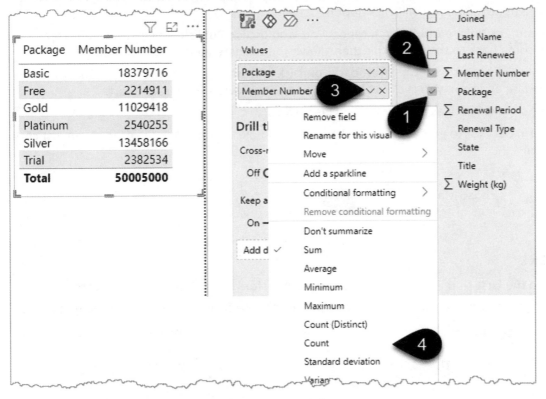

- Change the visual to a Clustered bar chart (1)

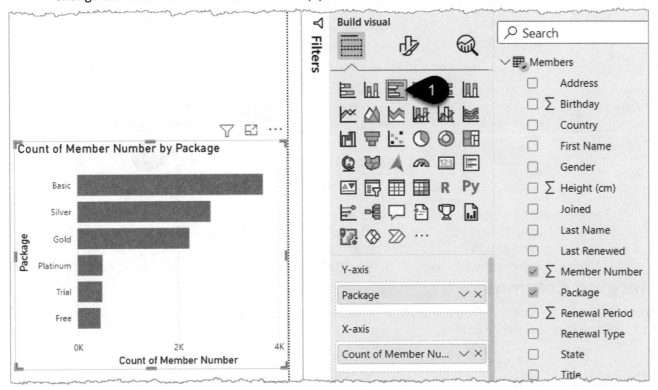

And now you have a chart showing count of members by package type. This is the start of your Power BI journey. From this point, you could then add more visuals to the page and build out your report.

To see my file at this stage open Solutions\Chapter 2 Gym Report Stage 1

You should save your file at this stage before you go any further.

- Click on File then Save As and call it Gym Report

There are 3 buttons you will use frequently when developing Power BI reports, see the image below. No need to click items 1 or 2 right now, but you will click option 3.

Publish (1). When you are finished building a report you would click Publish which saves your report to PowerBI.com. We'll come back to this later. This then allows you to share your report with others.

Refresh (2). To update the report with the latest data you click Refresh. This runs the Power Query Applied Steps, the visuals update and then you click Publish to replace the previously shared report.

Transform data (3). To make changes to your Power Query steps.

- Click Transform data (3) to go back into the Power Query Editor. Don't click the drop-down just click the big button

Cleaning Text

- Right-click on the First Name column (1) and choose Transform then Capitalize Each Word (2)
- Repeat this right-click → Transform action and this time choose Trim to remove the leading spaces (3)

💡 Trim removes all leading and trailing spaces from text but not spaces between words. e.g. " appl e " becomes "appl e". If you need to remove all spaces then you can use right-click then Replace Values and ensure the advanced options box that appears does not have a check in the box for Match entire cell contents. Type a space in the first box and leave the 2nd box empty.

Merging Columns

The next step is to Combine First Name, Last Name, and Member Number into a single column. The order you click the columns (while holding Ctrl) is the order they will combine.

- With the First Name column already highlighted (1) hold Ctrl and select Last Name (2) then Member Number (3)

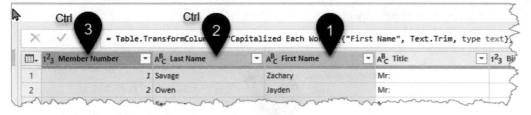

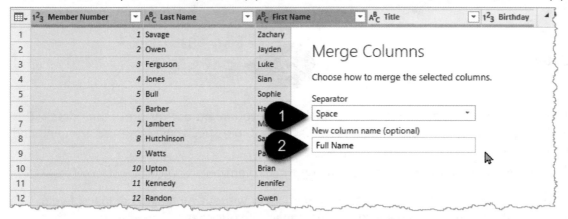

- Right-click on one of the column headings and choose Merge Columns
- Choose a Space for a separator (1) and set the new column name to be Full Name (2)

You will now have 1 column called Full Name. You will see a new step in the Applied Steps panel called Merged Columns (1) and the formula bar will include the "M" code that has been written for you. See the image below.

- Right-click on the applied step that is labelled Merged Columns (1) and choose Rename (2) then replace the current step name with the text "Created Full Name via merge"

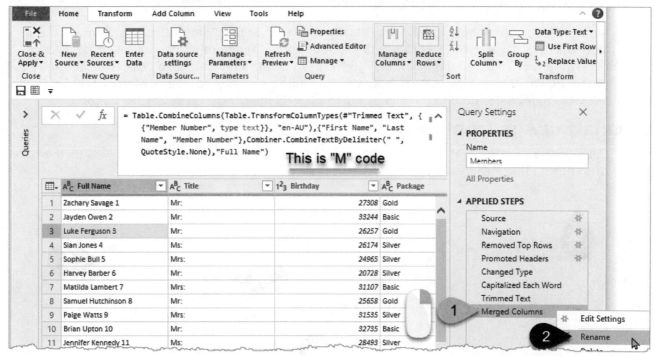

Giving your steps more meaningful names will help you or someone else to understand what steps have been used during the data clean-up.

Dates

The next column to fix up is the Birthday. It is currently being displayed as a number. This is a scenario many Excel users are all too familiar with. You can easily change it to a date by clicking on the 123 in the corner of the column (1) and changing it to date (2).

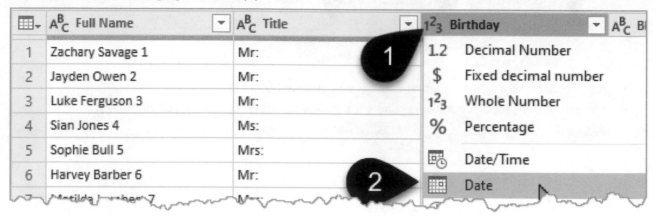

This "Date" setting is the "data type" and is not the final "style" you might use for presenting dates. This determines how Power BI stores the data in memory and treats it in a special way for auto grouping and filtering by year, month, etc.

Click the save icon in the top left corner and choose the Apply Later option

> 💡 Clicking Apply Later allows you to continue in Power Query without running a full load of your changes into the data model. If you want to see the impact of your changes on your report then you would choose Apply.

> ⚠ From now I won't remind you to save but do it regularly. Shockingly Power Query in Power BI does not have an UNDO option, so if you accidentally delete a step you will need to discard changes without saving and re-open to get it back.

> ☕ A curious fact, the whole numbers originally displayed in the Date of Birth column are the number of days since 31 Dec 1899. Oddly this start date is 1 day different from how "normal" Excel works. There was an original deliberate "bug" kept in Excel to match a leap year error in other software. Power Query dates do not have this bug but this means up until 1 March 1900 Excel and Power Query dates do differ. I'm guessing this is very unlikely to cause anyone a problem.

Calculating Age from Date

- Click on the heading of the Birthday column (1) then go to Add Column (2) followed by the Date drop-down (3) and choose Age (4)

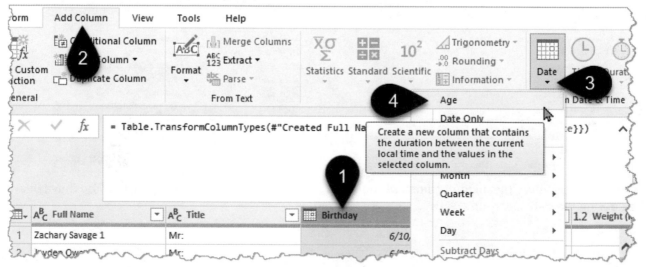

A new Age column will appear, which is great, but it is displayed in days.

- To convert it to years right-click on the Age column (1) and select Transform →Total Years (2)

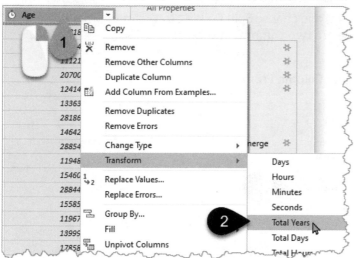

⚠ The "M" code formula that is generated simply divides the days by 365 (see 1 in the image below). This is a fairly blunt and inaccurate yet very simple approach.

- Round the decimals down to the nearest year by right-clicking on the Age column (2) and choosing Transform → Round → Round Down (3)

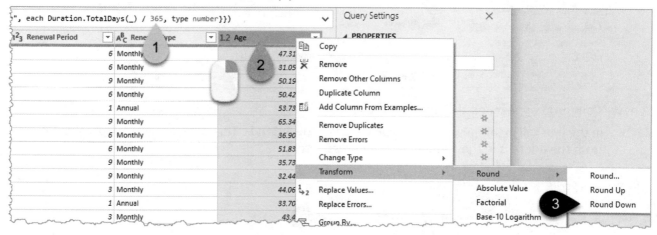

Extracting Text using Column from Examples

The Address column contains the postcode, you can easily extract it in one of two ways.

One option is to right-click on the Address heading (1) and choose Split Column by Delimiter. This would allow you to split the text into three columns since there are two commas in the address field.

The other option is magic!

- Right-click on the Address column (1) → Add Column From Examples (2)

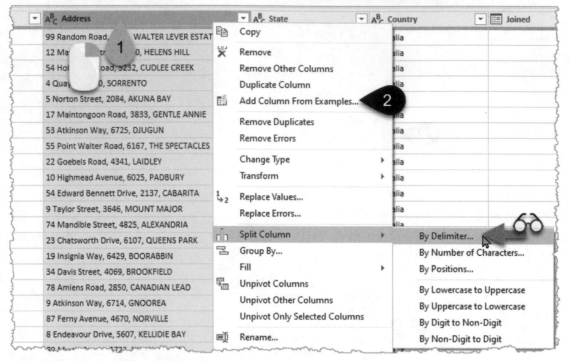

A new "Column1" appears on the right-hand side.

- In the first cell in this new column type the postcode 4856 (1). This is the postcode you want to extract from the address in the same row. Then press Enter

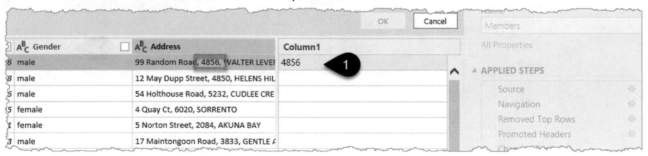

The postcode now spills down for every row! This is amazing!

Power Query has recognised a pattern and generated this formula for you (1) that extracts the data between the 3rd space and the subsequent comma.

```
Text.BetweenDelimiters([Address]," ", "," ,2, 0)
```

But wait, it's not quite right yet. Look at the screenshot and the items flagged with crosses.

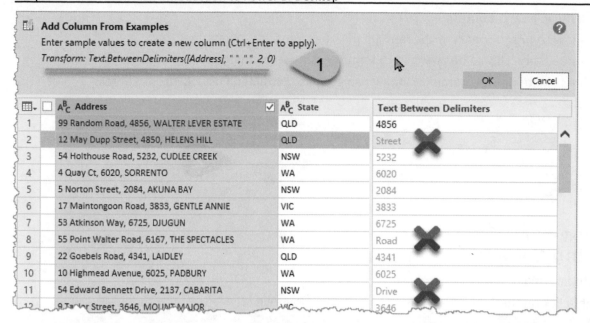

💡 The formula is saying extract the text between the space and the comma, skipping the first 2 spaces before starting to search, and skip 0 commas. That's the meaning of the two numbers at the end of the formula. You should always review the formula that has been generated. If it does not make any sense to you, don't trust it, and try a different approach.

To fix the wrong results you can provide another example to help Power Query learn the pattern.

- Type 4850 over the word Street underneath where you typed 4856 (see 1 in the image below) and press Enter

The formula (3) will have changed to

```
Text.BetweenDelimiters([Address],", " , ",")
```

This is extracting everything between the first "comma space" and the next comma. If Power Query doesn't recognise what you want to do after you enter the first example, then simply add more examples and it may then work it out. I'd admit defeat if it doesn't work after 5 examples.

- The final step is to rename this column as Postcode (2) by double-clicking on the word Text Between Delimiters and typing Postcode

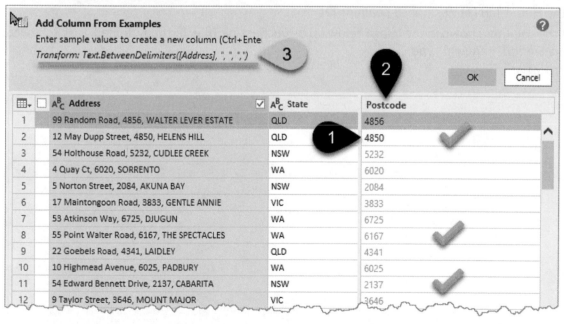

- Click the yellow OK button
- The new column appears at the far right of your screen.

The applied step name should be changed to something more meaningful.

- Right-click on the step name (1) and Rename (2) as "Extracted Postcode from Address"

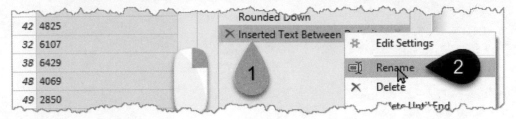

💡 You can also press F2 to rename a step.

Removing Columns

This next step normally surprises Excel users.

- Right-click on the Address column (1) and choose Remove (2)

"But won't I get #REF errors in the Postcode column if I do that?"

You'll see the Postcode column is fine. Think of each step as creating a completely new table, like a copy-paste values.

You can happily remove all columns that you don't need. It's strongly recommended to remove the columns you don't need for your report. It makes your reports faster to load and less confusing for someone inheriting the report from you.

💡 Selecting one or more columns and pressing the delete key works the same as right-click Remove.

To remove the other columns that you don't need:

- Click the Home Tab (1) → Choose Columns (2)
- Select the columns shown in the image below (3) by unchecking Title, Birthday, Joined, Last Renewed, Renewal Period, Renewal Type
- Click OK (4)

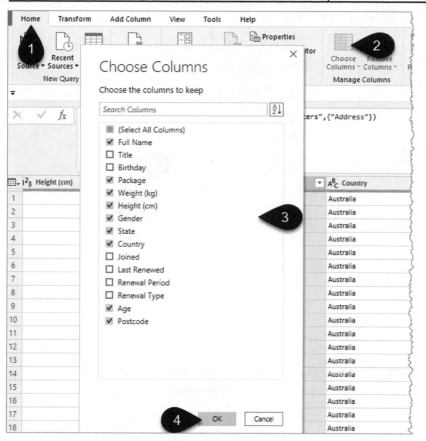

- Click Close and Apply on the Home Tab

The data will now re-load into your data model and your report/charts will update.

The first thing you will notice is your chart is no longer working because you no longer have a Member Number column you used for the Count.

- Remove Count of Members from the X-Axis box by clicking the small cross next to Count of Members (1)
- Drag Full Name into the X-Axis box (2), this should again give a simple count

☕ I rarely find that the "Fix this" button helps (3), but if you are stuck then give it a go. Just make sure you fully understand what fix has been applied. In this specific case it just removes the Count of Members field.

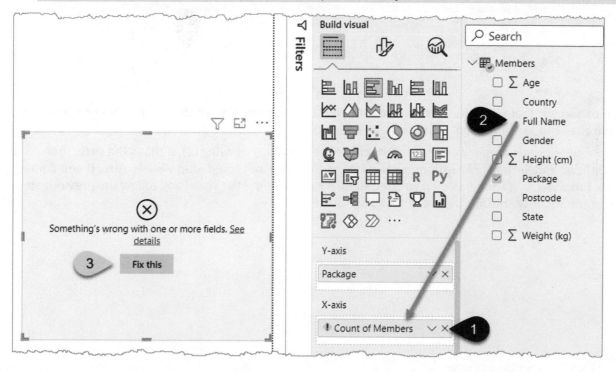

- Untick Package (1) and drag State into the Y-axis (2)

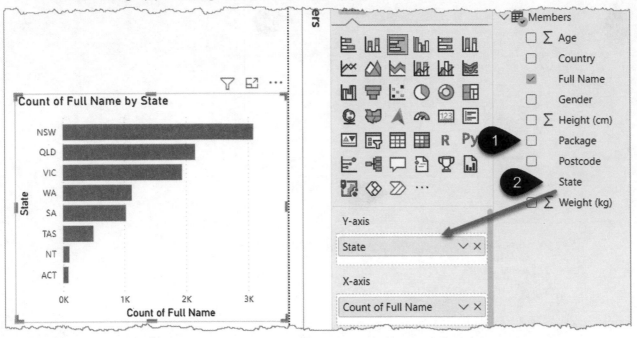

- Add data labels by clicking the formatting icon (1) and turning Data labels On (2)
- Click General (3) then expand Title and change Title text (4) to "Number of Members"

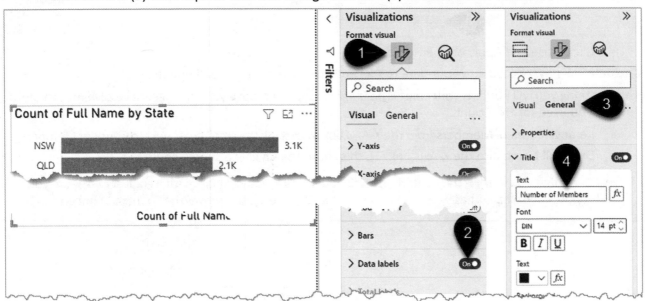

It's time to add another visual but **first, make sure you click on some empty space,** otherwise the clicks you make will alter the existing visual that you have selected.

You are about to create a map, but you may not have the map icon showing (1). If that's the case, then go to File → Options and Settings → Options → Security → Use Map and Filled Map visuals. Also, if you do have the visual but a warning appears when you add some data just delete the visual and follow the previous steps to change the security settings before proceeding further.

- Follow the 4 clicks in the image below to create a map visual. The "pitchfork" icon (4) is the expand down icon, which allows you to expand out from Country into Postcode level

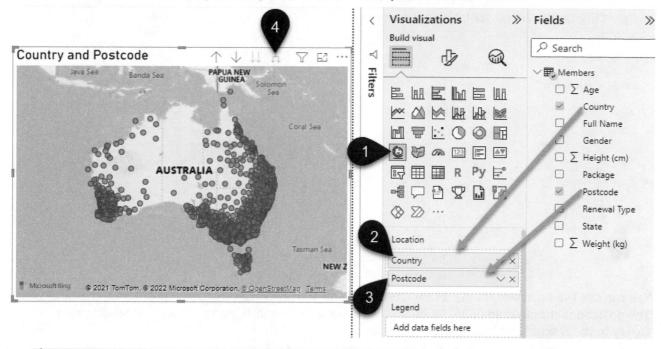

☕ I used to refer to the "pitchfork" as the "trident", but then on a training course once a student pointed out that it only has 2 prongs so I should call it a bident. We've never spoken since.

Now you can interact with the 2 visuals. By default, all Power BI visuals filter each other. You'll see later that you control this interaction on a per visual basis.

- Click the bar or word for TAS (1). The map zooms into the data for Tasmania
- Click on NT (2). Nothing happens, why?

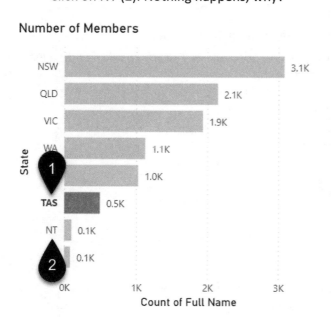

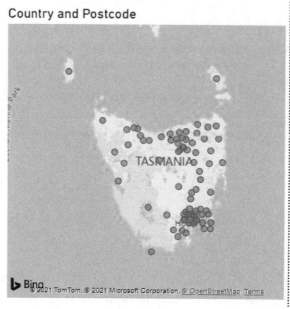

In this case, the problem is the postcodes for NT (Northern Territory).

- Click on some white space and then add a Table Visual (1) for Postcode (2)
- Click on the NT bar or label in the chart (3)

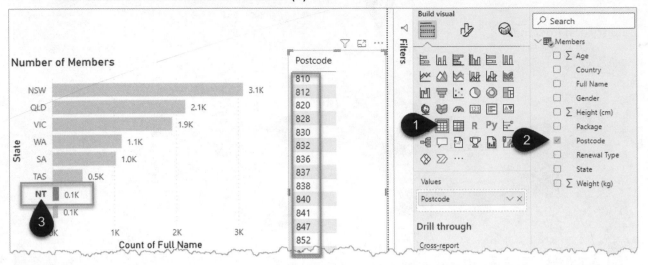

You can see the Postcode is only 3 characters long, but all Australian Postcodes should be 4 characters long. The postcodes should read 0836, 0838, 0839, etc. but unfortunately, we're missing the leading zeros. Power Query to the rescue!

Editing a Query and Adding a Formula

- On the Home tab click the Transform data icon (1) which will launch the Power Query Editor Window

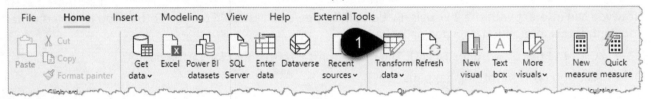

Look at row 135 in the Postcode column and you can see the three-digit postcode.

To fix this you will write a formula in Power Query to say "If the postcode is 3 characters long add a leading zero". This may be a familiar concept to the Excel folk reading this.

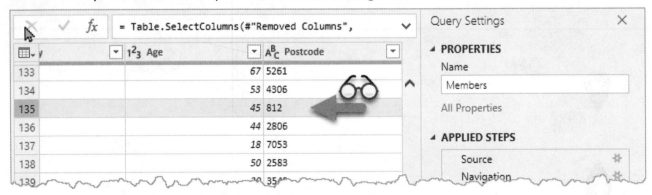

- Click the Add Column tab (1) → Custom Column (2) and a new formula window appears
- Type "Fixed Postcode" in the new column name box (3)
- Write your formula (4)

```
= if Text.Length( [Postcode] ) = 3 then "0" & [Postcode] else [Postcode]
```

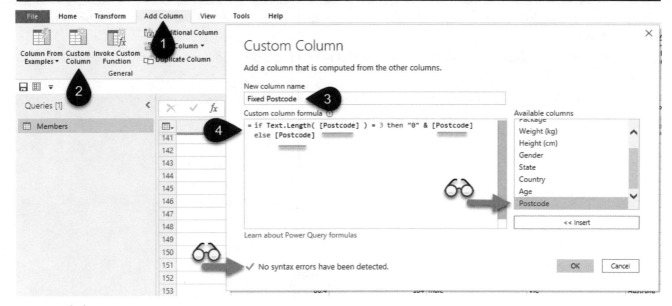

- Click OK

💡 Rather than typing [Postcode] each time you can simply double-click on the word Postcode in the right-hand panel.

While the formula syntax is familiar to Excel users it is different enough to catch you out. You must use lower case "if" and type "then" and "else" rather than use commas. "M" formulas are case-sensitive so always check for the green tick in the bottom left of the Custom Column input window.

💡 There is a "fancier" technique to fill out numbers with leading zeros, and that's to use the Text.PadStart function. In the above scenario you could replace the "if formula" with this =Text.PadStart([Postcode],4,"0"). This forces any text with less than 4 characters to "pad out" the start with as many 0s as required to make it 4 characters long.

If you need to make a change or you get an error then click on the cog next to that step, see (1) in the image below. This will bring you back to the formula editor window.

Remember to document your code as you go.

- Right-click on the Added Custom applied step (2) and rename as "Fixed Postcodes with missing 0" (3)
- Right-click on the step (2) and choose Properties (4)

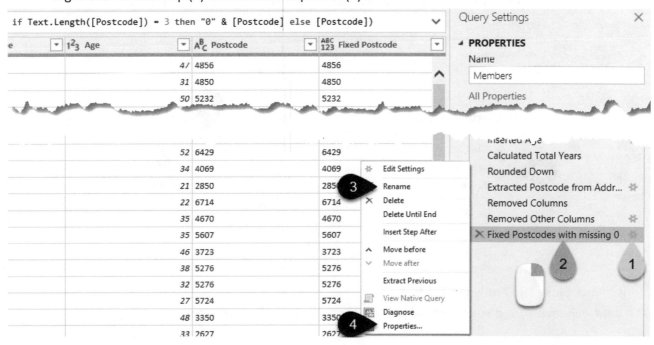

This properties window is where you should type the explanation of "Why I did this step". Your future self will thank you.

- Type into the description field (1) "Source data included 3 digit postcodes missing leading zero"
- Click OK

A small information circle (2) will appear next to the step indicating there is some extra information available. Hovering over the step also displays your description.

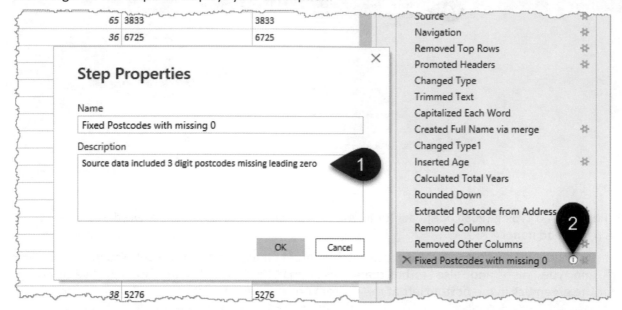

👆 I always confidently claim that the information symbol was added as a result of my submission to the Power BI ideas site here url.pbi.guide/infoi. I've no idea really if it was or not, but if anyone knows for sure that it wasn't then don't tell me as I like my tiny claim to fame. While we're on the topic of the ideas site I'd encourage everyone to check it out, add new suggestions and vote for ideas you agree with. For Excel fans, the equivalent site is the Microsoft Feedback Portal aka. ms/ExcelSuggestions.

- Right-click on the original Postcode column (1) and Remove it (2)
- Double-click in the heading of the Fixed Postcode column (3) and rename it as "Postcode"
- Click on the data type icon (4) and change to Text

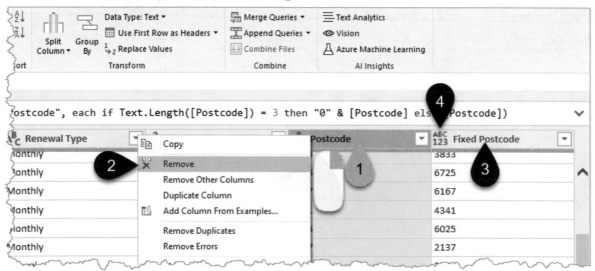

- Click Close and Apply (on the Home tab)

The data will refresh, and your map should now show Northern Territory locations.

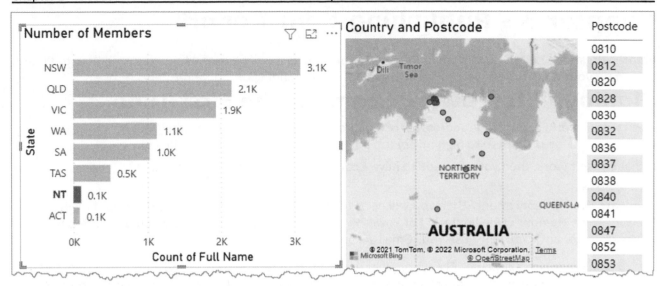

To see my file at this stage open Solutions\Chapter 2 Gym Report Stage 2

Summary of Your Introduction to Power Query

Power Query is an amazing tool for extracting data from a wide range of sources and then "cleaning it up" to help you build your reports. Each time you click refresh those "Applied Steps" in Power Query will run and your report will update. The goal is to create tables of data organised into columns that then allow you to summarise and filter your data easily in your report.

The crazy thing is that Power Query has also lived in Excel since the Excel 2016 version and only a minority of Excel users know about this. In chapter 10 of this book, you will see how to access this power in Excel rather than Power BI.

☕ I always recommend that new Power Query users head over to Oz du Soleil's YouTube channel, Excel on Fire. If you're looking for real-world Excel Power Query use cases presented in a highly engaging way then that's the place to go url.pbi.guide/whoop

Chapter 3 - Publishing Your Report

Before you start to learn how to build more complex reports it will be useful to understand how to Publish and share your report. Then you will have a general understanding of the "end-to-end" process.

Signing in to PowerBI.com for the First Time

If you type PowerBI.com into the address bar of your browser it should take you to https://powerbi.microsoft.com/ where you will be prompted to Sign In. Try to sign in with your organisation email address.

If that doesn't work, then you will need to have a conversation with your IT department to work out the best way forward.

If you **are** the "IT department" then you will need to go to PowerBI.com and follow the steps labelled "Start Free" or "Sign Up now". One limitation of Power BI is that you need an organisation email address to create a Power BI "tenant". You can't use your Gmail account for example.

> 💡 The tenant is your Power BI environment where your reports will be hosted and shared to report consumers. If you are not part of an organisation with a work email address and you want to set up a test tenant for a short period, then there are 2 resources that will help you. Firstly a video by Adam Saxton from the YouTube channel Guy in a Cube url.pbi.guide/YooO and then the official Microsoft documentation on how to sign up for a free E5 Trial url.pbi.guide/E5trial.

The PowerBI.com Experience (aka "the Service")

The Power BI web platform is referred to as "the service" and it could be an entire book on its own. This book will focus on the things you need to know immediately to get started as a user/report developer, it will not cover any of the Administrator settings. I've added a link in Chapter 14 for those of you interested in admin features.

> ☕ PowerBI.com is a service hosted in "the cloud". What this means is your reports are saved to a computer deep in some air-conditioned data centre. If you are signed in to Power BI.com and click on the ? in the top right corner of the screen and go to "About Power BI" it will tell you where in the world your data is stored. If you don't see the ? but do see 3 dots … then click those and go to "? Help and Support" → About Power BI.

Once you have signed in to Power BI.com, clicking on My workspace (1) shows you the free and empty space set aside for you to get started. This is where you can publish your first report to, and then you can share your report with others from here.

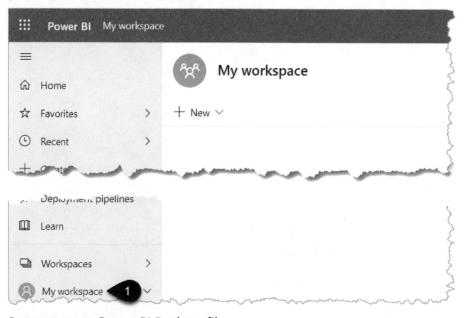

Return to your Power BI Desktop file.

- Click the Publish button (1), you may be asked to sign in. If you are prompted to sign in, then use the same email address you used to sign in to PowerBI.com
- Select My workspace (2)
- Click Select (3) and then read the next instructions before clicking anything else

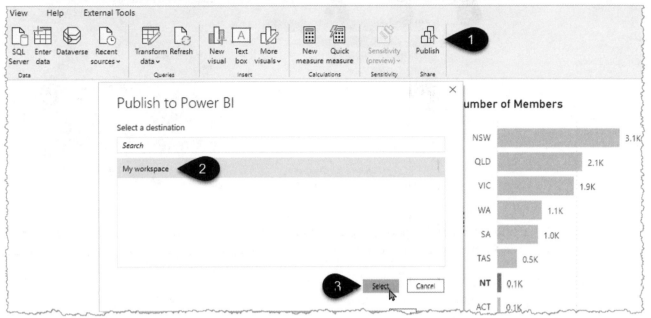

💡 You could also just have double-clicked My workspace.

After a few seconds, the image below should appear.

- Click on the blue hyperlink (1) to take you to your report in PowerBI.com

💡 If you accidently clicked Got it by mistake (many people do) then simply click publish, select your workspace, and this time you will be asked if you want to replace your report. Click yes, and then click the hyperlink as per the above image.

A copy of your report is now saved in PowerBI.com. This is a good time to explore items 1,2 and 3 flagged in the image below.

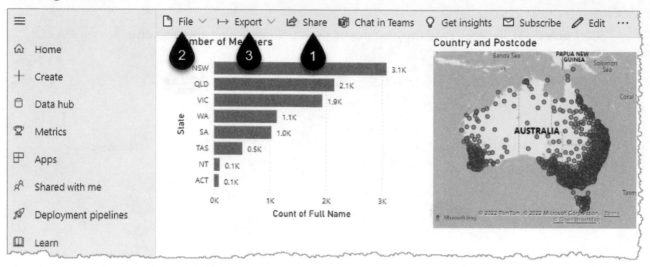

The Share icon (1) is one way that you share reports. You need a Power BI Pro licence to share reports. If you click it and you don't have a licence you may be fortunate enough to be offered a 60-day free trial. Go ahead, try free!

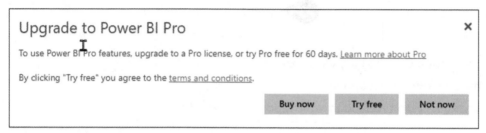

If you do not have this option, then you will need to contact your IT department for assistance. While Power BI Desktop and My workspace in PowerBI.com are free, the sharing of reports with others requires a licence. This book will cover the different licence types in a few pages time.

Sharing Your Report

Once you do have a Pro licence then the share button will allow you to share via a link.

My recommendation for people beginning their Power BI journey would be to share in the following way: click on the *"People in your organisations with the link can view and share"* (1) then choose *"Specific people"* (2) and untick the option *"Allow recipients to share this report"* and untick "*Allow recipients to build content with the data*" (3). That way you control exactly who has access to your report. Click Apply (4) and then type in email addresses (5).

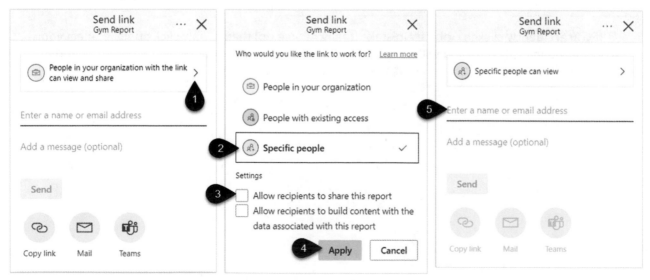

☕ I wouldn't be surprised if these options have changed by the time you read this book, as this experience is far from ideal in my view. Remember to check out the partner website for this book for updates and explanations of changes PBI.guide.

If you need to remove access from someone or make some change then click the share icon again but this time choose the … (1) in the corner of the window that appears and click Manage permissions (2).

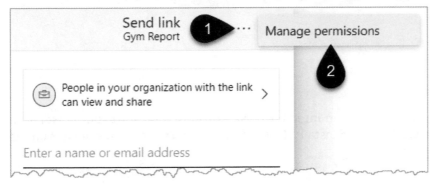

Later in the book, you will see that there are better ways of sharing but the method above is simple when you are just beginning to get a feel for how things work.

Under the File drop-down (1) there are several options including Download this file (2). This downloads an exact copy of your Power BI desktop file should you ever lose your copy or inherit someone else's report and you don't know where their desktop file is saved.

There is a more advanced Manage permissions screen (3), different from the simpler one mentioned above.

Another option that may appear under the File menu is Publish to web (4 above). This is often turned off by Organisation Administrators (recommended) as otherwise it allows you to publish your Power BI report publicly and anyone in the world can get access to the URL that is generated for you. This option is great for organisations that want to share public information and for companies that want to showcase their Power BI skills. If you didn't look at it already you can see the url.pbi.guide/FirstLook report that I have shared using this option.

☕ There are a couple of useful sites to see the reports others have developed and get some inspiration for your report. Power BI Partner Showcase url.pbi.guide/showcase and Power BI Data Stories Gallery url.pbi.guide/dsg1.

Export Options

The Export section (1) allows you to convert your report to screenshots in PDF or PowerPoint or create a linked Excel workbook via the Analyze in Excel option.

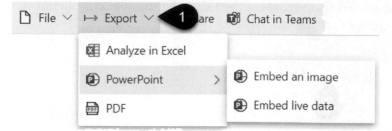

PowerPoint also comes with the option to embed an interactive live Power BI page into your PowerPoint slide. You can also start from within PowerPoint and install a Power BI app from the store. More information can be found here url.pbi.guide/PowerPoint.

Analyze in Excel

Given the title of this book I'd imagine the Analyze in Excel option will be of interest to you.

Clicking the Analyze in Excel button should prompt you to open an online Excel file saved to your OneDrive.

You may also get a warning about unsafe links, click OK

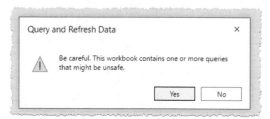

This Excel file will be linked to your data model and automatically create a place-holder PivotTable for you. You will then have PivotTable access to the dataset behind your published report.

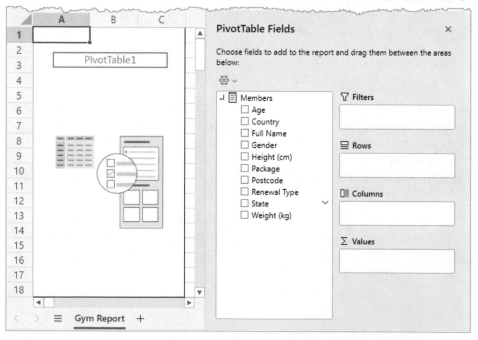

You can open this Excel file in the desktop version for the full user interface experience.

⚠ Depending on your version of Excel you may not be able to drag an item into the Values box. In more recent versions of O365 you can, but I strongly recommend you avoid it if at all possible. Everyone should create calculations known as "measures" to put into the Values box. The book covers this in Chapter 7. It really will help to future-proof your reports.

Analyze in Excel if you don't have OneDrive for Business

If you don't have Office 365 then Power BI won't be able to open the file in OneDrive so it will try to download a copy of the Excel file and it may prompt you to download and install some updates. But wait! Try clicking on the small blue text underneath the Download button (1). It says, "I've already installed these updates". Most computers these days already have the updates required.

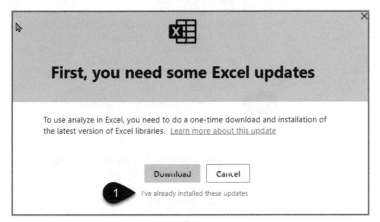

💡 Depending on how Office is installed on your machine the required components may already be there. To get a little technical here, installations of the type "Click to Run" have them by default while MSI installations do not.

Once you click *"I've already installed these updates"* then the Excel file download will begin, or you may have to click Analyze in Excel one more time. If it still doesn't work, then you may need to install the updates.

Depending on your browser the download file may appear in the top corner, and you can open it from there. If it doesn't appear then go to your downloads folder on your computer and open it from there instead.

Two consecutive yellow warnings will appear in your Excel file. You will firstly be prompted to Enable Editing and then secondly Enable Content (1). If you aren't signed in with Excel then a further warning may appear and then a Sign in option will require you to enter your credentials.

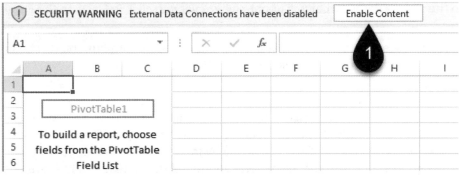

Connect to Your Power BI Dataset from Excel

Depending on the version of Excel you are using you may be able to connect directly to the dataset from Excel itself, rather than using the Analyze in Excel option. All up-to-date versions of Excel 365 and the web version of Excel will have this.

💡 You must have at least one report published for the following steps to work.

- Open an empty Excel file

- Click on Get Data (1) and a "From Power BI" option appears (2)
- Click on "From Power BI" (2) and a list of all the Power BI datasets you have permission to access will appear. A dataset is the data model part of your report.
- Click on the Gym Report Dataset (3) and a new PivotTable will appear

💡 The workspace name underneath Gym Report (3) is just your email address which represents reports published to "My Workspace".

Another method to connect to a dataset is via Insert (1) PivotTable (2) From Power BI (3). Note, this method also works in the web version of Excel.

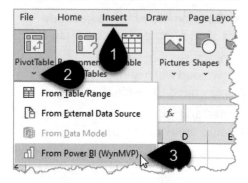

Regardless of whether you connect via the method above or via the Analyze in Excel option you end up with a PivotTable that is connected to the source dataset that will update whenever you click Refresh on the Excel Data Tab or open the Excel file.

This is fantastic since you now have a single data source to manage, maintain and update but you can build multiple Power BI and Excel reports from that same "single source of truth".

Creating a Workspace

For real-world reporting, you shouldn't use "My workspace" to store and share your reports. There are several very good reasons for this statement. Firstly, if you leave an organisation then your "My workspace" is removed and is no longer accessible to anyone. Secondly, if you are away from work when the report needs to be updated, then no one else has access. Finally, there are several additional useful features that are not present in "My Workspace" such as dataflows, access levels and the creation of Apps.

The solution is to create a new workspace and make at least one other person the Administrator of that workspace. Even if you're the only one in your organisation starting to use Power BI you should build your reports in a workspace that you will be able to grant access to in the future.

⚠ Creating a workspace requires a Pro or PPU (Premium Per User) licence. More on the difference between PPU and Pro later.

- Return to your Power BI session in the browser

- Click on the word "Workspaces" (1). If you don't see the word workspaces click on the 3 lines in the top left corner to expand out the menu. Those three lines are known as the "hamburger"
- Click on Create a workspace (2)

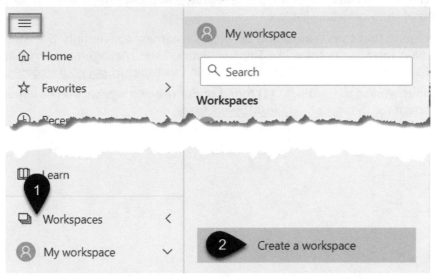

⚠ Many IT departments block the creation of workspaces and a warning may appear guiding how to request a new workspace. It can be a good idea for larger organisations to control the creation of workspaces so that only those who have had training and are aware of the organisations' Power BI rules and procedures are given workspace creation rights.

You need to give the workspace a name (1) and a description (2) and you can upload a small logo/icon if you'd like (3). Don't do this part yet, just read along, but stay on this screen.

Under the Advanced options (4) you will see that you have some licence options. Choose Pro unless you know you need Premium per user or Premium per capacity. More on those next.

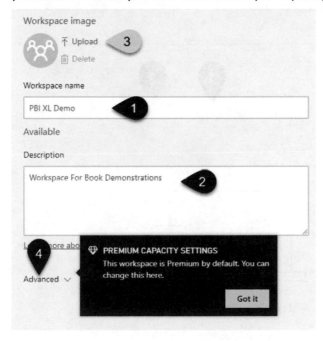

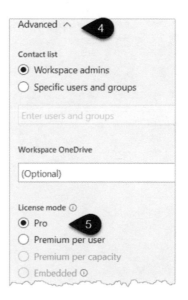

Workspace Naming

When you are just exploring and learning I'd recommend creating a workspace called something like "zTempTraining – Your Name". This can then be easily identified and removed at a later date. The z simply moves your workspace to the bottom of the workspace list.

For real-world workspaces, I'd recommend that the organisation agrees on a naming convention. One suggestion is always to begin with the main focus, something like Sales Analytics, Sales Management, Project A Executives, Project A External. Melissa Coates has an informative video on this topic url.pbi.guide/coates.

Also, look at the link "Learn more about workspace settings" (1) found under the Settings section or when you create a workspace. Here's a shortcut for that url.pbi.guide/MDworkspace.

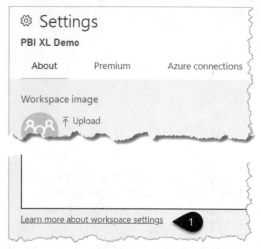

For this book, I'll name the workspace as PBI XL Demo and click OK.

- Name yours zTempTraining – *Your Name* and click OK

Once you've created your workspace you can change the name of it under settings (1) and importantly grant Administrator access to another person in your Organisation.

- Click the Access option (2)

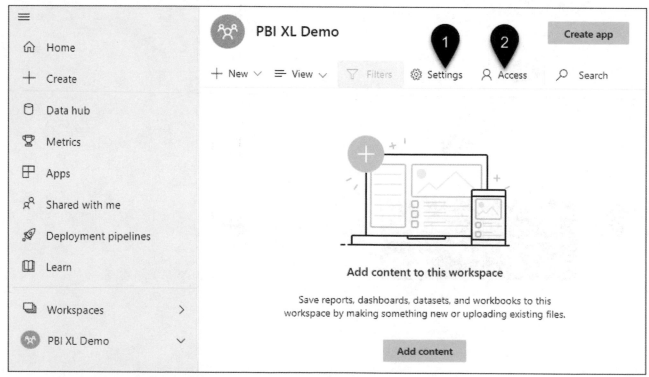

- Type the email address of a colleague (1) and change the drop-down (2) to Admin

⋏ Access
PBI XL Demo

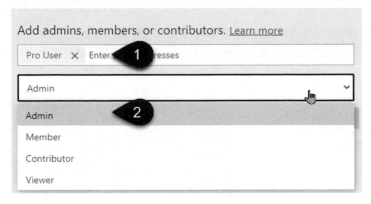

Add admins, members, or contributors. Learn more

💡 You should always add at least one colleague as an Admin of the workspace, so if you are on holiday or leave the organisation then they can take over easily.

1. An Admin can delete you from the role and even delete the entire workspace so make sure it's someone you trust!

2. A "member" cannot delete admins or delete the workspace but can add and remove reports and add/remove other members and publish/update Apps. More on Apps later.

3. Contributors can add and remove reports.

4. Viewers – well it speaks for itself.

💡 Granting Viewer access to the workspace is one way to share reports but it's not my recommended way. My preference is to think of a workspace as an environment for the report creators. Then the reports are best shared via something called Apps, which is covered in Chapter 12.

⚠ In Chapter 13 the book will cover Row Level Security which is a fantastic feature allowing you to secure the data that is displayed to individuals when they view the reports. This feature does not apply to anyone that is an Admin, Member, or Contributor i.e., they will see all data!

☕ Microsoft Docs information on roles can be found here url.pbi.guide/MDroles.

Publish Your Report to a Workspace

At the time of writing, there is no way to move an existing report between workspaces. Instead, you need to follow these steps:

- Return to your Power BI Desktop file
- Click Publish (1)
- Double-click on the name of the new workspace (2)

- Click the blue "Success!" hyperlink that appears to take you to the report
- To see the workspace content click on the workspace name (2). If you don't see the workspace name click on the "hamburger" (1) to expand out the side menu, and if you still don't see it then click on the word Workspaces and pick from there

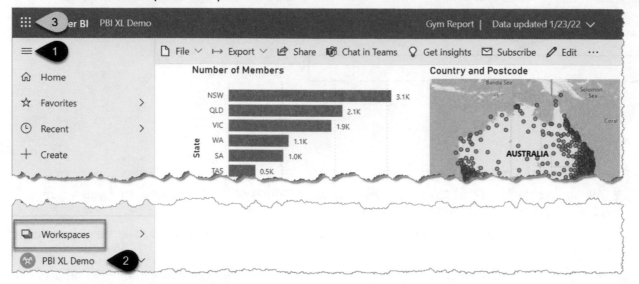

☕ The icon in the top left (3) is known as the "waffle" and just shows all your Office 365 applications.

In the workspace view, you can see all the reports and their associated datasets that are published to the Workspace.

The Reports are colour coded blue and the Datasets are orange.

- Hovering your mouse next to the Dataset icon shows the Schedule Refresh icon (1) which is covered later. Click on the three dots (2) and some additional options appear including Delete and create report (3).

💡 While you can create a report in the browser, I recommend building all reports in Power BI Desktop as it's a more complete experience. Deleting a dataset also deletes all associated reports.

- Click on the text "Gym Report" (3) next to the blue report icon to view the report

☕ Other "objects" can also be added to workspaces including "Dashboards", dataflows, datamarts (in Premium workspaces), and Excel workbooks.

For now, this will be enough of an introduction to the Power BI Service and the book will return to this topic later to demonstrate the best way to share reports with others via the use of Apps.

💡 To be organised about things and avoid confusion in future you should go back to the original "MyWorkspace" where you first published your report, and delete your dataset for Gym Report. Deleting a dataset will automatically delete the associated report.

Power BI Licence Options: A Brief Overview

Pro Licence

The base level of licence type is Power BI Pro. This is the licence required to share reports and create workspaces. If someone has shared a report with you then you will also need a pro licence to see that report unless the report has been shared from a "Premium per Capacity" workspace. More on that in an upcoming paragraph.

At the time of writing, the pro licence is USD$9.99 per user per month.

You can check what licence you have by clicking on the user profile image in the top right corner (1) of the PowerBI.com screen, you may even be able to Buy Pro now (2) from here. The IT departments of organisations normally manage licences via the Office 365 Admin portal or Azure portal.

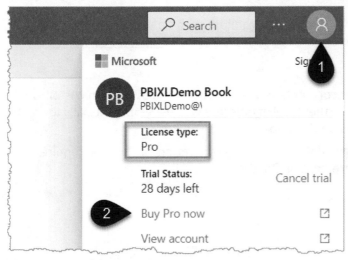

Premium Per User (PPU)

If you are presented with Premium Per User as an option when you create your workspace don't choose it unless you are sure you need it. It's a more expensive licence (double the Pro cost) with more features than Pro but only other Premium per user licence holders will be able to see the reports you share with them. A few reasons to opt for PPU include 48 refreshes per day rather than 8, datamarts, paginated reports, 100GB model size limit v 1GB and XMLA endpoint read/write connectivity, and additional dataflow functionality.

For more information see this "Power BI Premium Per User FAQ" page url.pbi.guide/PPUFAQ.

If you chose Premium Per User, then your workspace will have a diamond with a Person icon next to it. To change it to Pro click on the workspace (1) then the Settings icon (2) and choose the Premium menu (3) and click back on Pro (4).

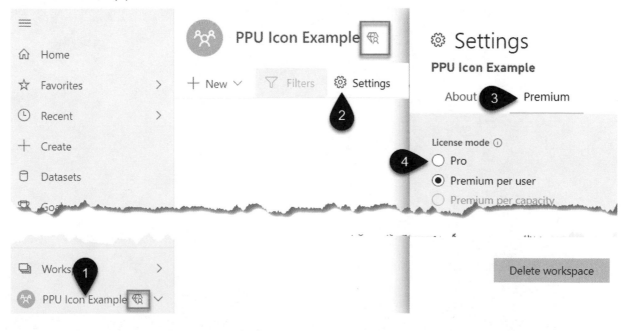

The other options which are likely greyed out are Premium per capacity and Embedded.

Premium Per Capacity

Premium per capacity is often referred to as Power BI Premium. Larger organisations often opt for this licence for a couple of reasons. The easiest of the benefits to understand is that report consumers don't need to have a pro licence to view a report that is shared with them from a "Premium Capacity" workspace. Imagine you have 2,000 report consumers paying USD $9.99 each to view the reports, this can get very expensive. With Power BI Premium, companies pay a fee starting from around USD $4,995 per month instead.

A premium workspace will have a diamond next to it. There are also additional performance enhancements and features that come with paying for Premium as per PPU. An important point to note is that report publishers still require Pro licences.

> ☕ If you are interested in finding out more about Power BI Premium then head to this article url. pbi.guide/PremFAQ. For the latest comparisons of features and pricing go to url.pbi.guide/PBIPrice.

Embedded

Embedded is used when an organisation wants to incorporate Power BI reports into their own custom-built websites for their customers to access. It requires a further level of different web development skills to create one of these solutions and is not something covered in this book.

Now it's time to change the focus back to connecting to data and building reports, and a common requirement to import data from Excel or CSV files stored in SharePoint or OneDrive.

Chapter 4 - Files Stored in SharePoint/OneDrive for Business

Every day more businesses are moving to saving their files on OneDrive and SharePoint. The technique for connecting to these files is different to the simple Get Data → Excel option and is not currently easy to discover. I'm hoping that by the time you read this book a much simpler and more intuitive technique will be available but if not then read on.

To demonstrate this technique, you will need to do the following:

- Set up a folder on your OneDrive for Business, the name doesn't matter, but if you'd like to copy this example then call it OneDrive Demo

💡 If you already have Power BI.com open you can quickly access OneDrive via the 9 dot "Waffle" icon in the top left corner.

- Upload the Membership Data.xlsx file into that folder

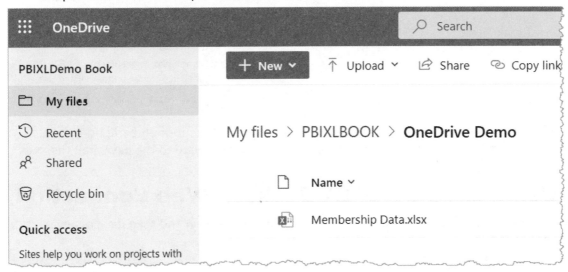

⚠ This technique does not work with OneDrive personal accounts.

Once you have saved your Membership Data to your OneDrive for Business folder you will follow these general steps which will be explained in more detail over the next few pages:

1. Copy the file path that you need to use in Power BI to connect to the file

2. Paste that file Path into the Power BI Desktop Get Data from Web connector

3. Pull the data into Power BI

4. Build a simple visual

5. Publish to your new workspace

6. Set up "Scheduled Refresh"

Step 1: Finding the Connection Path

As per the previous section you now have a file in a OneDrive (or SharePoint) folder.

- Place a tick against the file (1) then click the information symbol (2)
- Scroll down the right-hand panel (3) and click the Path symbol (4) to copy it.

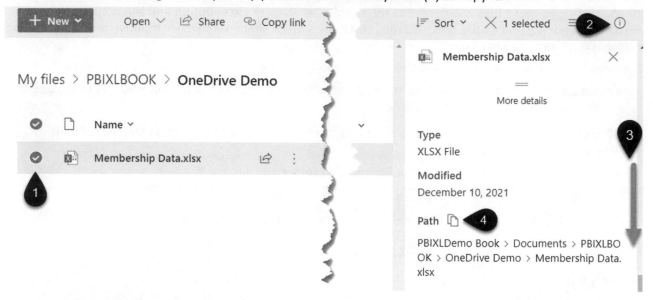

☕ Yes, this is crazy! How is anyone expected to discover this? As I mentioned earlier a simpler navigation experience is being developed by Microsoft, and I look forward to the day when these few pages are redundant.

Step 2: Using the Power BI Desktop Web Connection

- Go to your Power BI Desktop file and create a new file via File → New and then dismiss any startup screen that appears
- Click the Get data drop-down (1)
- Click from Web (2)
- Paste in the URL you copied (3) then click OK (4)

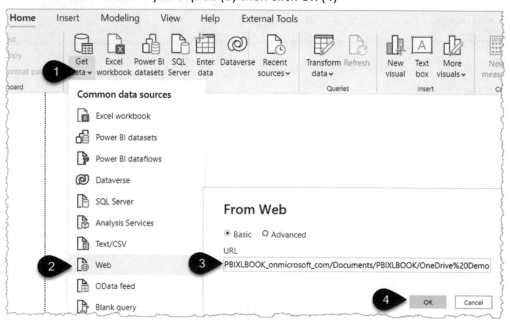

You'll then need to sign-in to your OneDrive account.

- Click Organizational account (1)
- Click Sign in (2) and you may need to pick your account and enter your password
- Click Connect (3)

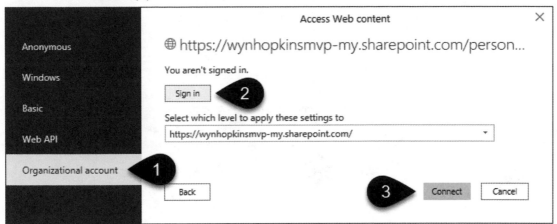

💡 Your credentials will be remembered on your computer ready for the next time you connect to a file in this OneDrive / SharePoint site. If it doesn't work then try going to the Transform data button drop-down, choose Data source settings, and clear any permissions related to SharePoint. Then try again.

You are now connected, and the Power Query navigation window should appear.

Everyone agrees that this process is overly complicated and hopefully a simpler method will be created by the Power Query team soon.

As a bit of additional information (just read along without clicking anywhere), there is an alternative method to finding the URL. Open the OneDrive file in the Excel desktop app. Then go to the Info section and copy the path (1).

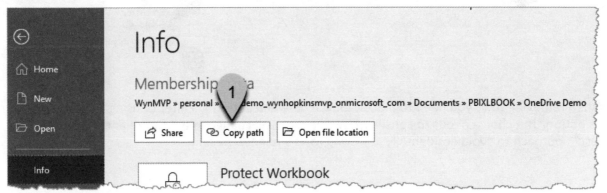

The important thing is to then delete `?web=1` after you paste the URL into the box.

Step 3: Pulling the Data into Power BI

Whichever method above you use will take you to the Navigator window.

- Right-click on the sheet name "Members" (1)
- Choose Transform Data (2)

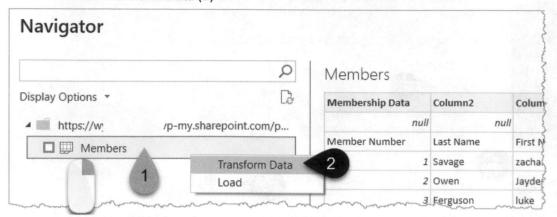

Power Query will try to be helpful and automatically add 2 steps, but in this scenario, it's done the wrong thing.

- Delete the 2 applied steps starting with Changed Type (1) then Promoted Headers (2)

You then need to remove the top few rows that are showing null.

- Click the drop-down for Column2 (3) and click Remove Empty (4)

⚠ When removing rows you need to make a choice between applying a filter or using the Remove Rows option. The choice needs to consider how the data will change in the future and what is the "safest" approach to avoid accidentally removing rows you need to keep.

Now, with the top rows filtered out, you can promote the headers and pick the columns you need to keep.

- Click Use First Row as Headers (1)
- Click Choose Columns (2)
- Deselect all columns (3)
- Tick Member Number (4) and Package (5) then click OK

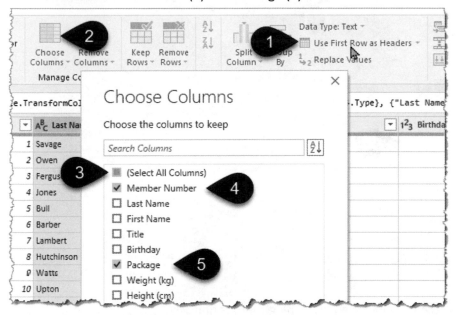

- In the Home menu click Close and Apply

You will then be taken to the Report view.

Step 4: Build a Simple Visual

- Tick Package (1)
- Then also drag Package into the Values Box (2) and change to Count (via 3 and 4)

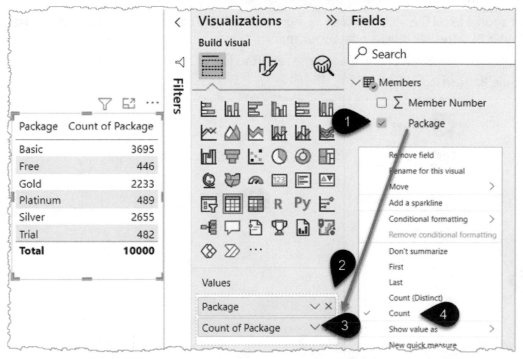

- Save the file to your exercises folder, or wherever you like, and name it "OneDrive Demo"

Step 5: Publish to Your New Workspace

- Publish (1) to the workspace you created
- Click on the blue hyperlink (2) to open the report

> 💡 If you only have MyWorkspace available then publishing there is fine.

Now that you have a report published that is connected to an online data source it's a good time to demonstrate how to set the report to refresh automatically. By doing this, the report is kept up to date without you having to manually open Power BI desktop, click refresh and click publish each time.

Step 6: Set up a Scheduled Refresh

You can now set up your report to refresh multiple times per day. "Refresh" means reconnecting to the source data and pulling in the data again and updating all the report visuals.

This means that if your source Excel file on OneDrive has more rows of data added to it, or if any of the data changes then when Power BI refreshes it will update your report.

- Click on the name of the workspace you loaded the report to (1)
- Click the Schedule Refresh icon (2)

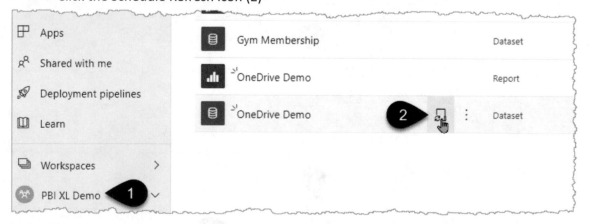

- Click Edit credentials (1) to permit Power BI to connect to your OneDrive file
- Choose the OAuth2 option (2) and then None for Privacy Level Settings (3)

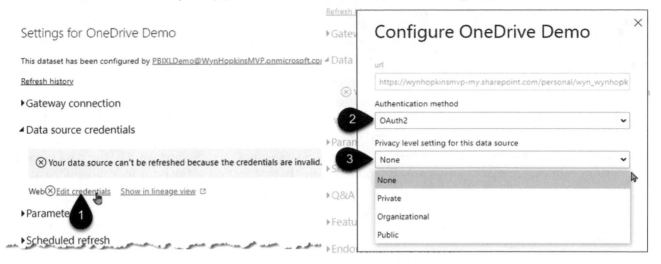

💡 The Privacy levels relate to how different data sources in your model might "interact" with each other when refreshes happen. You may not want Payroll data from one data source being exposed to the Database Admin of another data source when queries refresh. For most Excel users choosing None for all sources or Organizational for all sources is good enough but if you are dealing with sensitive data then you should read up more on this topic starting with this Microsoft Docs article url.pbi.guide/MDpriv.

- Click Sign In, you may need to select your email and enter your password
- Expand Scheduled refresh (1) and click Keep your data up to date (2)
- You can add different times of day to refresh (3)
- Then click Apply

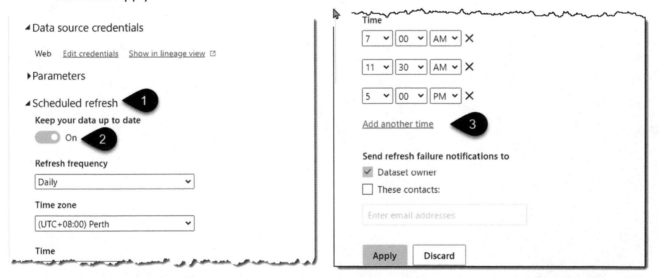

💡 With a Power BI Pro licence you can set up to 8 refresh times per day. If your workspace is set as a Premium Workspace using PPU or Premium Capacity then 48 refreshes are available to you.

You can test if you've got this working properly by opening your Excel file that you saved to OneDrive, changing some data, and then saving the file. Return to this report after your scheduled time of refresh to check if it has been updated.

You can review the last time your report was refreshed by clicking on the name of your workspace in the left-hand panel and reviewing the refresh times.

	Name	Type	Owner	Refreshed ↓	Next refresh
	OneDrive Demo	Report	PBI XL Demo	3/5/22, 5:34:59 PM	—
	OneDrive Demo	Dataset	PBI XL Demo	3/5/22, 5:34:59 PM	3/5/22, 6:00:00 PM

💡 I've found that the scheduled refresh won't happen exactly on time and may even be 10 to 15 minutes late.

Towards the end of chapter 12 it shows how scheduling a refresh is not so straightforward if your data is not an online source. In that scenario, a Gateway is required. Refer to that section of the book for more information.

Chapter 5 - Creating a Power BI Model

You have now seen the end-to-end process of connecting to data, building a few visuals, and publishing your report to a new workspace ready to share with others.

It's now time to tackle a more complex data scenario that uses multiple sources of data and introduces the concepts of Fact Tables, Dimension Tables, the Data Model, and DAX.

- Close your browser and any Power BI desktop files you have open
- Open a new Power BI Desktop file and dismiss any start-up screen

One "helper" feature that you should now disable is the Auto date/time feature which builds hidden date tables with Year, Month, Quarter hierarchies for people who haven't learned about Calendar tables. You're about to use a Calendar table so turn off the auto date/time feature as follows:

- Go to File → Options → Options and Settings
- Untick Auto date/time for new files (1)
- Click OK

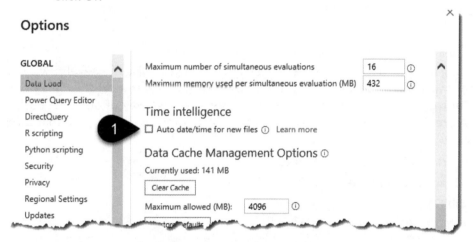

- After making this change close down Power BI Desktop completely

Using a Template File with a Pre-built Calendar Table

- Go to your exercises folder and double-click on the Power BI Template file named "Empty File with pre-built Calendar.pbit"

> 💡 A template file opens as an "Untitled" file which means you don't accidentally save over the original. You can create a template file via File → Export → Power BI Template, this is covered in Chapter 9.

- Immediately save this file with a new name via File → Save As → name it Coffee House Report
- On the Home ribbon click the Excel Workbook icon and navigate to Exercises\Data Sources\Coffee Sales\Coffee Sales Data.xlsx and select that file by double-clicking on it
- Right-click Sheet1 and choose Transform Data

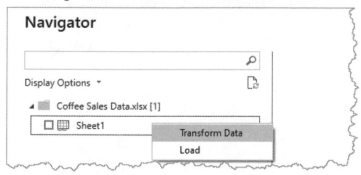

- In the Applied Steps panel on the right-hand side of your screen delete the Changed Type step
- Follow the bullet points below the image to manually change the data types to look like the screenshot

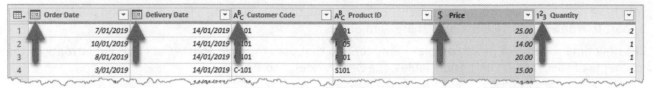

- Change the Order Date and Delivery Date to Date type by using the tip below

💡 Hold Shift while clicking on Order Date and Delivery Date then continue holding Shift when you click on the ABC123 Data Type icon on either column, and change them to the Date option. Both columns are now changed in one go. Date formats will appear based on your Windows System Settings.

- Change the Customer Code and Product ID Data Types to Text
- Change the Price to fixed decimal. This then stores the data with 4 decimal points. Unless you need more than 4 decimals of accuracy the fewer decimals you store in the model the better performance will be if you have huge datasets (millions and millions of rows)
- Change Quantity to whole number
- Re-name the table as SalesData via the Name box in the right-hand panel

Now you're going to do something that will have many experienced Power BI users raise their eyebrows. You are going to add a column that calculates Price x Quantity. The reason for the eyebrow raise is that when you are dealing with millions of rows of data there is a more "memory-efficient" way of doing this using something called a SUMX measure. We'll touch on this later in the book, but for most users, the following approach is simpler to understand:

- Click the heading of the Price column to highlight it (1)
- Hold Ctrl and click the Quantity column heading (2)
- Click the Add Column tab (3)
- Click the Standard button (4) and choose Multiply (5)

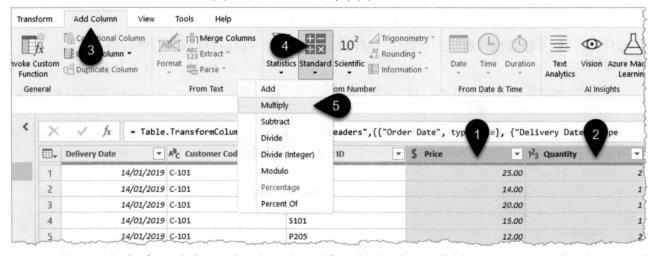

- Click inside the formula bar and replace the red font "Multiplication" (1) with the words "Sales Amount"

💡 To rename the column as Sales Amount you could have double-clicked on the column heading and typed over it. This is fine and adds a new step, but you can "show off" and simply go to the formula bar and replace the red font as you did above.

- Right-click on the "Inserted Multiplication" step (1) and choose Rename (2) Alternatively, you can click on it and press F2
- Rename it as "Calculate Sales Amount "

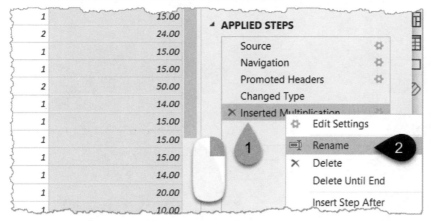

- Click Home → Close and Apply

You should now be in the report view.

- Tick Sales Amount from your SalesData table (1) and it will appear as a column chart
- Drag month from the Calendar table into the X-axis box (2)

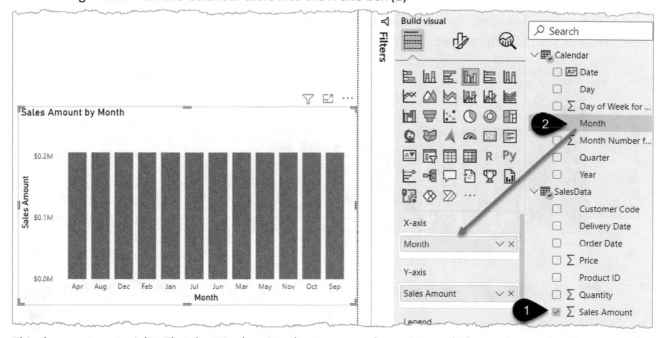

This does not seem right. The chart is showing the same number repeatedly for each month. The reason for that is you haven't yet connected the Calendar to the SalesData. This means the month "filters" in the axis of the chart don't filter the underlying sales data so the Sales Amount being displayed is simply the total of all sales being repeated over and over again.

Creating Relationships Between Tables

- Go to the model view (1)
- Drag Order Date from SalesData to Date in the Calendar table (2) to create a "relationship" between the two tables

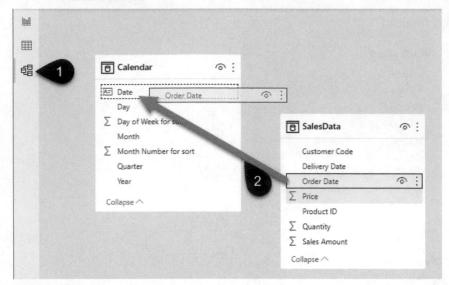

Now go back to your chart and it will look different, this is because the months from the Calendar are now filtering the SalesData table. How this works will be explained in more detail in a few pages time, but for now, you'll finish off fixing up this chart.

- Turn on the data labels via the Format icon → Data labels on (1)
- You can see the value for Sep is $21.8k.

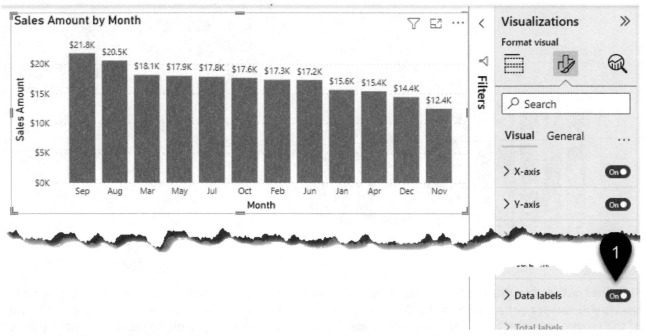

Managing Sort Order

Unfortunately, the chart is currently sorted by Sales Amount in descending order, but it would make more sense to display it in month order.

To force any text label to sort in the order you want there is a special "Sort by column" button.

- Click on the **word** Month in the Fields panel (1). Note that this is **not** the same as ticking the checkbox next to the word
- On the ribbon click Sort by column (2)
- Click Month Number for sort (3)

Nothing will change

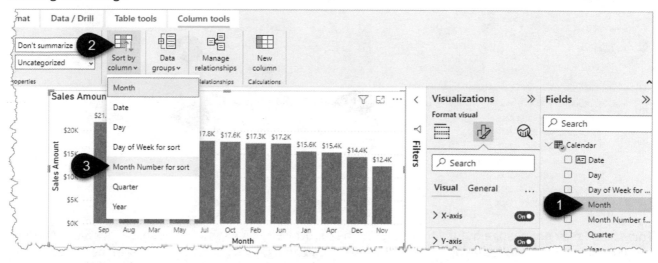

Because you created the chart before you set the Sort By column preference the chart has not changed. Any new chart you create **will** be sorted correctly.

The quickest way to fix the existing chart is to remove the month from the axis by unticking it, then immediately drag month back into the X-axis box. Try it out, you will need to click the icon to the left of the Format icon to show the X-axis fields box.

💡 Remember to set your sort orders before starting to build any visuals!

To understand this sort-order feature:

- Click on the data view icon (1) and select the Calendar table (2)
- Click on the Date Column drop-down (3) icon and click Sort ascending (4)

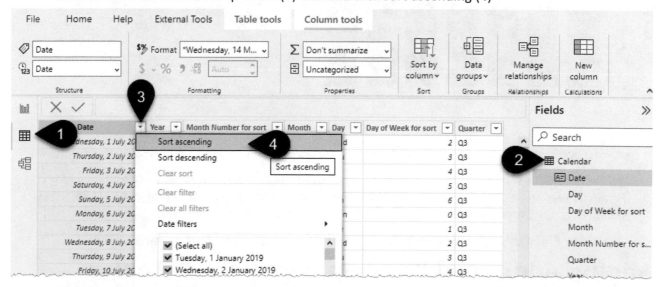

💡 Any sorting or filtering you do in this screen, other than using the Sort by column button, has no impact on anything in your report, it's purely for you to explore your data as the report developer. The people you share the report with via PowerBI.com will not see this screen.

Look at the column "Month Number for sort" and scroll down. You'll see there's a number that corresponds to each calendar month. This is your "Sort by" column.

There is one more sort column available in this view. "Day of Week for sort" is there so that you can ensure your days don't display alphabetically.

- Click on the heading of the Day column to highlight it (1)
- In the Ribbon click Sort by column (2)
- Choose Day of Week for sort (3)

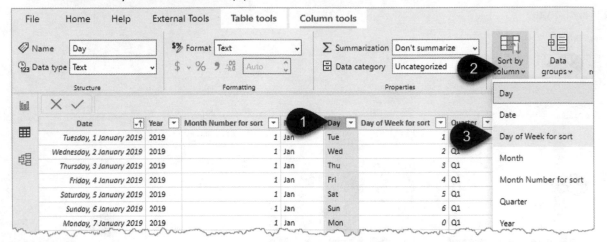

This screen may not change but if you now go to the report view, click some white space, tick Sales Amount from the SalesData (1) followed by ticking Day from the Calendar (2) your chart will display in the correct order.

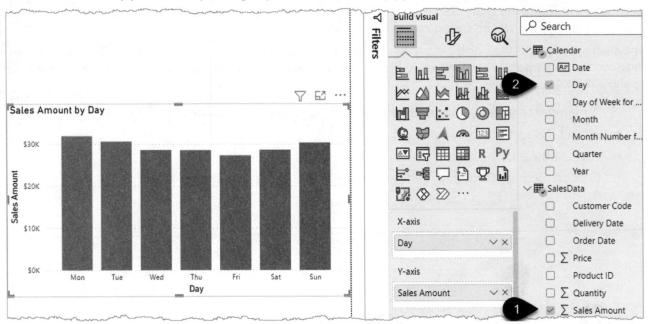

- You don't need to keep this chart so delete it by clicking on the chart and pressing the delete key

💡 This date table has been pre-built for this exercise. A more complete and flexible calendar including Financial Year and a choice of which day of the week is the "start", has been included under Exercises\ Other Files\Calendar File.pbix and we will look at how to use this in Chapter 8.

To see my file at this stage open Solutions\Chapter 5 Coffee House Report Stage 1

Adding Additional "Lookup/Dimension" Tables

A matrix visual is the Power BI equivalent of a Pivot Table and can have labels in rows and columns. Let's add one now:

- Click on some white space and then tick the Matrix Visual icon (1)
- Tick Customer Code (2) and tick Quantity (3)
- Click on the heading Quantity (4) to sort the list in descending order

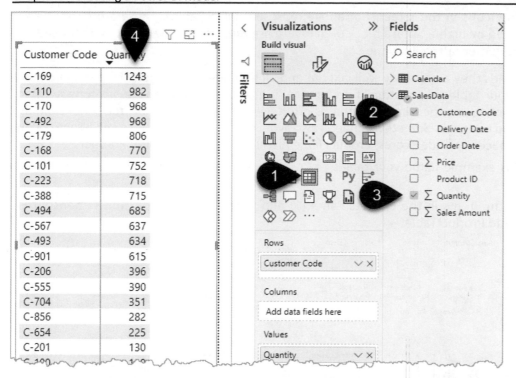

You can see that customer C-169 bought the most items but who is that?

If this was Excel you'd go to the trusty old VLOOKUP, INDEX MATCH, or even better XLOOKUP to "look up" this code from another table containing a list of customer codes, customer names, and maybe other details such as customer location. These tables are often referred to as lookup tables, mapping tables, or dimension tables.

The fantastic thing about Power BI is that you don't need to use any formulas to do this lookup, it's as simple as a drag and drop.

Firstly, you need to pull in the customer and product lookup tables.

- On the Home Tab click the Excel Workbook button and navigate to the Data Sources\Coffee Sales\ Lookup (Dimension) Tables.xlsx file and double-click on it
- Tick tblCustomer and tblProduct (1) then click Transform Data (2)

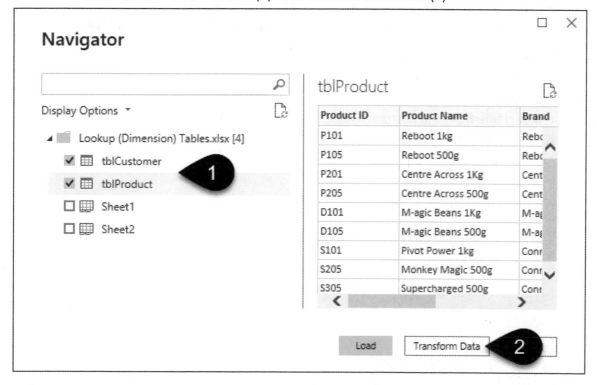

👆 The blue heading icons in the screenshot above represent Excel Tables. These are structure tables in Excel created by highlighting a block of data and pressing Ctrl+T. The Sheet1 and Sheet2 icons are the sheet names in the Excel file.

Looking at the 2 new tables they are already well laid out and all that needs to be done is to rename them. The name you use for your tables is a matter of preference, but whatever you choose, be consistent and be descriptive, I prefer not to use the Dim prefix that is often used in databases (short for dimension) and generally name my lookup tables as "*Something*Table". I also avoid naming my tables the same as any column and prefer not to have spaces or underscores, ProductTable just flows better than Dim_Product.

To follow along with this example name your tables as CustomerTable and ProductTable by following the step below:

- Double-click on the items in the Queries Panel (1) and rename them as per the screenshot i.e. CustomerTable and ProductTable

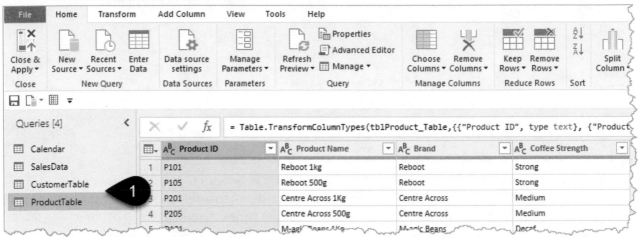

The most important thing is that your Column Data Types are all set correctly (no ABC123 data types) and that your ID/code columns are the same types as your code columns in your SalesData table. They should be fine so you shouldn't need to click anything.

👆 For those of you Excel users that have experienced the fun of wasting half an hour trying to figure out why your VLOOKUP doesn't work only to discover one value is text and one is number you know the issues of having mismatched data type columns. If Customer Code is Text (ABC) in the CustomerTable make sure that Customer Code in the SalesData table is also Text (ABC).

- Click Close and Apply on the home menu
- Click on your Matrix Visual (1) so that it is "active"
- Remove Customer Code by unticking it (2)
- Drag Customer Name from the Customer Table into the Rows (3)

Your matrix should now display by customer name.

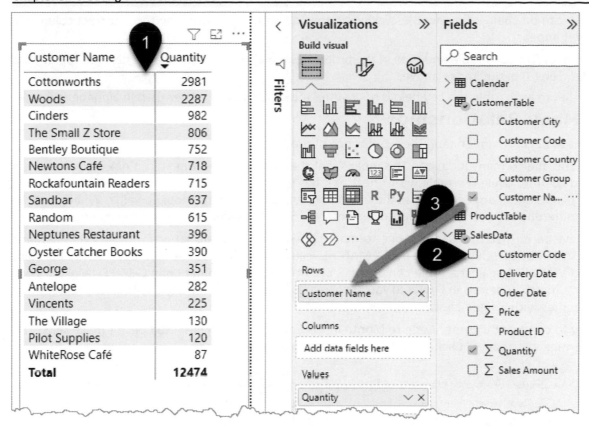

How does this work?

- Click on the Model icon (1) and you should see 4 tables with 3 of them connected to SalesData. If you can't see all 4 then click the autofit icon in the bottom right corner

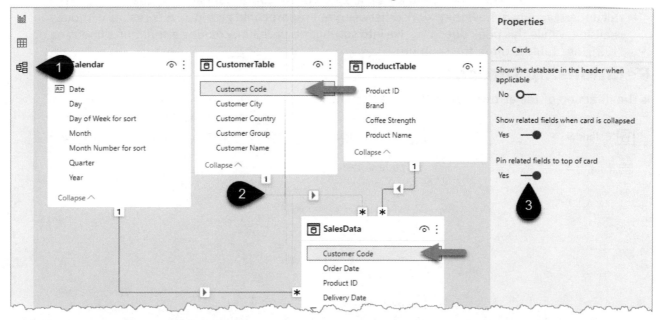

By default, autodetection of relationships is turned on and Power BI was clever enough to recognise that Customer Code in the CustomerTable has common values with the Customer Code in the SalesData table, see (2) above.

The name of the columns are relevant, but it's the common data in those columns that helps the most with the autodetection of the relationship between the 2 tables.

Power BI doesn't always autodetect relationships, or when it does it doesn't always get it right so you should hover over each line to ensure the correct fields have been joined, see (2) above.

A relationship line can be deleted by right-clicking on the line and choosing delete.

A relationship can be changed by double-clicking on the line and then clicking on the 2 correct columns in the tables that appear.

- Click away from any table and then in the properties panel change "Pin related fields to top of card" to Yes, see (3) in the image above.

You will see that in each table the key field is now at the top of each table rather than in alphabetical order.

One to Many Relationships

It's important to begin to understand the significance of the 1 and * icons.

The 1 to * is the one-to-many indicator. This means that the table with the 1 next to it has unique values in its connected column, while the table with * next to it has many occurrences of the key field. For example, the customer code C-169 appears once in the CustomerTable as it's a unique lookup value. While there are hundreds of different occurrences of sales to customer C-169 in the SalesData, this is the many side.

Excel users have performed thousands of one-to-many type relationship calculations without ever hearing of the concept. VLOOKUPS, XLOOKUPS, and INDEX MATCHES can be thought of as one-to-many type relationships. If you write a VLOOKUP against a table containing 2 occurrences of customer code C-169 Excel would only return the first match, whereas in Power BI you are given the option to create a Many-to-Many relationship. This option comes with a significant warning.

e.g. if you try to connect Customer Code to Month in the Calendar, which I realise doesn't make sense, the following warning will appear. Click Cancel if you tried this yourself.

> ⚠ This relationship has cardinality Many-Many. This should only be used if it is expected that neither column (Customer Code and Month) contains unique values, and that the significantly different behavior of Many-many relationships is understood. Learn more

⚠ Until you are an advanced user, avoid Many to Many relationships at all costs. When you do become advanced, still avoid them ☺. Seriously though, you should avoid them until you have a full understanding of how they work otherwise your report could give incorrect results without you realising. While this book doesn't delve into solving this problem, creating a common dimension or "bridging" table is often the solution.

Relationship Direction

Is the direction of the arrows between the tables important?

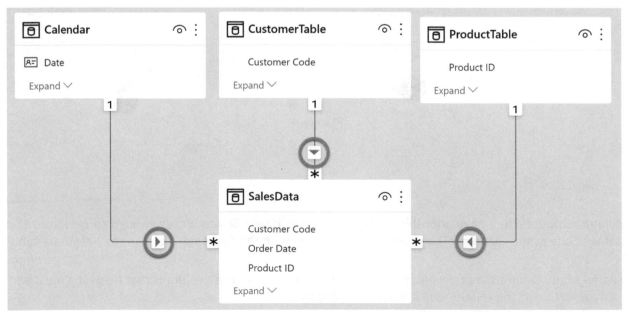

Yes. This is the reason why many people, including me, prefer the method of having our lookup tables "up" at the top of the screen and our fact/transaction tables (the many side) down at the bottom. It's easier to see that the arrows are pointing down towards the Fact tables.

Why is this important? These arrows represent the direction that the filters are flowing, and by this, it means that the items such as City or Customer Name from the CustomerTable can then be used to filter the SalesData.

To help explain this further return to the report view.

- Click on the existing Matrix visual and remove Customer Name (1) by unticking it
- Drag Customer City into the Rows instead (2)

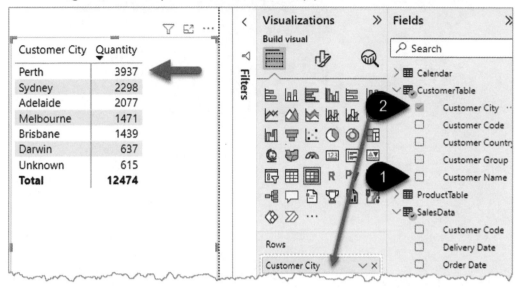

How does Power BI generate the figure of **3937** for Perth?

A key concept to understand early on in your Power BI journey is that it's all about filters.

Row labels in a table or matrix are filters.

Let that sink in.

I'll repeat it.

Row labels in the visual are filters.

Also, the axis of a chart, for example, month or day, is a series of filters.

This is a very different concept to traditional Excel, although PivotTable users have been using this without realizing it for many years.

You can demonstrate this by manually replicating how that figure for Perth of **3,937** is arrived at.

- Click on the Data View icon (1)
- Click on the CustomerTable (2)
- Apply a filter to just show Customer City of Perth (3)

👆 Remember that any "playing about" you do in this view has no impact on your report, this is purely a screen for you to explore your data. In contrast, applying a filter in the Power Query Editor window will remove data from your report.

The Customer Codes are the things to focus on as it's this column that is connected to our SalesData table in the model view. It is these codes that "flow down" the line to the SalesData table and subsequently filter it.

Now replicate these filters impacting the Sales Data by following these steps:

- Go to the Data View (1)
- Click on SalesData (2)
- Filter Customer Code for the 5 Perth Codes (3) C-101, C-110, C-168, C-223, C-388 then click OK

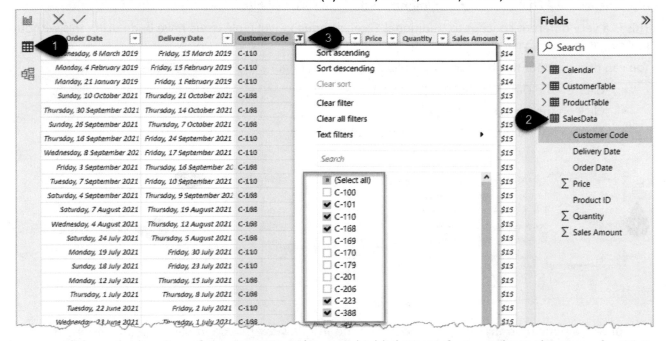

- Click on the heading of the Quantity Column to highlight it. Unfortunately, at the time of writing, Power BI does not show you the SUM of this column, just that there are 3,026 filtered rows
- Right-click and copy the column and paste it into Excel and you will see if you add the values they total to **3,937!**

This filtering happens because of the relationship that was created between the CustomerTable and the SalesData.

To recap, when the values are being calculated in the Matrix visual, the Power BI "engine" performs the following steps:

1. filters the Customer Table for Perth

2. the Perth Customer Codes filter the SalesData table

3. then the SUM of the Quantity column is calculated

This process then gets repeated for each city displayed in the matrix visual.

Customer City	Quantity
Perth	3937
Sydney	2298
Adelaide	2077
Melbourne	1471
Brisbane	1439
Darwin	637
Unknown	615
Total	**12474**

The Total of 12,474 is simply the result if you don't filter for Customer City.

If you turned the matrix into a chart, you'd get the same numbers as the same process is happening in the background. The axis of the chart provides the "filter context" to filter the SalesData before triggering the calculation that "sums" the Quantity column.

> ☕ The true way that Power BI creates the model and related tables behind the scenes via the Power BI "Vertipaq" engine are worthy of entire chapters in a book. It would be wrong of me not to call out "The Definitive Guide to DAX" as a book that covers this granular in-depth explanation for those who love to "get into the weeds". Alberto Ferrari and Marco Russo of SQLBI.com are the undisputed masters in this area and I highly recommend you check out their website and YouTube videos when you are a bit more advanced in your Power BI journey.

You can then add multiple "filters" to a visual.

- Add Year from the Calendar table to the Matrix Visual Columns field (1)

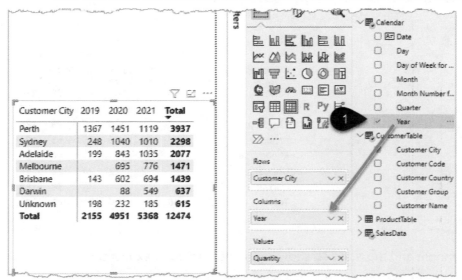

The values are now being calculated after being filtered by both the Year and the Customer City.

- Drag Month underneath Year in the columns field box (2)
- Click the bident (2) to expand out the visual

💡 The bident and other icons may appear below your visual if it is positioned against the top of the screen.

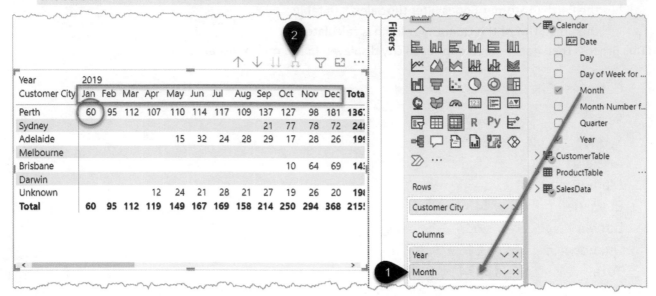

The number 60 for Perth Jan 2019 is being calculated after 2 sets of filters are being applied.

1. The Customer Codes for Perth city filtering the SalesData via the Customer Code column
2. The 31 dates in the Calendar table for Jan 2019 filtering the SalesData via the Order Date column

After the 2 filters above are applied to the SalesData table the Order Quantity column in that filtered table is then summed up to give 60.

To see my file at this stage open Solutions\Chapter 5 Coffee House Report Stage 2

Adjusting Power BI Visuals

Displaying Year and Month on a Chart Axis

The chart you built earlier showed Sales Amount by Month. There was no filter for year, so it was actually displaying 3 years' worth of January results. If you click on the bar for Jan in the chart you will see the Matrix visual shows 3 Jan's – one for each year.

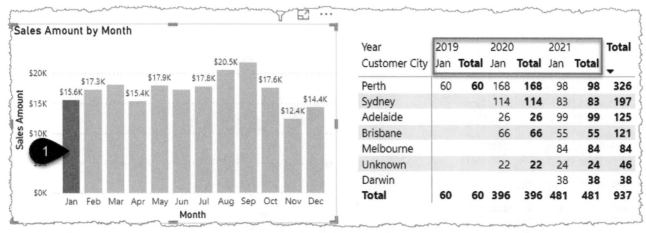

💡 The chart is showing $ Amount and the Matrix is showing Quantity so don't expect the numbers to match.

Add Year to the Chart axis by following the steps below:

- Click on the chart
- Drag Year into the X-axis box above Month (1)
- Click the bident to display Year and Month (2)

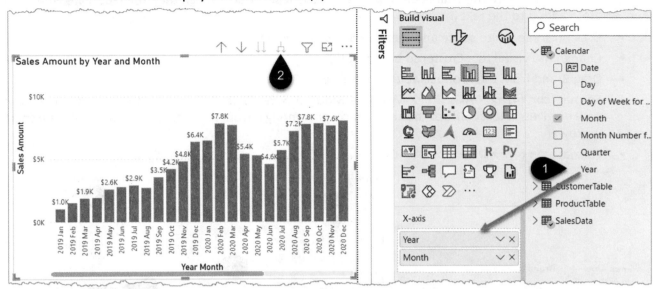

💡 Occasionally the chart doesn't appear as above, instead, Years are grouped together. If this happens click the 3 dots in the top right corner of the chart and choose the Sort Axis → Year Month option.

- Click Format icon (1) → X-Axis (2) → Concatenate labels → Off (3)

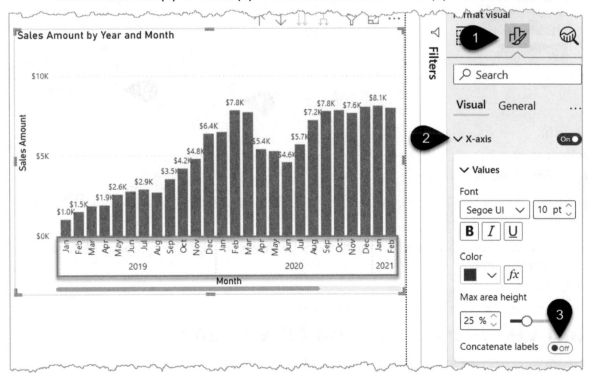

💡 Occasionally you will see a warning sign in the formatting pane. Don't worry nothing is wrong, it is just flagging that your desired text size will not display properly in the space you have given your visual. Making your chart bigger will cause the icon to disappear but if the font looks fine then there's no need to make any change.

Displaying the Full Axis Label in Your Bar Chart

It's good to know how to prevent the horrible truncating of text in your axis label.

For example, if you create the chart below and don't have it set wide enough then the labels are truncated and 3 dots ... added to the text instead.

- Click on some white space and then tick Sales Amount (1)
- Change the visual to a Clustered bar chart (2)
- Drag Brand from the ProductTable into the Y-axis (3)
- Format icon (4) → Y-Axis (5) → Max area width → 50% (6). It's this part that means your label will now be given at least 50% of the chart space, preventing it from truncating when you make the chart narrower
- Format icon (4) → Data labels → On

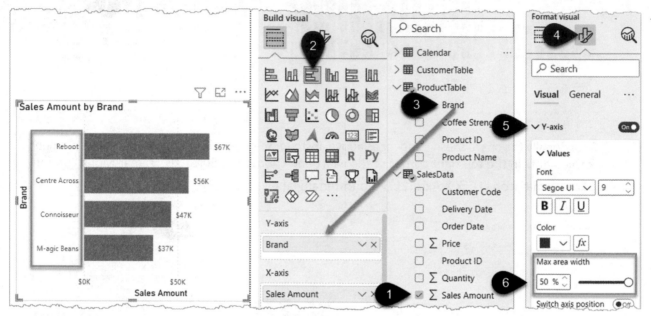

And a final touch:

- Format icon → X-Axis → Title Off
- Format icon → turn off the X-Axis

☕ I hope that one day a fix is applied so that turning off the X-Axis or Y-Axis automatically turns off the Axis Title.

Try out the interaction of the visuals you have built so far by clicking on the different parts of the different visuals and see how they impact each other.

You can hold Ctrl to multi-select.

Click on a selected item a second time to turn off the filter.

Filtering via Slicers and the Filter Panel

There are 2 main ways to allow users to easily apply a "semi-permanent" filter to a page.

Option 1 is the Slicer, which is the most obvious and intuitive to use for report consumers. Option 2 is the Filter Panel, which will take up less screen space and can even be hidden completely from the report consumer.

Slicer

- Click on some white space and click the icon for the slicer visual (1)
- Tick Year from the Calendar table (2)

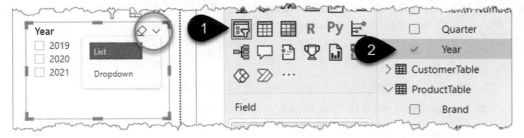

The slicer will appear as a list or you could use the small icon in the corner to change it to a Dropdown. Year is currently set as a "text data type" in Power Query and text slicers default as a list.

Note that if the Year had been set as a number data type, then the slicer would guess that you want a slider style and it would look like the image below. In a scenario where you get the slider style slicer, you can change it via the small v drop-down in the top right corner. Annoyingly the small drop-down will not appear if the "height" of your slicer is not sufficient. If you can't see the v in the top right corner, then make the visual "taller" by dragging the grab handle.

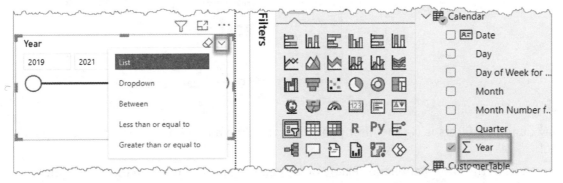

💡 To prevent a slicer defaulting to the slider in the future, either set the number as a text data type in Power Query or click on the word Year in your Fields Pane and select Don't summarize from the summarization drop-down on the Ribbon. You'll see the ∑ disappears and Power BI will no longer try to treat it like a number.

Often the list is exactly what you want, but sometimes it is easier for report consumers to have nice big buttons.

To convert a List into buttons:

- Click on the slicer then click Format icon
- Slicer settings (1)
- Orientation → Horizontal (2)

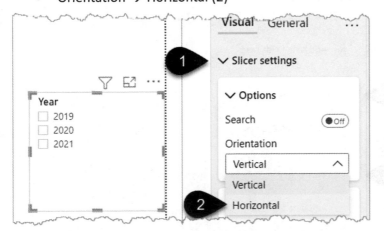

The buttons can now be dynamically re-sized by dragging the corner of the slicer as required. If you just want a single row of icons as per the image below then drag the bottom right corner up and to the right until a single row appears.

☕ Discovering this option is far from intuitive. It still confounds me that this isn't one of the slicer drop-down options. Maybe this will be an option by the time you read this book. It's important to remember that the slicer must be set as a List before this Vertical/Horizontal formatting option can be selected.

Under the Slicer settings, you can also force Single select and enable a Select all button.

To change the size or colour of the font you need to look in the Values section.

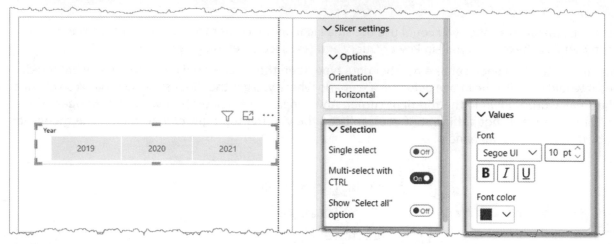

Filter Panel

The alternative way of adding filters is via the filter panel, you can drag any column from your fields panel into the Filter Panel.

There are 2 main sections in the Filter Panel: the "Filters on **all pages**" (1) and "Filters on **this page**" (2). A 3rd section, "Filters on this visual" (3), appears at the top when you click on a visual on your page.

- Click on some white space then drag Coffee Strength from the ProductTable into the "Filters on this page" box (1)
- Tick "Strong" from within that filter panel (2)

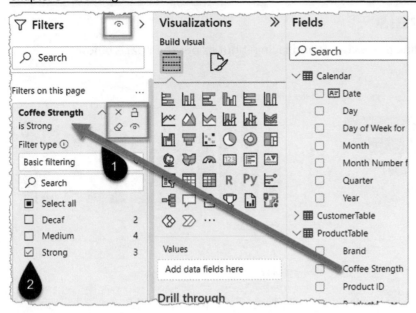

Every visual on that page is now filtered to just show "Strong" coffee. If you want to filter every page in your report just to show strong coffee, then you would put the filter in the "All Pages" box instead.

The Filter Panel includes several options that impact how the report consumer can interact with the filters. You can hide the entire panel, hide specific filters, or lock filters so the report consumers can see them but cannot change them.

The choice of whether to use slicers or filters is a personal design choice and depends on the scenario.

If you are not sure what filters are being applied to one of your visuals simply hover over the filter icon in the top (or bottom) corner of the visual (1) and it will display the filters affecting it.

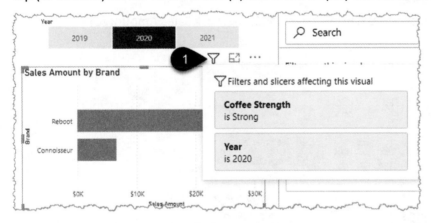

- Remove the Filter for Coffee strength by returning to the filter panel, hover over the title "Coffee Strength" and click the small x (1) next to the padlock symbol

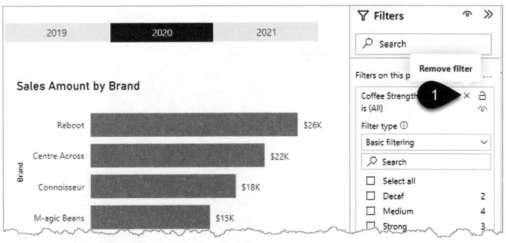

Exploring More Visuals

You'll now complete your report by adding more visuals and laying it out as per the image below.

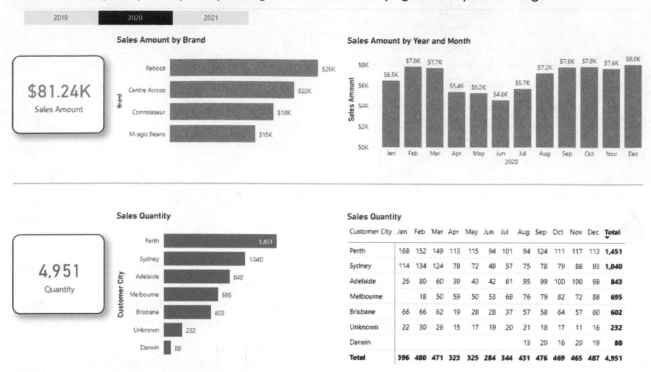

Create a Card Visual for Sales Amount

- Click on the Year 2020 in your slicer
- Click on some white space then click the Card Visual Icon (1) then tick Sales Amount (2)
- Click the Format icon (3)

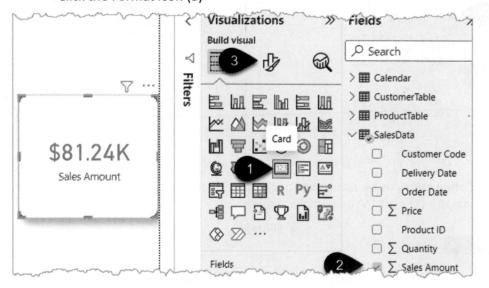

- Click Callout value → Color → Blue (1) and Font 30 (2)

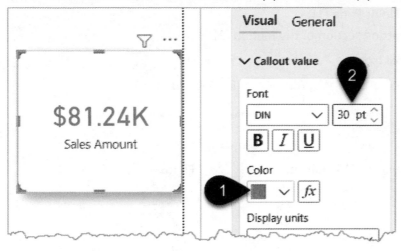

- General (1) → Effects (2) →
  - Visual Border On (3) & Rounded Corners 15 px
  - Shadow On (4)

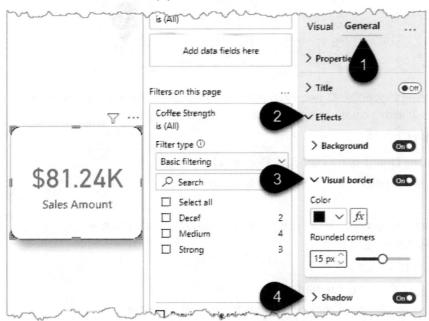

Create a Card Visual for Quantity by duplicating the Sales Amount Card as follows:

- Copy Paste the existing Card Visual (Ctrl+C Ctrl+V)
- Remove Sales Amount by unticking it from the Fields Pane and then tick Quantity
- Format icon → Visual section → Callout value → Color → Orange

Change the default number format to have a comma separator for thousands as follows:

- Click on the word Quantity in the Fields Pane (1)
- Click the Comma icon in the Formatting section of the Ribbon (2)

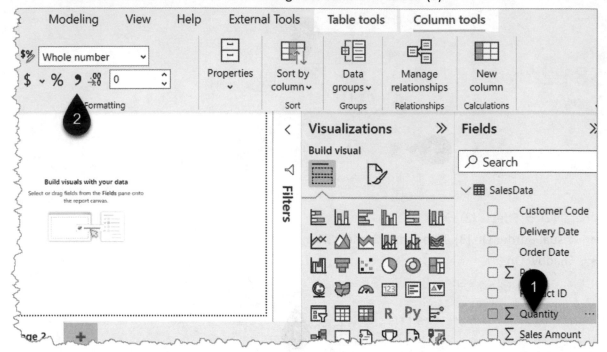

This is now the default number formatting whenever Quantity is used in a visual. You will see that the number in the Card visual and the totals in the Matrix visual are also now displaying with commas.

Format the Matrix Visual

- Click on the Matrix showing sales Quantity by Year and Month (1)
- Remove Year from the columns by unticking it from the Fields panel
- Click on the Format icon (2)
- General (3) →Title On → expand drop-down and type "Sales Quantity" in the Text box
- Visual (4) →Style presets (5) → Minimal
- Grid (6) → Border → Orange
- Grid→ Options→ Row Padding → 6 (this is the name for row height)
- If your Total (7) isn't sorted Max to Min then click on the word Total (7) to sort it

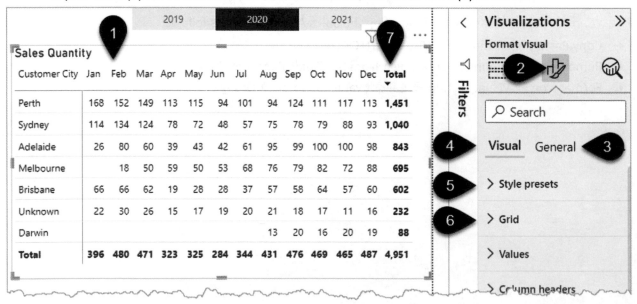

Add a Bar Chart for Sales Quantity

- Click on white space and click Clustered Bar Chart icon (1)
- Tick Quantity (2)
- Drag Customer City into the Y-axis (3)
- Click Format Icon (4) and turn Data Labels On
- Data Labels → Values → Display Units → None (this stops larger numbers displaying as 'k)
- Bars → Colors → Orange
- X-Axis → Title Off, then turn the X-Axis Off
- General → Title → type "Sales Quantity" in the Text box

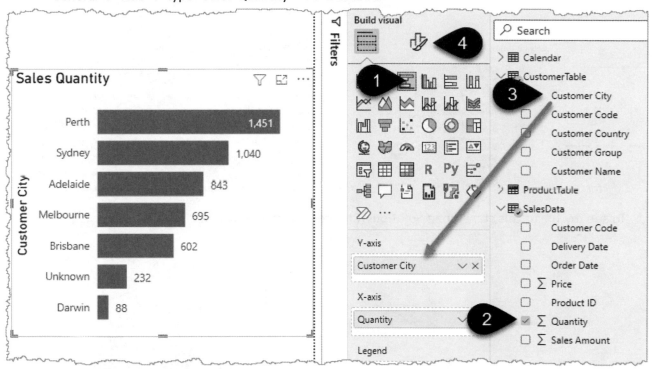

Insert a Line Correctly

- Click on the Insert Ribbon → Shapes → Line
- Drag the corner of the image to resize and position it to split the page horizontally
- Ensure the height of your line visual is as reduced as possible to save it overlapping other visuals

- To change the colour, click on the line, go to the Format shape menu that appears on the right, and choose Style → Border → Color and pick a light blue with Transparency of 20%

☕ Needing to set the border colour for a line is not intuitive and again is one of those little things that I hope the Power BI team fix one day. Similarly, to draw a vertical line, you need to choose Format Icon → Rotation → All 90. And yes, that does seem overly complicated for such a common need.

You should now have a page that looks like the screenshot from a few pages earlier.

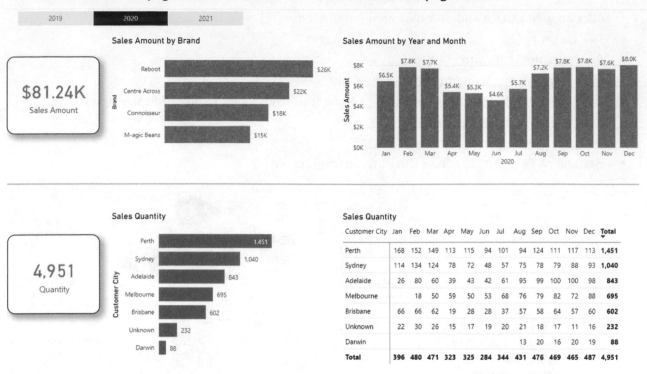

To see my file at this stage open Solutions\Chapter 5 Coffee House Report Stage 3

Chapter 6 - Getting Your Data into the "Right Shape"

A key part of making your life easier when it comes to analysing your data is to realise that it's all about using correctly structured tables of data. Each "type of thing" in your table needs to be a single column. For example, Customer Code is a single column, Sales Amount is a single column, Delivery Date is a single column, you get the idea.

Often, however, it's up to you (and Power Query) to convert the source data from a less useful layout into a shape that is good for Power BI. When you start writing formulas, which are covered in a Chapter 7, you'll find that overly complex formulas are often a result of not structuring your data in the ideal way to begin with.

The classic example of incorrect data layout is when the source data is laid out like a matrix with months or years running across the columns.

The screenshot below is from the Adelaide Budget file which can be found in Exercises\Data Sources\Coffee Sales\Regional Budgets\

	A	B	C	T	U	V	W	X
1	Customer City	Customer Name	Customer Code	202005	202006	202007	202008	202
2	Adelaide	Sandbar	C-567	430	430	390	390	
3	Adelaide	The Small Z Store	C-179			190	830	
4	Adelaide	Woods	C-493	560	570	160	220	
5	Total			990	1000	740	1440	1.
6								
7								

You can see that Year and Month are laid out in columns. This is a very common layout. It is easy to type in and read data in this format but if you have ever tried to create a PivotTable from data like this you will know it's a bad experience. You need to drag all the months individually into the Values box, some of them change to "Count" and trying to total them by year is horrible!

Look at the image below, don't do this!

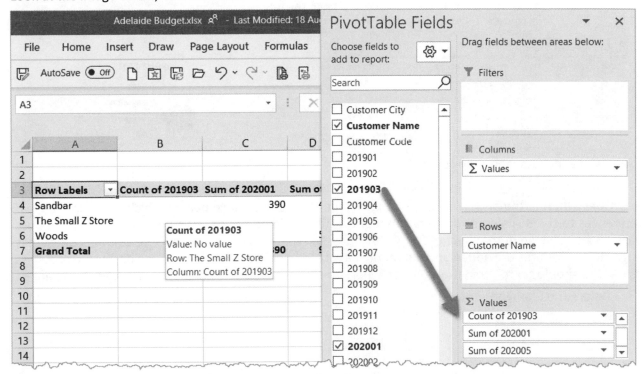

The fantastic news is that Power Query can solve this issue with a few simple clicks.

Power Query's Two Best Features in One Chapter!

Power Query's 2 best features, in my opinion, are:

1. "Unpivot Other Columns" - the ability to take a wide matrix style layout and flip it into a narrower longer table with correctly structured columns

2. The ability to consolidate multiple files from a folder

> ☕ When I first saw how easily Power Query could convert data from a matrix type layout into a useful data structure I was blown away and knew it was something that I had to learn more about. Then a few years later when the automatic file consolidation feature was added it was a true "drop-the-mic" moment for me.

To illustrate this, you will first learn how to "Unpivot Other columns" on one budget file. Then you will take this knowledge a step further and use it while combining all the budget files in a folder into one beautifully structured budget table.

⚠ If you opened the Adelaide Excel file make sure you now close it otherwise Power Query may not be able to connect to it.

Unpivoting Other Columns

- In your Coffee House Report Power BI file click the Excel Workbook button on the Home ribbon
- Find the Adelaide Budget Excel file under Exercises\Data Sources\Coffee Sales\Regional Budgets\ and double-click on it
- When the navigation window opens, right-click on Sheet 1 and select Transform data
- Click on the Changed Type step (1) and expand out the formula bar (2) you will see that Power Query has tried to be helpful and work out the data types, but referencing all these unnamed columns at this stage is not what you need

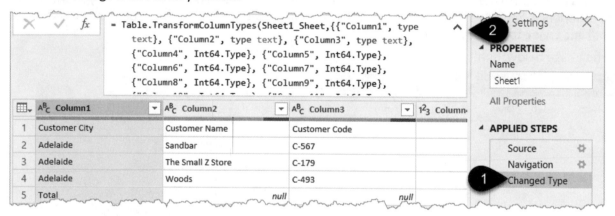

- Delete the Changed Type step
- Click Use First Row as Headers (1 see image below)

Power Query then automatically adds a Changed Type step (2 see image below) which now "hard codes" in references to the 36 columns of years and month. This would be fine to leave if those column names are never going to change in that budget file, but it's possible that in the real world these column names may change as new months are added and old months are removed. To make your solution as "future proof" as possible you should try to avoid the situation where the formula refers to column names that may change.

- Delete the Changed Type step (2)

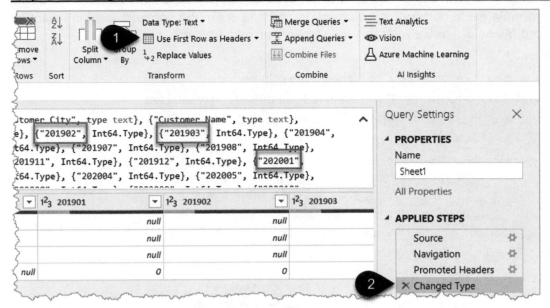

You don't need the Total row in the Custom City Column.

- Right-click on the word Total (1) and select Text Filters → Does Not Equal (2)

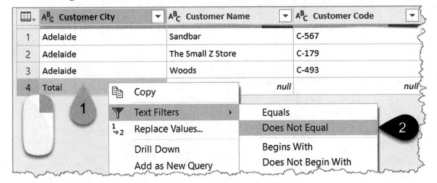

A new step will be added labelled "Filtered Rows". Rename this as "FILTERED OUT Totals"

> 💡 I'd recommend using CAPITAL LETTERS for your Filtering steps as it helps them to stand out. I have found that it's very useful to be able to scan down a set of steps and spot the ones that are removing (filtering out) items.

You may be wondering why you didn't just click the drop-down for Customer City (1) and "untick" Total (2) as per the screenshot below. Look at the resulting formula in the screenshot below, it would have been ="Adelaide" rather than <> "Total".

The below screenshot is just for information, there's no need to replicate it.

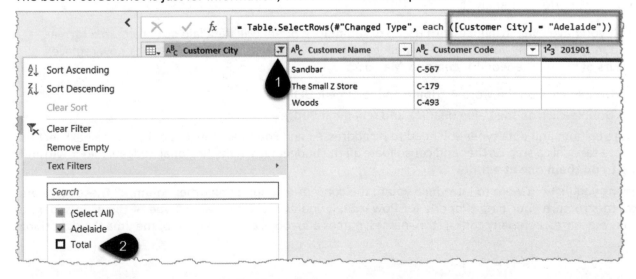

Always review the formula to check it is doing what you intend it to do. In this scenario, we don't want to hard code in the word "Adelaide" as we want this code to work on data from other cities.

Now comes the magic.

- Click on the heading "Customer City" to highlight the column
- Hold SHIFT and click on "Customer Code" so that 3 columns are now selected
- Right-click on one of those headings (1) and choose Unpivot Other Columns (2)

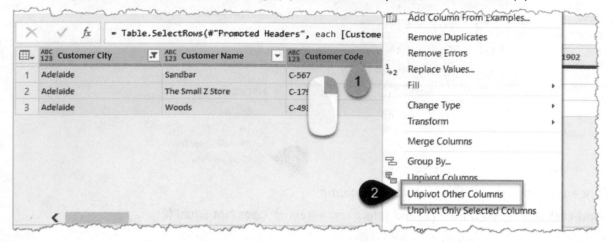

Your data should now look like this:

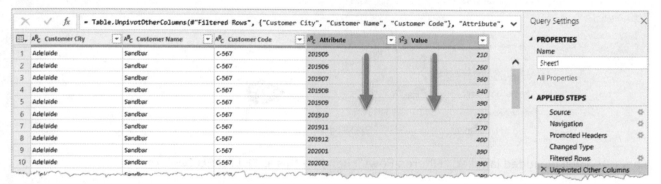

So what just happened?

The 36 individual date columns were converted into a single column of dates called "Attribute" and all the corresponding numbers are now in a column called Value.

For customer Code C-567 there are now 32 rows of dates. Wait, why not 36 rows? The reason is that the first 4 columns of dates for C-567 had "null" in them as there was no data for those months, the Unpivot Other Columns feature removes nulls.

This is almost perfect for analysis.

> ☕ If you have ever struggled with trying to summarise or analyse data laid out in a matrix format you may be shaking your head in disbelief at how easy that was. A single right-click now replaces hours of manual re-work or complex Macros.

- Double-click on the word Attribute and rename it Date
- Double-click on the Value heading and rename it Budget

The Date column and data types still need to be addressed and you'll see how to do that in the next section where we take this a step further and consolidate **all** the budget files in the Regional Budgets folder **without having to do them one at a time!**

The steps you just did were to introduce you to the concept of **Unpivoting other columns**. These steps are critical to structure your data properly for Power BI. If you ever see the same "type of thing" in separate columns e.g. dates, company codes, store names, names of people, etc. then most of the time the right thing to do is unpivot the data. In this exercise Customer City, Customer Name, and Customer Code were already structured in their own columns so you highlighted those first and then "Unpivoted **Other** columns".

You don't need to keep this single Adelaide table for the rest of these lessons.

- Right-click on Sheet1 in the left-hand queries panel (1) and Delete it (2)

⚠ Remember there is no undo in Power Query so don't delete the wrong one!

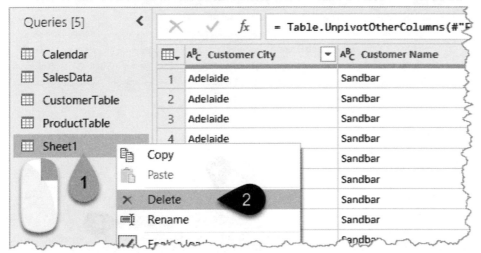

- Click Close and Apply
- If a yellow bar appears indicating Pending Changes click Discard Changes

Consolidating Multiple Files from a Folder

Building on what you've just learned, now it's time to take it up a step and consolidate all the budget files in the Regional Budget folder, unpivoting each one as they are "sucked in" to Power BI.

💡 Power Query can consolidate Excel, Text, and CSV files and pretty much any type of file it can connect to via the Get Data experience.

- Click the Get data button (1). Just click the button itself, not the drop-down
- Double-click on Folder (2)

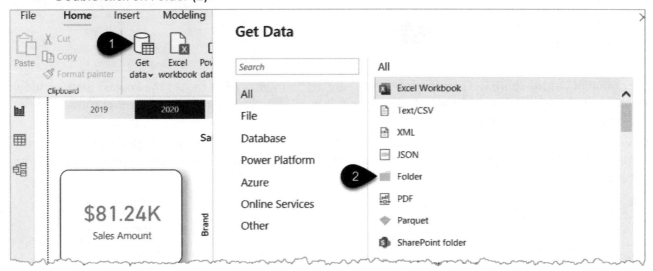

- Click the Browse button and navigate to the folder Exercises\Data Sources\Coffee Sales\Regional Budgets and click OK to select it and then OK again on the next screen
  - On the screen that appears click the drop-down on the Combine button (1)
  - Click Combine & Transform Data (2)

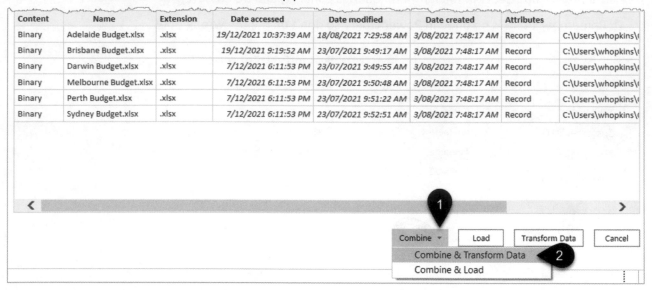

- In the next window that appears right-click on Sheet1 (1)
- Click Transform Data (2)

At the time of writing there is a bug that's been around for many years that causes the Power Query window to become hidden behind your Power BI window at this point. Simply minimize your Power BI window to see the Power Query editor window.

You will see that all your files have been combined and stacked (appended) on top of each other, which is very promising, but the layout is bad with repeated heading rows and the months are in that horrible multi-column matrix layout style.

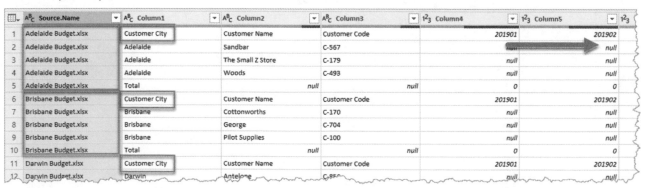

In order to convert and unpivot each file before the append happens you need to create a set of "clean-up" rules to apply to each file as they are being imported.

- Click on the Transform Sample File (1)

This shows the first file in your folder and is part of 4 "helper" elements that the Combine from Folder step automatically created.

You will now repeat the clean-up steps you did earlier on the Adelaide file.

- Click the Use First Row as Headers button on the home tab
- Delete the Changed Type step to avoid hard coding the references to the different months
- Right-click on the word Total (1) and select Text Filters → Does Not Equal (2)

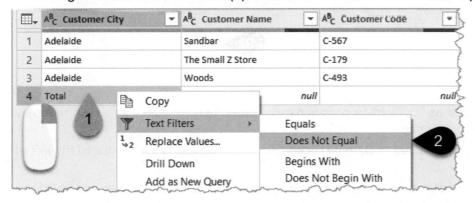

- Click the heading Customer City and hold Shift and Click Customer Code in order to select the first 3 columns
- Right-click on the Customer Code heading (1) and choose Unpivot Other Columns (2)

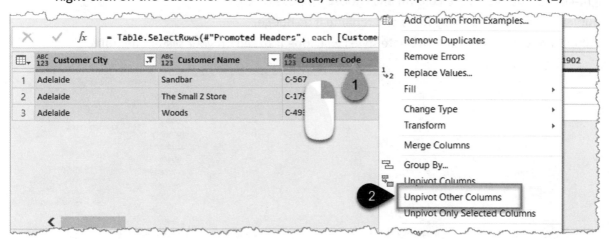

The Attribute needs to be converted to a date from its current format of 201905, 201906, etc. You could use the very clever right-click Add Column from Examples to add a 01 to each Year and Month, however, for learning purposes, you will use the Custom Column option instead to add 01 to then end of each "date" to make 20190501, 20190601 etc:

- Click the Add Column menu then the Custom Column button (1)
- In the New column name box type Date (2)
- Double click on the word Attribute in the right-hand window (3)
- Type & "01" (4)

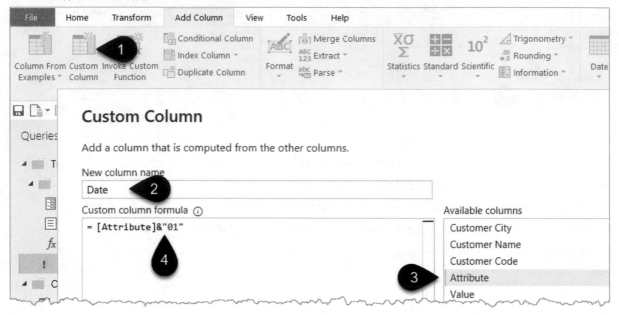

- Click OK
- Rename your applied step as "Convert to proper date". Remember, you can edit a step name by pressing F2 or via right-click Rename.
- Change the Data Type from ABC123 to Date by clicking on the small ABC123 indicator to the left of the word Date
- Change the Date to the end of the month by right-clicking on the Date column and choosing Transform → Month→ End of Month.

☕ I love the simplicity of this End of Month feature!

- Right-click on the Attribute column and choose Remove
- Double-Click on the heading Value and rename it as Budget

Your table should now look like this. The date styles will appear based on your system defaults.

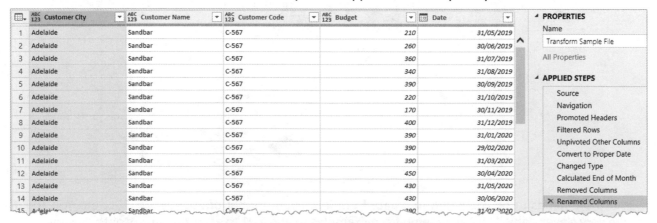

💡 There is no need to change the Data Types for all the columns in the Transform Sample File, in fact, at the time of writing, those data types do not flow through into the final consolidated table.

- Click on the Regional Budgets query (1) and you will get an error

This often happens after cleaning up the Transform Sample file. It's normally simply a case of deleting the Changed Type Step.

- Delete the Changed Type step (2)

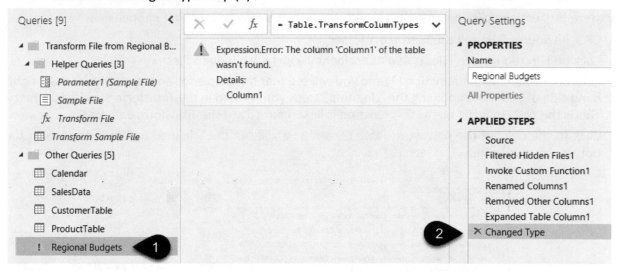

You should see all your data magically unpivoted into a perfect table structure as per the image below. The set of instructions you just created in the Transform Sample File is applied to each file in the folder.

You can now either manually set your Data Types one column at a time by clicking each ABC123 icon or alternatively use this shortcut:

- Select any column or click on any "cell" in your table
- Press Ctrl+A to highlight All columns
- Click the Transform tab followed by the Detect Data Type button (1)

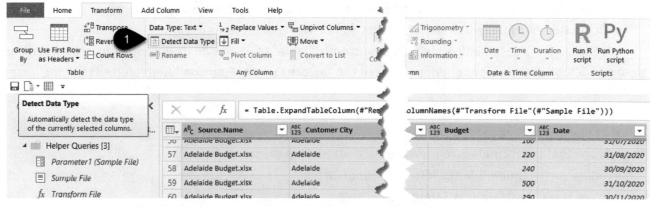

- Right-click on the first column called Source.Name and click Remove
- Rename your query from Regional Budgets to BudgetData (1)

AB C Customer Code	1²₃ Budget	Date
C-567	210	31/05/2019
C-567	260	30/06/2019
C-567	360	31/07/2019
C-567	340	31/08/2019
C-567	390	30/09/2019
C-567	220	31/10/2019
C-567	170	30/11/2019
C-567	400	31/12/2019
C-567	390	31/01/2020
C-567	390	29/02/2020
C-567	390	31/03/2020
C-567	450	30/04/2020

What are these other steps in the BudgetData query highlighted in the orange box above?

For those keen to understand the magic of what just happened please read on, or for anyone else feel free to skip the rest of this section and live with the simple joy that this magic just works ☺.

Follow these instructions clicking on each applied step one at a time to see what happens:

- Click on Source: Lists all the files in the folder
- Click on Filtered Hidden Files1: Avoids accidentally including hidden files
- Click on Invoke Custom Function (1) and you will see that this step adds an extra column to the right-hand side of your data applying the "clean-up" steps you created in the Transform Sample File query. This is the truly magical bit, as this function is linked directly to the Transform Sample File
- Click to the right of the first word Table (2) and you will see the "cleaned up" data appears at the bottom of your screen

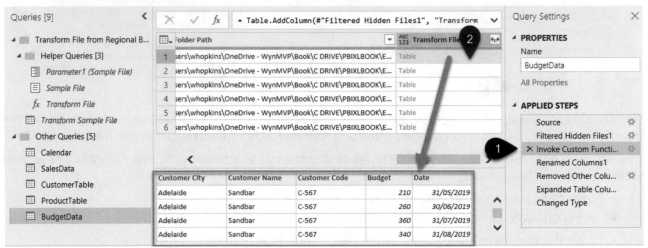

- Click Renamed Columns1: A simple rename of the Name column to Source.Name
- Click Removed Other Columns1: Leaves Source.Name and the Transform File column
- Click Expanded Table Column1: Opens up each "Table" to display all the information inside each one

Now take a look at the helper queries that feed the "Invoke Custom Function" step referred to in the image above.

- Click on Transform Sample File (1)
- Click on the Source Step (2)

You will see that the formula is referring to Parameter1 (see the image below).

- Click on Parameter1 in the left-hand panel (3)

You will see it simply references Sample File.

- Click on Sample File in the left-hand panel (4)

You will see it references =Source{0}[Content]. This means it is taking the first file from the folder. Power Query refers to the first record as 0 and the 2nd as 1 etc. This is confusing for new users.

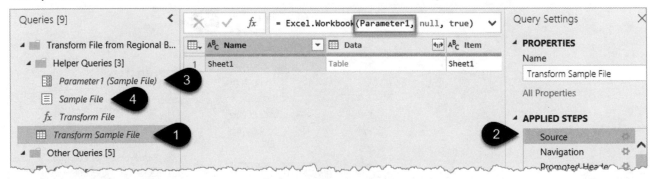

- Click on the Transform File function (1) per the image below

This function is magically linked directly to the Transform Sample File query so that any transform steps you make to the Transform Sample file automatically get converted into this function.

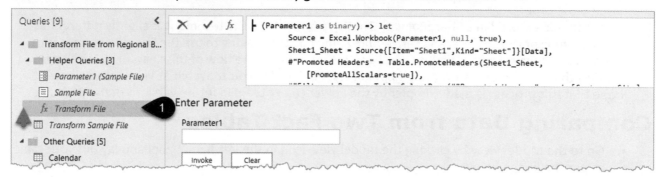

⚠ If you ever try to make changes directly to the function you will receive a warning that the link between the query and the function will be permanently broken.

For those of you that skipped that explanation, we resume our story here…

Organising Power Query Elements into Folders

There is one more thing you can do to make your code easier to understand in the future and that is to put your BudgetData query and the Transform Helper Queries into a single folder that you then rename as "Budget from Files in Folder".

- Right-click on the BudgetData Query in the left-hand panel
- Move to Group → New Group (1)

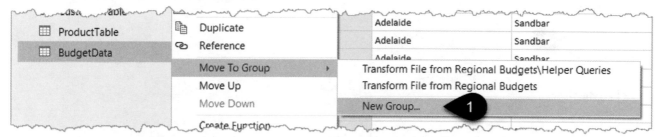

- Name that Group as "Budget from Files in Folder" and click OK
- Drag the folder called Transform File from Regional Budgets into that new folder

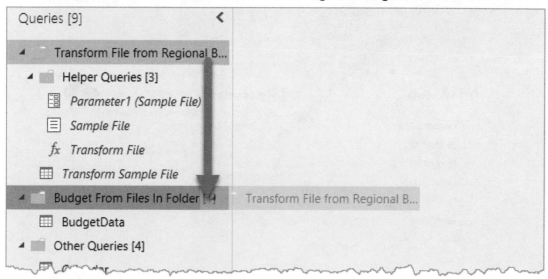

💡 This is purely a way of keeping your related queries organised together. It has no impact on how Power Query works.

- Click Home→ Close and Apply

☕ If you had to minimize the Power BI Desktop screen earlier on because the Power Query window was not showing, then you will need to click on the Power BI desktop icon on your taskbar to display the report.

If your files are stored in a SharePoint or OneDrive folder then the technique is slightly different at the beginning of the process, and can require some minor tweaking to use the SharePoint.Contents connector rather than SharePoint.Files. I don't want to break the flow of this chapter so I will share a video that I made on this topic url.pbi.guide/SPFolder for you to watch at your convenience. I hope that this process is made simpler by the Power Query team in future versions of the product.

Comparing Data from Two Fact Tables

- Go to the Model view by clicking the model view icon in the left-hand panel and lay out your tables as per the image below
- Note that a relationship has been auto-detected between the BudgetData and the Customer table. Hovering over the line shows you that the Customer Code fields have been connected.

Linking the Facts to Common Dimensions

- An important point to note is that you should avoid directly linking two Fact Tables to each other. It would be tempting to link Customer Code from BudgetData to Customer Code in SalesData but the best approach is to link them to a common Dimension Table instead. Trying to link Fact Tables to each other could lead to confusing Many to Many relationships or could result in errors in your report due to codes in one table not existing in the other table.

- Drag Date from the BudgetData to Date in the Calendar (1) to connect those two tables

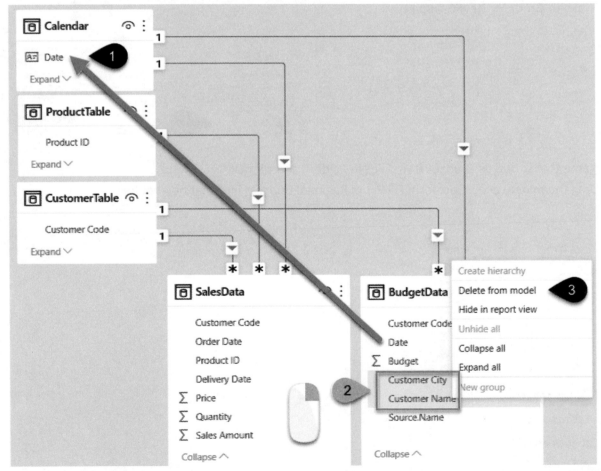

Looking at the BudgetData we can see we have Customer City and Customer Name, but these fields already exist in our CustomerTable, so we don't need them in the BudgetData.

Remove Customer City and Customer Name from the BudgetData table in a single step as follows:

- In the BudgetData table, as per the previous image, click on Customer City, hold Ctrl, click on Customer Name
- Right-click (2) per the previous image. Delete from model (3)

Removing unnecessary columns can make your reports work quicker and avoids confusion with repeated columns containing similar information in different tables.

Removing columns this way adds a step to Power Query. To see this follow these steps:

- Click on the Transform data button in the ribbon
- Click on BudgetData from the left-hand panel and you will see a new "Removed Columns" step has been added
- Close the Power Query window to return to the report

💡 There is no product information in the BudgetData, it's purely a Customer Level budget so there will be no connection to the ProductTable.

To see my file at this stage open Solutions\Chapter 6 Coffee House Report Stage 1

Visualising the Data

- Return to the Report View by clicking the Report icon in the left-hand panel
- Add a new Page to your report (click the yellow + next to page 1)
- Rename it by double-clicking on the name "Page 2" and typing Actual v Budget

Create the chart shown below by following these steps:

- Click the Line and Clustered Column chart icon (1)
- Drag Year and Month from the Calendar table into the X-axis (2)
- Drag Sales Amount from the SalesData table into the Column y-axis box (3)
- Drag Budget from the BudgetData table into the Line y-axis box (4)
- Click on the "bident" icon on the chart to drill down into Months (5)

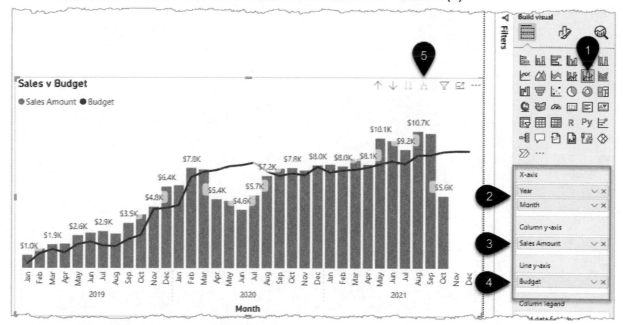

Add some additional formatting to the chart above:

- Click the Formatting Icon
- Click General→ Title and type in Sales v Budget
- Click Visual→ X-axis and turn off the X-Axis Title and turn off Concatenate Labels
- Click Visual → Y-axis and turn the Y-axis Title off and then turn the Y-axis Off
- Click Visual → Data labels on

You will see that the labels looked crowded as the chart is showing values for the Sales and the Budget.

- Under the Data labels drop-down change "Apply settings to" and choose Budget → Show data labels → Off

Now that you have the base data imported and nicely structured it is time to start adding some calculations such as Sales Variance, Cumulative Year to Date Sales, and Actual Sales v Prior Year.

Calculations in Power BI are called measures. Measures are written using a formula language called DAX.

Strap in as the power is about to turn up to 11...

To see my file at this stage open Solutions\Chapter 6 Coffee House Report Stage 2

Chapter 7 - DAX (Data Analysis eXpressions)

Rather than some long preamble describing what DAX is and how it works let's just jump "feet first" into a few examples and explain things along the way.

The first goal is to create a calculation for Sales Variance which will be the difference between the Actual Sales and the Budget Sales. DAX calculations are known as "measures" and every measure is given a name.

To make the Variance "measure" as simple as possible you should first create 2 simple base measures, one for Actual Sales and one for Budget Sales. The Variance measure can then refer to these two other measures.

Writing Your First DAX Measure

- Right-click on the SalesData table in the Fields pane (1) and choose New measure (2)

A formula bar will appear. You can use Ctrl and the mouse wheel or Ctrl + to make the text bigger

- Type over "Measure =" with the following formula (3)

```
Actual Sales $ = SUM( SalesData[Sales Amount] )
```

- Press Enter or click the tick to the left of the formula (4)
- Format the measure by clicking on the $ (5) and 0 decimals (6)

☕ If you noticed extra spaces in my formula, then full marks for being eagle-eyed! I'm in the habit of using spaces liberally in my formulas. I do the same thing when writing Excel formulas. I find it easier to read and see where the square/round brackets end. Don't however try to use SalesData [Sales Amount] as that space between the table name and column name is not valid.

You will see that the measure appears in the SalesData table in the right-hand fields panel with a calculator icon next to it.

- Click on some white space on the canvas
- Click the Card Visual (1) and then tick your new measure (2)

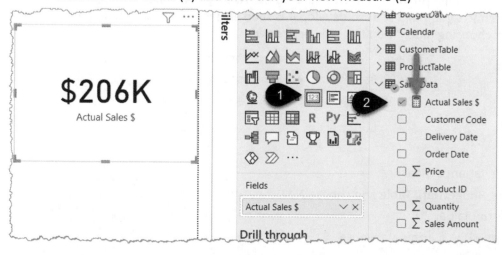

Now repeat this for Budget Sales $ by following these steps:

- Right-click on the BudgetData table and choose New measure
- Type over "Measure ="

  ```
  Budget Sales $ =SUM( BudgetData[Budget] )
  ```

- Press Enter then format as $ and 0 decimals

The new measure appears in the BudgetData table.

- Add this new Budget Sales $ measure to a Card visual

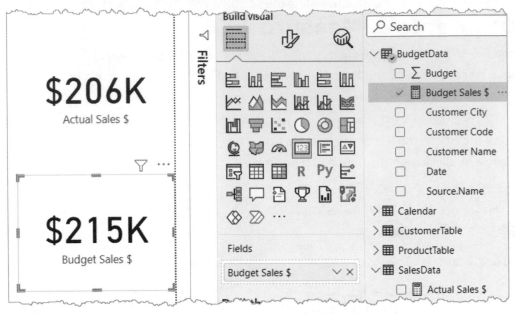

Having a column in your BudgetData table called "Budget" could be confusing, even more so if you had also named your table as Budget.

Imagine your Budget measure being `Budget = SUM( Budget[Budget] )` !!!

- Right-click on the word ∑ Budget in your BudgetData table and rename it as "Budget Column" to flag it as a column

  💡 This change automatically adds an extra step into your Power Query process.

  ⚠ A measure cannot (and should not) have the same name as a column in the same table. I'd also recommend avoiding Table names having the same name as columns or measures. Product[Product] or Date[Date] just seems a little confusing to me.

You will also see people recommending that you immediately hide your "Budget Column" once you've created a measure to avoid accidental use. I however wouldn't hide things until you've finished building your report, especially when you are new to writing measures. The reason for this is it's a useful reference to see that source column if you need to build further measures such as the Average or Max. However, once you are more confident and the reports you build start to develop it is seen as good practice to hide those columns by clicking the 3 dots and choosing hide. *Don't do this right now*

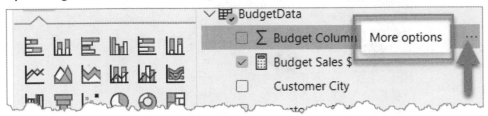

Now it's time to write the Variance measure.

- Right-click on your BudgetData Table and choose New measure
- Type this in the formula bar

  ```
  Variance Sales $ = [Actual Sales $]-[Budget Sales $]
  ```

💡 You will see that "IntelliSense" shows your existing measures as soon as you type the square bracket [.

- Press Enter
- Format it as $ with 0 decimals
- Add this new measure to a Card Visual
- With the new Card visual selected click the Format Icon (1) followed by Callout value (2) and change the Display units to Thousands (3)

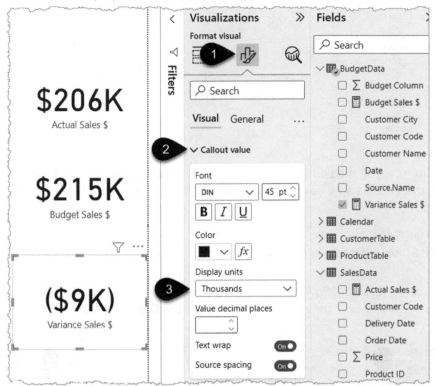

- Click on the Year 2019 in the Axis of your chart (1) and see the card values change
- Click on 2020 and see what happens (2)

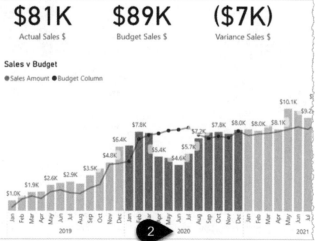

- Click on some white space in the chart to turn off the filter

You'll now add one more visual and then we'll pause for some explanations and best practice recommendations.

- Click on some white space and choose the Table Visual (1)
- Tick Customer City from the CustomerTable and then tick Actual Sales $, Budget Sales $ and Variance Sales $

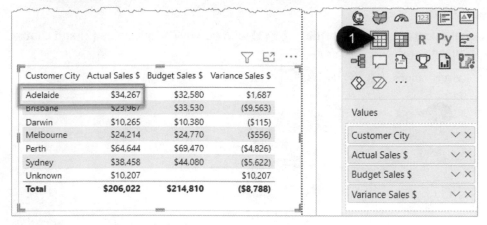

We will focus on Adelaide and explain how the measure for Actual Sales $ is working to give the figure of $34,267. If you don't see that figure, then makes sure you don't have any bars highlighted on the charts you created in the previous exercise.

The Actual Sales $ measure is `Actual Sales $ = SUM( SalesData[Sales Amount] )`

Remember it's all about the filters. The label Adelaide in our Table visual is a filter on the CustomerTable for the Customer City = Adelaide (1).

The 3 Customer Codes relating to Adelaide (2) then "flow down" the relationship to the SalesData table and filter that table to the corresponding items and only then does the measure SUM the Sales Amount column to give $34,267.

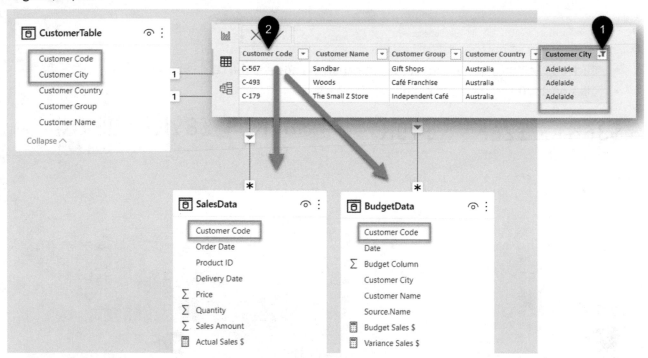

The same filtering process then happens to the BudgetData table and the Budget Sales $ SUMs the filtered Budget Column to give $32,580 for Budget Sales for Adelaide.

Finally, the Variance Sales $ measure simply subtracts one result from the other.

A Common Question – Why do we Need Measures?

I often get asked why you should bother with the Actual and Budget measures since earlier you simply dragged Sales Amount and Budget onto the canvas to build your charts.

There are 2 main reasons to write "explicit" measures for **all** values displayed in a report rather than relying on the "implicit" measures created by dragging columns onto the canvas.

1. Re-usability

2. Future-proof your report

Re-usability is highlighted by our Variance measure:

```
Variance Sales $ = [Actual Sales $]-[Budget Sales $]
```

This is simpler and clearer compared to the alternative:

```
Variance Sales $ =
SUM(SalesData[Sales Amount]) - SUM(BudgetData[Budget Column])
```

As your reports grow and become more complex the technique of referencing other simpler measures becomes even more critical in generating reports that are easier to maintain and update.

Future-proofing is all about making it easy for you or someone else to make a change in the future and have that flow through to all the right places. For example, if you discover that Actual Sales $ needs to reference a different column such as "Sales including Taxes" then it's one simple change to the Actual Sales $ measure and the visuals and dependent measures will automatically update.

> ☕ I cannot stress how important it is to only use measures in visuals from now on. While you can get by for a while simply dragging in columns and having Power BI automatically sum or count the values, I can confidently say that if you do that you will be caught out one day having to spend hours re-building a report when something unexpected changes.

A third, potentially important, reason to use Measures is if you are intending to use the Analyze in Excel feature you saw earlier. At the time of writing this book, only the beta of desktop Excel will allow columns to be used in the values box of a connected "Analyze in Excel" Pivot Table.

Change the chart showing Actual Sales v Budget to use the measures instead of the Sales Amount column and the Budget Column by following these steps:

- Click on the chart and untick Sales Amount
- Drag Actual Sales $ into the Column y-axis (where Sales Amount was previously)
- Untick Budget Column
- Drag Budget Sales $ into the Line y-axis (where Budget Column was previously)

You will need to customise the data labels again and turn off the labels for the Budget Sales $.

- Click the Format Icon (1) followed by the Data labels drop-down (2)
- Choose Budget Sales $ (3)
- Turn off the Data labels (4)

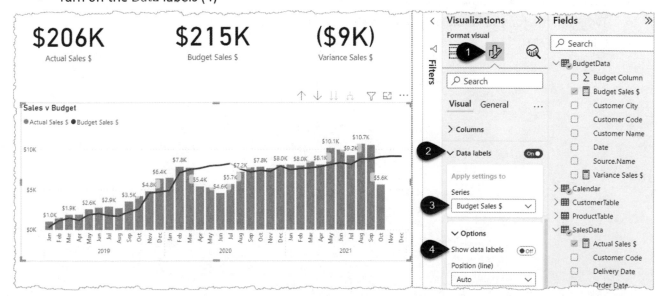

Naming Conventions when Referencing Measures or Columns

Here's the rule:

- Never put a Table name in front of a measure name
- Always put a Table name in front of a column name

In the Actual Sales $ measure you could have written

```
Actual Sales $ = SUM( [Sales Amount] )
```

but instead, you wrote this longer recommended formula that includes the Table name of the column you are referencing

```
Actual Sales $ = SUM(SalesData[Sales Amount])
```

The first version would only work because the measure is stored inside the SalesData table.

ALWAYS include the table name when referring to a column. One reason why will become apparent shortly.

In the Variance measure you could have written:

```
Variance Sales $ =
SalesData[Actual Sales $] - BudgetData[Budget Sales $]
```

But you should NEVER put a table name in front of a measure name.

The main way to identify columns and measures in DAX formulas is to stick rigidly to these 2 rules and you won't go wrong. This is a really key point, so we'll state it again:

- Never put a Table name in front of a measure name
- Always put a Table name in front of a column name

> 💡 The formula bar does subtly identify measures with a purple colour while columns and tables are a dark blue.

> To see my file at this stage open Solutions\Chapter 7 Coffee House Report Stage 1

Storing Measures in their Own Dedicated Table

A measure can be stored in any table. It does not impact how it works providing you stick to the naming rules mentioned in the previous section. My preference has always been to create at least one separate "Measures Table" to store all my measures in. I just find it easier to manage that way, however, others will prefer to keep their measures in the tables they relate to just like you currently have Actual Sales $ in the SalesData table and Budget Sales $ in the BudgetData table.

To create a table to store your measures in follow these steps:

- Click the Enter data button on the Home ribbon (1)
- Type a name for your table. MyMeasures is commonly used (2)
- Click Load (3)

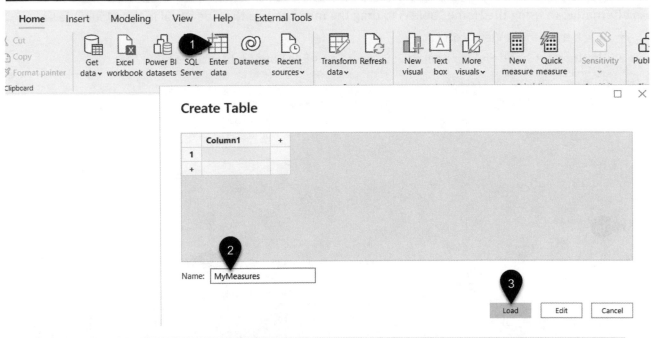

☕ You can name your table anything you want except for "Measures" as that word is protected. Random Excel fact: You can't name an Excel worksheet "History". Try it.   There was/is a special use for a History sheet in the old legacy "Track Changes" feature.

The MyMeasures table will appear in the Fields panel to the right.

⚠ Don't delete Column1 (1) until you add at least 1 measure to this table as otherwise, the table disappears.

• Click on your Actual Sales $ measure (2) and then move it by choosing Home table (3) MyMeasures (4)

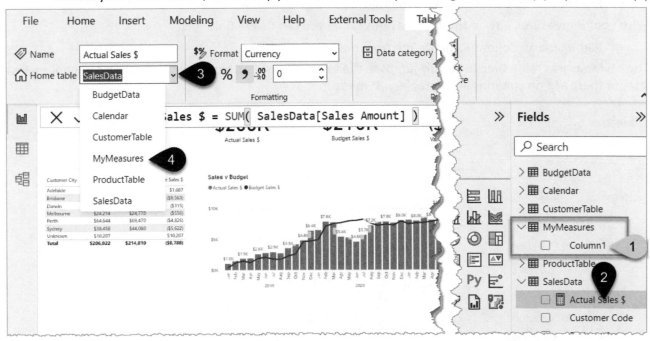

☕ At the time of writing, you cannot simply drag your measures into this table, however, try dragging a measure into it anyway as I imagine this is something that will be fixed one day "soon".

An alternative to using the Home Table is to drag the measures via the side panel in the Model View:

- Click the Model View icon (1)
- In the right-hand Fields panel drag Budget Sales $ to your MyMeasures table (2)

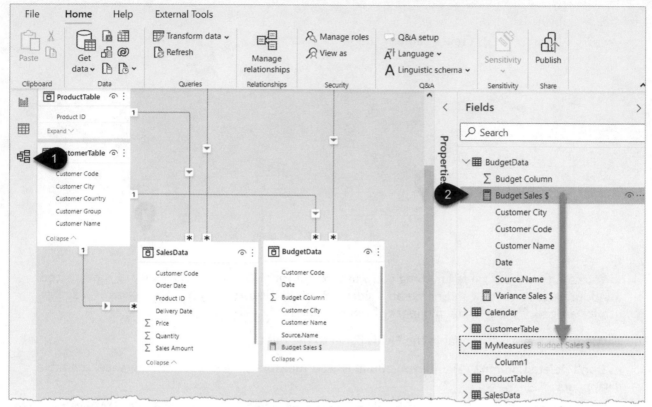

- Repeat for the Variance Sales $ measure

With your 3 measures now in the MyMeasures table, you can delete Column1.

- Right-click on Column1 and Delete from model

The MyMeasures table then magically jumps to the top of the list and has a special calculator symbol against it since there are no columns in this table, just measures.

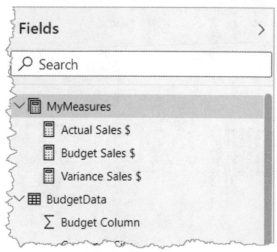

- Click on the Report view icon to go back to your charts and visuals
- Create a new page in your report and name it More Measures

⚠One small downside of adding measures to a dedicated measures table is that if you use Analyze in Excel then the double-click drill down capability in a PivotTable is lost. My approach is to use a Measures Table most of the time and then move measures back to source tables in the few scenarios when this drill down functionality is required.

Year to Date Measure

Writing the DAX formula to create a running total for the year is simple but it is a tricky concept to understand.

Add this Year to Date measure to your MyMeasures table by following these steps:

- Right-click on MyMeasures and choose New measure, and then type in this formula:

```
Actual Sales $ YTD = TOTALYTD( [Actual Sales $], 'Calendar'[Date] )
```

- Format it as $ and 0 decimals

👆 In the formula the table name Calendar automatically gets quotes ' ' around it. This is because there is also a DAX function called CALENDAR and this differentiates them.

Add a table containing Year, Month, Actual Sales, and YTD Sales by following the steps below:

- Click on some white space
- Click the Table Visual icon (1)
- Tick Year followed by Month from the Calendar table and then tick Actual Sales $ and Actual Sales $ YTD (2)

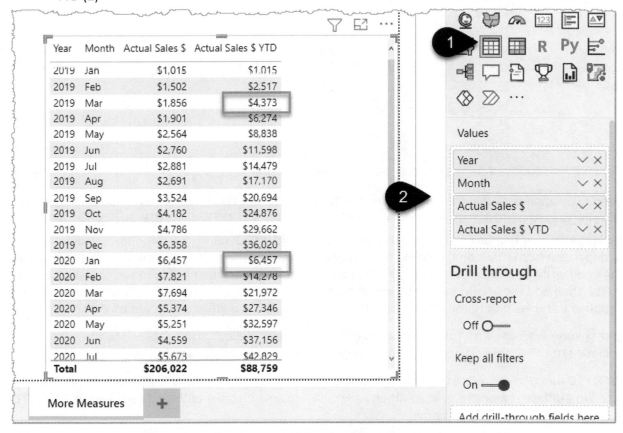

Notice how the Sales YTD figure builds up during 2019 and then resets for Jan 2020.

This is great! But how does it work? Always remember it's all about the filters.

Focus on the 2019 Mar figure of $4,373. The table is supplying a filter to the Calendar Table of 2019 and Mar, so that's 31 dates that are ready to flow down the relationship and filter the SalesData table.

However, TOTALYTD is a function that can modify this date filter.

In the measure you included Calendar[Date], this tells the TOTALYTD function to not only filter the Calendar for dates in Mar 2019 but to also include the dates from the beginning of that year i.e. 1st Jan 2019. There are then 90 dates that flow down the relationship and filter the SalesData table.

After the filtering happens, you apply the [Actual Sales $] measure which then simply sums the Sales Amount column while the SalesData table is in that filtered state.

In other words, the TOTALYTD function modifies the filters impacting the Calendar table. It defaults to un-filtering as far as 1st January.

To further illustrate this, create a measure called Days YTD as follows:

- Right-click on the MyMeasures table and choose New measure then type this:

```
Days YTD = TOTALYTD( COUNTROWS('Calendar'), 'Calendar'[Date])
```

- Add this measure to your Table visual

You used COUNTROWS('Calendar') since the Calendar table has 1 row for each day, therefore COUNTROWS gives us the number of days.

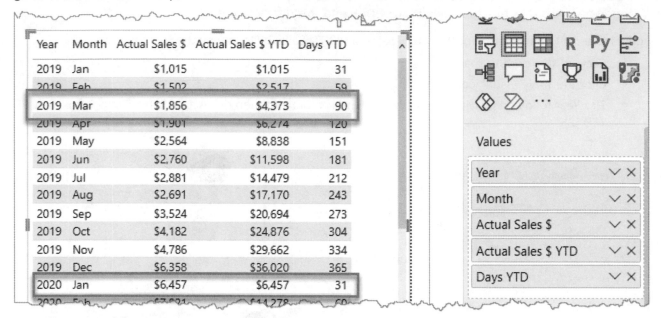

The same logic applies to this measure. Looking at March 2019 the TOTALYTD function modifies the filter from filtering only March 2019 to all the dates from 1st of Jan 2019 and 31st March 2019. Hence 90 rows/days.

The challenge with writing DAX formulas is that you must picture in your mind how this filtering will work. This is a big departure from traditional Excel where you physically select the cells as you are writing the formula. With DAX you write formulas that reference Tables and Columns without being able to see or pick particular values. You then add those calculations to visuals such as a chart or a Table visual which will result in filters being applied to tables before the calculations are performed. This is a difficult concept to learn.

> ☕ It's when we deal with formula languages like DAX that you can truly appreciate the simple brilliance of the Excel grid and its formula language. But DAX is very powerful.

The TOTALYTD function defaults to "un-filter" the data as far back as 1st of January, however, if your reporting year starts in a different month e.g. 1st July then you could add an optional month-end date to your TOTALYTD function as follows: *Don't do this now*

```
Actual Sales $ Financial YTD = TOTALYTD( [Actual Sales $], 'Calendar'[Date],
"30/06" )
```

This means that your Calendar will be unfiltered as far as 1st July, however, to use this function successfully you will need a Calendar table that has a Financial Year and Financial Month Sort column.

A calendar table with these fields has been provided under Exercises\Other Files\Calendar File.pbix and this is covered later in this book in Chapter 8: The Calendar Table.

Time for another example to help your understanding of DAX.

Prior Year Comparison and the CALCULATE Function

You can quickly compare a month of sales with a prior year using this measure.

- Right-click on the MyMeasures table and add this measure pressing Shift-Enter after the equals sign to start the 2nd line of code

```
Actual Sales $ Prior Year =
CALCULATE( [Actual Sales $], DATEADD( 'Calendar'[Date],-1,YEAR )  )
```

```
1 Actual Sales $ Prior Year =
2 CALCULATE( [Actual Sales $], DATEADD( 'Calendar'[Date],-1,YEAR )  )
```

> DATEADD(**Dates**, NumberOfIntervals, Interval)
> Moves the given set of dates by a specified interval.

- Format the measure as $ and 0 decimals

Breaking this down into its 2 parts:

Part 1: Microsoft should have named the CALCULATE function as "CHANGEFILTER" as that is essentially what it allows you to do. Its purpose is to modify the filter that is being applied in some way. You will use CALCULATE a lot as your use of Power BI grows. Writing DAX is all about applying and modifying filters in various ways so this "CHANGEFILTER" function is very useful.

Part 2: The DATEADD function is then telling the CALCULATE what filter to change. In this case, it takes any date filter being applied via your visuals, removes those dates, and then reapplies the dates for 1 year prior.

> 💡 The first part of the DATEADD function asks for Dates. When any function asks for Dates it's always your Calendar[Date] field that you type in here. These time intelligence functions may not work correctly unless you use a Calendar table.

- Add this new measure to your Table visual

Year	Month	Actual Sales $	Actual Sales $ YTD	Days YTD	Actual Sales $ Prior Year
2019	Jan	$1,015	$1,015	31	
2019	Feb	$1,502	$2,517	59	
2019	Mar	$1,856	$4,373	90	
2019	Apr	$1,901	6,274	120	
2019	May	$2,564	$8,?38	151	
2019	Jun	$2,760	$11,59?	181	
2019	Jul	$2,881	$14,479	212	
2019	Aug	$2,691	$17,170	?43	
2019	Sep	$3,524	$20,694	2?	
2019	Oct	$4,182	$24,876	304	
2019	Nov	$4,786	$29,662	334	
2019	Dec	$6,358	$36,020	365	
2020	Jan	$6,457	$6,457	31	$1,015
2020	Feb	$7,821	$14,278	60	$1,502
2020	Mar	$7,694	$21,972	91	$1,856
2020	Apr	$5,374	$27,346	121	$1,901
2020	May	$5,251	$32,597	152	$2,564
2020	Jun	$4,559	?37,15?	18?	$2,760

Removing Filters

It can be useful to compare the Actual YTD Sales $ at a particular date against the Budget for the full year to see how much budget remains. This requires us to write a measure for Full Year Budget. We cannot simply add the Budget Sales $ measure to our Table visual as it will be filtered by the Year and Month that we are using in that visual. The new measure must be able to ignore the month filter.

Before creating this measure add a Drop-down Slicer for Year by following these steps:

- Click on some white space
- Click the Slicer Icon (1) and then tick Year (from Calendar)
- Click the small v (2) in the corner and choose the Dropdown option (3)
- Choose 2020

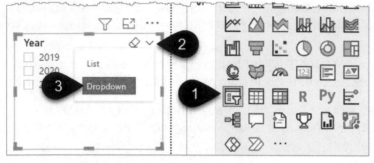

- Create the Full Year Budget measure in the MyMeasures table as follows:

```
Budget Sales $ Full Year =
CALCULATE( [Budget Sales $], REMOVEFILTERS( 'Calendar'[Month] ) )
```

- Format it with $ and 0 decimals

💡 You will also see people using ALL instead of REMOVEFILTERS. In this context, they do the same thing. REMOVEFILTERS was a relatively recent addition to Power BI as a clearer alternative to ALL. You can write DAX formulas in Excel, and the book will cover this later, but unfortunately, EXCEL is missing many of the newer functions including REMOVEFILTERS. A useful resource to see which functions are available in the different products is https://dax.guide

- Click on some white space and add a Card visual then tick this new measure to add it to the Card
- Click on some white space again and add another Card visual adding Budget Sales $. Be careful not to pick Budget Sales $ **Full Year** by mistake.
- Click on Mar 2020 in the Table visual (1) and you will see the card with Full Year doesn't change. Click on a few different months and none should impact the Full Year visual.

The Budget Sales $ will change to $7,510 but the Budget Sales $ **Full Year** measure REMOVES this Calendar[Month] filter and it, therefore, remains at $89k.

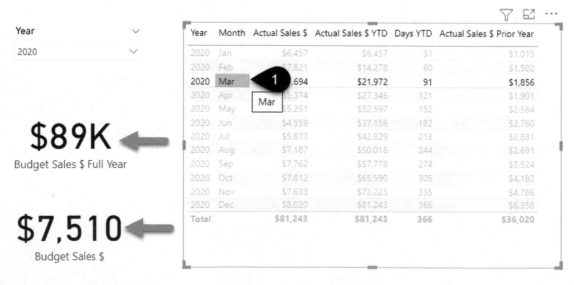

The next example hopefully won't put you off using DAX but will flag a "feature" that you should be aware of. This is essentially a bug so being aware of it can save you wasted hours in the future.

- Click on the Table visual and remove Actual Sales $, Days YTD, and Actual Sales $ Prior Year. All that should remain is Year, Month and Actual Sales $ YTD
- Add Budget Sales $ (1)
- Add Budget Sales $ Full Year (2)

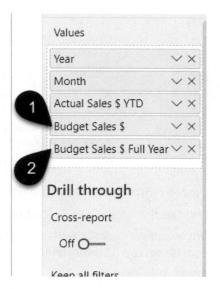

Year	Month	Actual Sales $ YTD	Budget Sales $	Budget Sales $ Full Year
2020	Jan	$6,457	$4,920	$4,920
2020	Feb	$14,278	$7,100	$7,100
2020	Mar	$21,972	$7,510	$7,510
2020	Apr	$27,346	$7,660	$7,660
2020	May	$32,597	$7,950	$7,950
2020	Jun	$37,156	$8,040	$8,040
2020	Jul	$42,829	$8,230	$8,230
2020	Aug	$50,016	$7,550	$7,550
2020	Sep	$57,778	$7,200	$7,200
2020	Oct	$65,590	$7,400	$7,400
2020	Nov	$73,223	$7,260	$7,260
2020	Dec	$81,243	$7,920	$7,920
Total		$81,243	$88,740	$88,740

Shouldn't Budget Sales $ Full Year REMOVE the filter for Month?

Yes, it should. The figure should be $88,740 all the way down. It worked when you displayed the number in a Card Visual. So why is it not working when displayed in the Table visual?

This bug is caused by the fact that you had to apply a sort column to the Month to force the months to display in number order rather than alphabetically. Power BI considers this sort column as another filter that needs to be removed. This is a bug, and not something you can discover without a lot of web searches.

> ☕ I actually got caught by this "feature" while delivering a training session. I couldn't work out what had gone wrong, so during the break I "Googled" the issue and my own Tweet from 6 months earlier explaining the issue appeared! The posts and videos I create are as much for my own benefit than anyone else ☺.

To fix this you need to include Calendar[Month Number for Sort] into the REMOVEFILTERS statement.

- Click on the name of your measure "Budget Sales $ Full Year" so that the formula bar appears
- Edit your measure as follows:

```
Budget Sales $ Full Year =
CALCULATE (
[Budget Sales $],
REMOVEFILTERS ( 'Calendar'[Month], 'Calendar'[Month Number for sort] ) )
```

> 💡 The formula above has been separated into different rows to make it easier to read. You can do this in the formula window by pressing SHIFT + Enter. This has the added benefit of auto-indenting your formula.

The figure of $88,740 should now appear over and over, this is correct, it is now ignoring the Month filter.

Year	Month	Actual Sales $ YTD	Budget Sales $	Budget Sales $ Full Year
2020	Jan	$6,457	$4,920	$88,740
2020	Feb	$14,278	$7,100	$88,740
2020	Mar	$21,972	$7,510	$88,740
2020	Apr	$27,346	$7,660	$88,740
2020	May	$32,597	$7,950	$88,740
2020	Jun	$37,156	$8,040	$88,740
2020	Jul	$42,829	$8,230	$88,740
2020	Aug	$50,016	$7,550	$88,740
2020	Sep	$57,778	$7,200	$88,740
2020	Oct	$65,590	$7,400	$88,740
2020	Nov	$73,223	$7,260	$88,740
2020	Dec	$81,243	$7,920	$88,740
Total		**$81,243**	**$88,740**	**$88,740**

A better way to display this would be using a chart.

- Change the Year Slicer Drop-down to be 2019 (1)
- Copy and paste your table by clicking on it and pressing Ctrl+C and Ctrl+V. Often the copy appears exactly on top of the original so just drag it somewhere else on the page
- Remove Budget Sales $
- Change the visual to a Line and Clustered Column Chart (hover over the chart icons to see the descriptions and pick the right one)
- Change the layout to match the image below
- Click the "bident" (2) after moving Year and Month to the Shared axis box

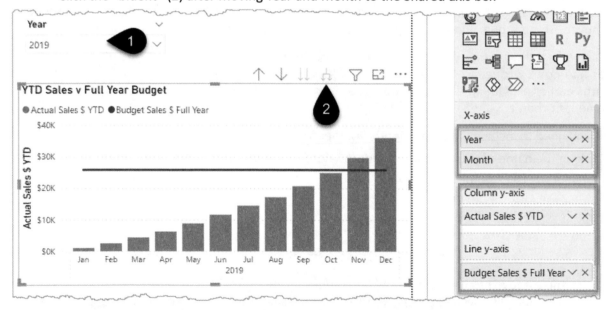

- Change the Title to YTD Sales v Full Year Budget via the format icon

💡 I'd also recommend changing the X-axis concatenated labels to off and turning off the X and Y-axis Titles.

Formatting Your DAX

As a useful side note, you can use a website called DAX Formatter to format your longer DAX formula automatically. Copy a formula and go to https://www.daxformatter.com/ then paste your code there, click format, and copy the nicely formatted code back to your Power BI report.

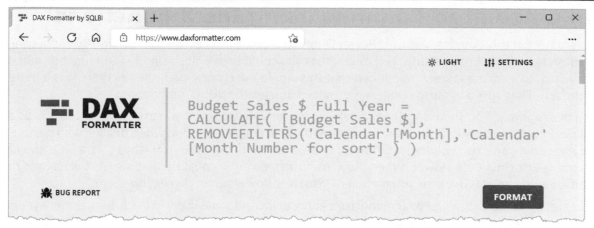

Ratios and Percentages Using DIVIDE

You are going to add this Matrix Visual to the page which shows the Actual Sales $ as a % of the Budget.

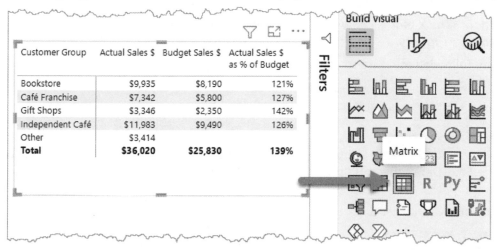

Note that the slicer on this page is set to 2019 per the previous exercise.

- Click on the icon for the Matrix visual. I'm now assuming you're remembering to click on some white space first
- Drag Customer Group into the Rows box and then tick Actual Sales $ and Budget Sales $

The remaining calculation you need to create is the Actual Sales as % of Budget.

- Right-click on the MyMeasures table and write the following formula:

```
Actual Sales as % of Budget =
DIVIDE( [Actual Sales $] , [Budget Sales $] )
```

- Format it as % with 0 decimals
- Add this to the Matrix Visual

💡 You can make columns in a Table or Matrix narrower by hovering the mouse between 2 columns until a double-headed arrow appears then click and drag.

You could perform the division by writing = [Measure1] / [Measure2] but the DIVIDE function can handle the scenario here where there is no denominator value, e.g. if you wrote =[Actual Sales $] / [Budget Sales $] then this would not work in this Matrix as "Other" has no budget and you would be trying to divide $3,414 by a blank. In this scenario, the visual would error out.

If the Budget was 0 rather than blank then =[Actual Sales $]/[Budget Sales $] would result in the word "Infinity" displaying. No one wants to be infinity over budget! The DIVIDE function also handles that scenario by showing a blank rather than that word.

To see my file at this stage open Solutions\Chapter 7 Coffee House Report Stage 2

Virtual Calculated Columns using the X Functions

Back at the very start of this exercise, you used Power Query to create the Sales Amount column by multiplying the Price column by the Quantity column. This meant that you could then write a simple SUM function when creating the Actual Sales $ measure. I mentioned that this would raise a few eyebrows as there was a more efficient approach. That approach is to create a measure that uses the SUMX function.

Before doing this example, you should feel comfortable in the knowledge that if you use Power Query to add a column that performs a calculation you are not doing anything wrong. It's just that when dealing with millions of rows of data, adding an extra column of relatively unique numbers can make refreshes take a little longer and reports may perform a little slower. When I say "perform slower" it could be that visuals take longer to appear when a page is selected, or the interaction of visuals is slower when clicking on them.

If you find no performance issues and your model isn't going to increase massively in the future as more years of data are loaded, then don't worry about it.

The alternative to adding "physical" columns permanently to your model is to use special functions in your measures that can create temporary columns to calculate the result. These temporary columns then disappear once the calculation is complete.

SUMX is one of these functions. The X part is known as the "iterator" part. It allows your formula to be run against every row in the table you specify.

To demonstrate this, add the following measure to your MyMeasures table:

```
Alternative Sales $ =
  SUMX( SalesData,  SalesData[Quantity] * SalesData[Price] )
```

and format as $ with 0 decimals

Think of it like this, SUMX allows you to create a temporary column on your SalesData table where the formula runs down every row in the SalesData table multiplying each Quantity by each Price and then at the end SUMs that temporary column.

Drag this new measure into your Matrix Visual.

Customer Group	Actual Sales $	Budget Sales $	Actual Sales $ as % of Budget	Alternative Sales $
Bookstore	$9,935	$8,190	121%	$9,935
Café Franchise	$7,342	$5,800	127%	$7,342
Gift Shops	$3,346	$2,350	142%	$3,346
Independent Café	$11,983	$9,490	126%	$11,983
Other	$3,414			$3,414
Total	**$36,020**	**$25,830**	**139%**	**$36,020**

As you can see you end up with exactly the same result as the Actual Sales $ measure because in essence, they are doing the same thing. The original one is a measure referencing a physical column in your data model taking up memory while the other only gets calculated as needed when it is displayed or interacted with in a visual.

The approach you use is up to you. As a beginner, it's simpler to add a new column in Power Query. But, and there is a but, this is possibly not the most efficient method. As you advance in your Power BI journey or if you deal with multi-million-row data sets you will likely move more towards SUMX. There are also other very useful iterator functions such MAXX and CONCATENATEX that operate in the same way of running down every row in a table performing some function.

☕ You can also create calculated columns using DAX in the Data View screen of Power BI Desktop. There's a button called New Column and clicking it allows you to write DAX formulas. My recommendation is that if you need to add a calculated column then use Power Query instead, or if possible, get it added to your data source. Follow Matthew Roche's Maxim of Data Transformation which is "Data should be transformed as far upstream as possible, and as far downstream as necessary." Read more about that on Matthew's blog url.pbi.guide/ffsM.
Only add DAX calculated columns if you need to use a Measure in that calculation or have progressed your understanding of DAX to a level where you know it's the right thing to do.

To see my file at this stage open Solutions\Chapter 7 Coffee House Report Stage 3

Dealing with Multiple Date Fields in Your Fact Table

In the SalesData table, we have an Order Date column that is connected to our Calendar table. All the charts and visuals we have built so far have therefore been reporting on Actual Sales $ by the **date ordered**.

However, looking at the SalesData table, there is also a Delivery Date column. What should you do if you also want to build some visuals showing Quantity Delivered each month?

- Create a new Page called USE RELATIONSHIP (1)
- Create a simple measure in MyMeasures called Quantity Ordered

  ```
  Quantity Ordered = SUM( SalesData[Quantity] )
  ```

- Format it by clicking the comma and ensuring 0 decimals is displayed
- Copy and Paste the Sales Amount by Year and Month chart from Page 1 to this page using Ctrl+C Ctrl+V
- Remove Sales Amount and add your new Quantity Ordered measure instead
- Change the columns to Orange via Format Icon → Visual → Columns (2)
- Change the title to "Quantity" via Format Icon → General (3) → Title

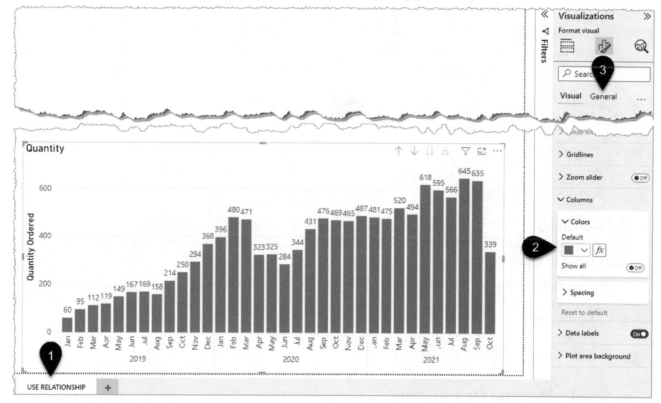

To add Quantity **Delivered** to your report you need to do 2 things, firstly set up an inactive relationship between your Calendar and the Delivery date, then write a measure that uses this relationship.

- Go to the Model View (1) and hover over the line between Calendar and SalesData (2). You can see that Date from the Calendar is filtering Order Date in the SalesData table
- Drag Delivery Date (3) from SalesData and drop it onto Date in the Calendar. This creates an "inactive" dotted line relationship between the two tables which has no effect until you write a special measure

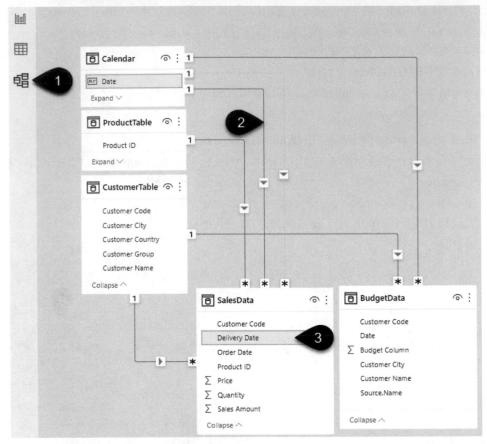

If you decide later that you would prefer to make Delivery Date the default active relationship then double-click on the Order Date line first, make it inactive, and then double-click on the Delivery Date line and make it active.

- Return to the Report View and add the following measure to MyMeasures:

```
Quantity Delivered =
CALCULATE(
  [Quantity Ordered],
   USERELATIONSHIP('Calendar'[Date], SalesData[Delivery Date] )
   )
```

- Drag this measure onto your chart

Annoyingly, at the time of writing, Power BI changes your chosen colour for Quantity Ordered

- Change the colours to orange and light blue via Format Icon (1) → Columns → Colors (2)
- Add a slicer for year and select 2021 (3)

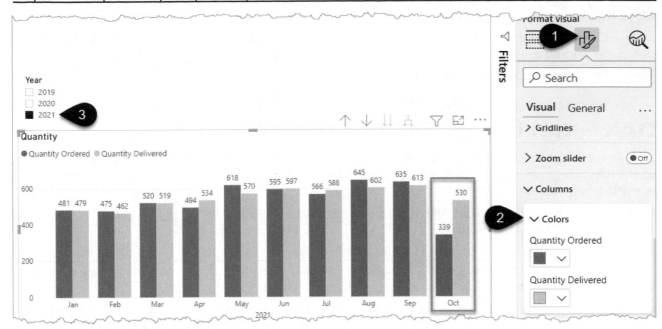

You should see clear differences each month.

It's important to understand how this works. Focus on October 2021. The chart axis is coming from the Calendar table and therefore Oct is filtering the Calendar table to those 31 dates.

For the orange bar (Quantity Ordered) those 31 dates then flow down the solid "active" line and filter the Order Date column for the corresponding 31 dates and then the Quantity Ordered measure simply SUMs the Quantity column in this filtered table and it totals 339.

For the light blue bar (Quantity Delivered) the CALCULATE function tells the measure to change the filter and that the 31 dates should flow down the dotted line relationship and filter the Delivery Date column. The measure then SUMs the Quantity column in this filtered table, and it totals 530.

The USERELATIONSHIP function must be paired with CALCULATE and the dotted line must exist. Similarly, the dotted line is ignored until called by the CALCULATE USERELATIONSHIP combination. You can have as many inactive relationships as you like, and this comes in very useful for things like employee start and end dates, arrivals & departures, etc.

Organising Measures into Folders

As a final "housekeeping" exercise you can group your measures into folders.

- Click on the Model view icon (1) and focus on the right-hand Fields panel
- Click Quantity Delivered, then hold Ctrl and click Quantity Ordered (2) then type Quantity in the Display Folder box (3) and press Enter. This creates the folder.

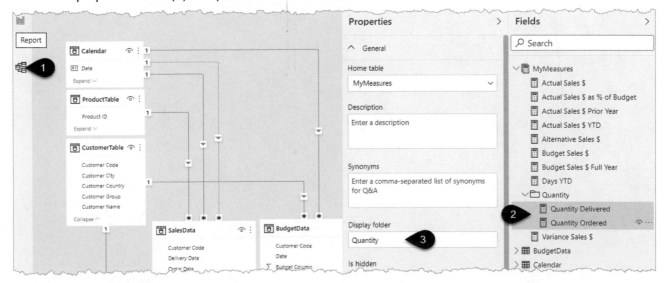

Move the other measures into a Sales Folder by following these steps:

- Click on Actual Sales $, hold Shift, click on Budget Sales $ Full Year and then type Sales $ in the display folder and press Enter
- Drag Variance Sales $ onto the new Sales $ folder

To see my file at this stage open Solutions\Chapter 7 Coffee House Report Stage 4

DAX – Next Steps in Your Learning

That's it for DAX in this book, it's a huge topic in its own right. There are excellent resources out there. Learning about using variables in your measures, understanding filter context, and context transition are next steps in the learning journey.

I would highly recommend Matt Allington's book "Supercharge Power BI" url.pbi.guide/scharge as a next step to extend your DAX knowledge.

In the spirit of full disclosure, Matt is a friend of mine and we both first learned our DAX from the Rob Collie book "DAX Formulas for Power Pivot" published in 2013. Matt has taken all his years of practical experience since then to hone a well-thought-out approach to helping people understand DAX.

When you progress even further in your learning journey it would be worth considering investing in a copy of "The Definitive Guide to DAX" by Alberto Ferrari and Marco Russo. Do not start with this book! As they say in the foreword "if you are a casual user of DAX then this book is probably not for you".

Alberto and Marco also provide great content on their SQLBI blog and YouTube channel https://www.sqlbi.com/. They are also behind https://dax.guide/ and https://www.daxformatter.com/. That's plenty of content to keep you learning DAX for a few years.

Chapter 8 - The Calendar Table

As you have seen from the examples so far, the Calendar table is a critical part of building flexible reports. It's fully worthy of its own chapter.

Since a Calendar table, also referred to as a Date table, is so important it still surprises me that there is no in-built functionality to create the ideal Calendar for your reports. Power BI can automatically create simple date hierarchy tables, but these are limited in their scope and usefulness. In fact, it is highly recommended that you turn off the automatic date table creation feature and never use it again because this functionality creates a "hidden" date table for every individual date field in your data. The number and size of these "invisible" date tables can bloat your Power BI model and slow down your report.

Turning Off Auto Date/Time for New Files

Back in the Chapter 5 "Creating a Power BI Model" you were encouraged to turn off the auto-date time feature. If you didn't do it then do it now.

- Go to File → Options and Settings → Options → In the Global Data Load section go to Time Intelligence → **Untick** Auto date/time for new files → Click OK

The Calendar table you used in the previous exercise is a good starting point, however, it's time to look at a more flexible Calendar table, how it works, how to adjust it, and how to copy it to other reports as needed.

- Close and save any other Power BI Files
- Open Exercises\Other Files\Calendar File.pbix

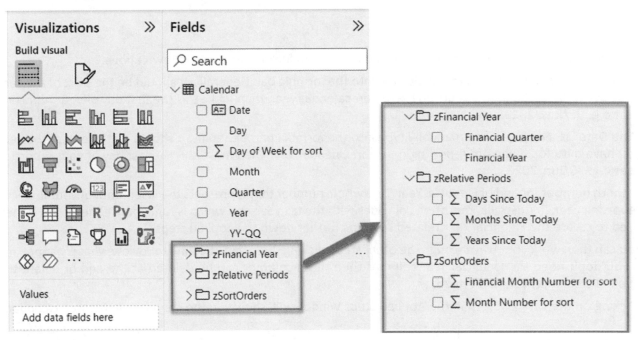

This Calendar table has a few folders to organise the columns. They were created in the same way that you created the Measures folders earlier. The names have been prefixed with z to force them to display at the bottom of the list.

The next section explains how this Calendar table works and what changes you can make to it.

- Click on the Transform data button on the Home ribbon
- Scroll to the top of the Applied Steps and then click on the "Today" step and look at the formula:

```
=Date.From(DateTime.LocalNow())
```

This generates the date per your computer, it's a bit like the =NOW() function in Excel. It updates every time the data is refreshed. It is used in later steps when calculating the relative periods such as Days Ago, Months Ago, etc.

To help you understand the purpose of each of the steps in the screenshot I've added notes below the image.

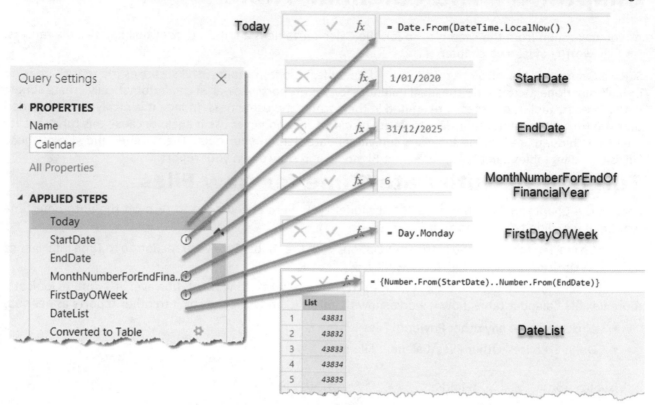

Click on the following steps one at a time and look at the formula or text as shown above.

"StartDate" is a date you can manually type into the formula bar. Generally, it should be the start of the year you have data for. If you are reporting on a non-calendar year, then make this the first day of your reporting year e.g. 01/July/2022.

"End Date" is a date you can manually type into the formula bar. Generally, it should be the end of the year you have data for. If you are reporting on a non-calendar year then make this the last day of your reporting year e.g. 30/Jun/2023.

"Month number for end of Financial Year", is a whole number that represents the last month of your financial reporting year. In Australia, this often coincides with the tax year-end which is June, hence the 6. This is then used to create the Financial Year related columns further down the applied steps.

You can then work your way through the other steps clicking them one at a time to review what is happening. If you don't need the Financial Year columns then these columns can be deleted at the end or delete the applied steps that you don't need.

Clicking on the very last step in the Applied Steps window will show you the complete generated calendar.

Power Query Advanced Editor

Click the Advanced Editor button on the Home Tab. You will then see all the Power Query Applied steps in one window. It looks a little scary.

Calendar   Display Options ▾   ❓

```
let
    Today = Date.From(DateTime.LocalNow() ),

    // Change start date to begining of year
    StartDate= #date(2021, 7, 1),


    EndDate = #date(2025, 12, 31),


    //set this as the last month number of your fiscal year : June = 6, July =7 etc
    MonthNumberForEndFinancialYear = 6,

    // Change to Day.Sunday or Day.Tuesday etc to impact the sort order number so you can then
    display your days in your visuals in the preferred way
    FirstDayOfWeek = Day.Monday,


    DateList = {Number.From(StartDate)..Number.From(EndDate)},


    #"Converted to Table" = Table.FromList(DateList, Splitter.SplitByNothing(), null, null,
        ExtraValues.Error),
    #"Named as Date" = Table.RenameColumns(#"Converted to Table",{{"Column1", "Date"}}),
    #"Changed Type" = Table.TransformColumnTypes(#"Named as Date",{{"Date", type date}}),
    #"Inserted Year" = Table.AddColumn(#"Changed Type", "Year", each Date.Year([Date]), type
        number),
    #"Inserted Month Number" = Table.AddColumn(#"Inserted Year", "Month Number", each Date.Month(
```

There are 2 things that make Power Query "M" language appear more complicated than it really is.

1. Any step names with spaces in the words end up getting wrapped in #"   ". So, you will see DateList does not have those elements but #"Converted to Table" does because there are spaces between words

2. Each step normally refers to the previous step, unless you manually change this in the formula bar or in the advanced editor

If you look at this line

```
#"Named as Date" =
Table.RenameColumns(#"Converted to Table",{{"Column1", "Date"}}),
```

you can see that the 'M' Code refers to the previous step #"Converted to Table" and this pattern is repeated for each step.

If you do delete a line, or multiple lines in the advanced editor the key thing to remember is that you will need to edit any remaining steps to ensure they refer to valid existing steps. Don't do this now, but if you were to delete the highlighted section below, which is the Financial Year section, then you must also change the bottom remaining step to refer to #" ◄ Dates Since Today" rather than the #" ◄ Financial Year Calcs" step it currently refers to.

```
YearsAgo = Table.AddColumn(MonthsAgo, "Years Since Today", each [Year] - Date.Year(DateToday ), Int32.Type),
#"◄ Dates Since Today" = YearsAgo,
#"►Financial Year Calcs" = #"◄ Dates Since Today",
#"FY Month Number" = Table.AddColumn(#"►Financial Year Calcs", "Financial Month Number", each if [Month Number
    -MonthNumberForEndFinancialYear  else 12-MonthNumberForEndFinancialYear+[Month Number]),
#"Changed Type1" = Table.TransformColumnTypes(#"FY Month Number",{{"Financial Month Number", Int64.Type}}),
#"Financial Year End" = Table.AddColumn(#"Changed Type1", "Financial Year End", each if [Financial Month Numbe
#"Fiancial Year Start" = Table.AddColumn(#"Financial Year End", "Financial Year Start", each [Financial Year E
#"Changed Type5" = Table.TransformColumnTypes(#"Fiancial Year Start",{{"Financial Year End", type text}, {"Fina
#"Added Financial Year Range" = Table.AddColumn(#"Changed Type5", "Financial Year", each Text.End( [Financial
#"Removed FY Start End Helpers" = Table.RemoveColumns(#"Added Financial Year Range",{"Financial Year End", "Fi
// To work out Financial Quarter
#"DivideFinancialMonth by 3" = Table.AddColumn(#"Removed FY Start End Helpers", "Financial Qtr Number", each [
#"Rounded Up to get Quarter" = Table.TransformColumns(#"DivideFinancialMonth by 3",{{"Financial Qtr Number", N
#"Added Financial Quarter" = Table.AddColumn(#"Rounded Up to get Quarter", "Financial Quarter", each "FQ-"&Text
#"Removed FYQ Helper" = Table.RemoveColumns(#"Added Financial Quarter",{"Financial Qtr Number"}),
#"Changed Type6" = Table.TransformColumnTypes(#"Removed FYQ Helper",{{"Financial Quarter", type text}, {"Financ
#"Renamed FY Month Sort" = Table.RenameColumns(#"Changed Type6",{{"Financial Month Number", "Financial Month N
#"◄ Financial Year Calcs" = #"Renamed FY Month Sort",
#"Renamed Month Sort Column" = Table.RenameColumns(#"◄ Financial Year Calcs",{{"Month Number", "Month Number f
in
    #"Renamed Month Sort Column"
```

💡 The ►◄ symbols are a technique I use to indicate related steps with an opening ► and a closing ◄. You see all the steps related to the Financial Year Calcs are flagged between the opening step named ►Financial Year Calcs and the closing step ◄Financial Year Calcs. I add these in the applied steps panel using the blue emoji symbols ►◄ by pressing the Windows key and the full stop key then picking the right symbol. At the time of writing, you can't add emojis directly in the advanced editor.

This book will not be exploring M code in-depth. Check out the official Power Query website for documentation around the Power Query interface and "M" language https://powerquery.com.

I'd highly recommend 2 books for people wanting to learn more about Power Query. Firstly "Master Your Data" by Ken Puls and Miguel Escobar is a great book dedicated to Power Query url.pbi.guide/myd. The first edition version of this book was called "M is for Data Monkey" and was where I began my Power Query learning journey.

The second book is "Collect, Combine, and Transform Data Using Power Query in Excel and Power BI" by Gil Raviv. url.pbi.guide/gilra

This is a great technical book and I'd recommend it to people who are a bit further along in their Power Query learning journey.

☕ As with my recommendation on Matt's book on DAX, I consider Ken, Miguel, and Gil as friends I'd happily share a beer with so take my recommendation with that in mind. Ken even did the tech review on this book! But seriously they all inspired me to write this book and I've been recommending their books for years. I even interviewed them in my Power Query podcast series called "Power Query Magic". Podcast url.pbi.guide/MagicPod and YouTube url.pbi.guide/MagicVid

Copying Queries Between files

It is very simple to copy this Calendar table into any other file.

- Right-click on the Calendar table in the left-hand panel (1) and choose Copy (2)

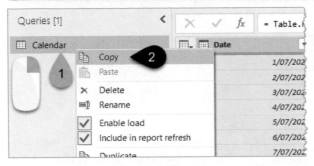

- Close this Power Query editor window
- Open a new Power BI Desktop file via File → New
- In the new file click the Transform data button on the Home Tab
- Right-click in the left-hand panel (1) and Paste (2)

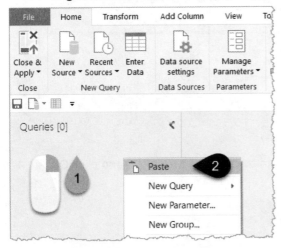

Your Calendar should magically appear. Keep this new file open, you'll come back to it in a few pages time.

You can even copy and paste queries between Power BI and Excel!

- Right-click copy the calendar
- Open a new, empty, Excel file
- Click the Data menu (1) → Get Data (2) → Launch Power Query Editor (3)

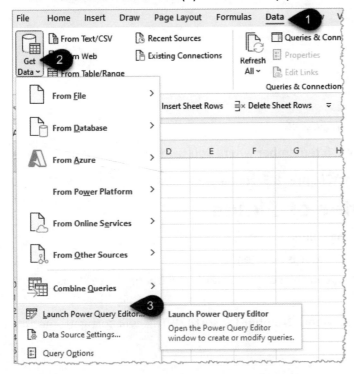

The Power Query Editor window will then open.

- Right-click in the left-hand Queries panel and paste. Your Calendar should appear (1)
- Click the drop-down for Close and Load (2)
- Select Close & Load To...(3)

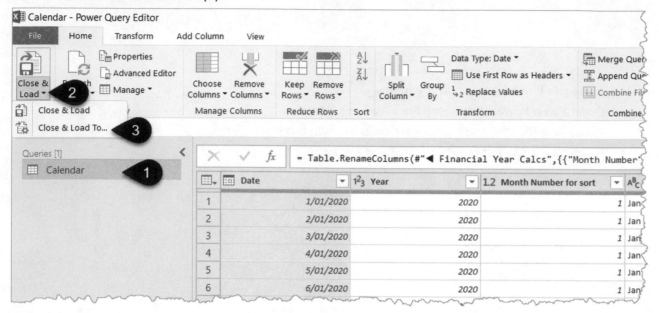

- Choose Only Create Connection (1) and tick Add this data to the Data Model (2) and click OK

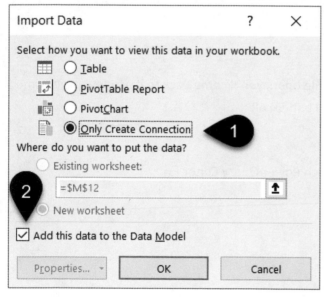

- Save this Excel file as Excel Calendar and then close it.

⚠ You will return to this file in the next chapter so remember where you save it!

To see my copy of the Excel file open Solutions\Chapter 8 Excel Calendar.xlsx

Changing the Display Order of Fields

Return to the new empty Power BI file you copied the calendar into.

- Click Close and Apply and you will see the Calendar is now loaded

You should immediately sort Month and Day to display in the correct order by following these steps:

- Click on the word Month (1)
- From the Sort by column drop-down choose Month Number for sort (2). This will sort your months in January – December order

💡 If you need to report on a Financial Year and want your months to display by July to June then choose Financial Month Number for sort instead (3). *Don't click this now*

- Click on Day (4)
- From the Sort by column drop-down choose Day of Week for sort (5)

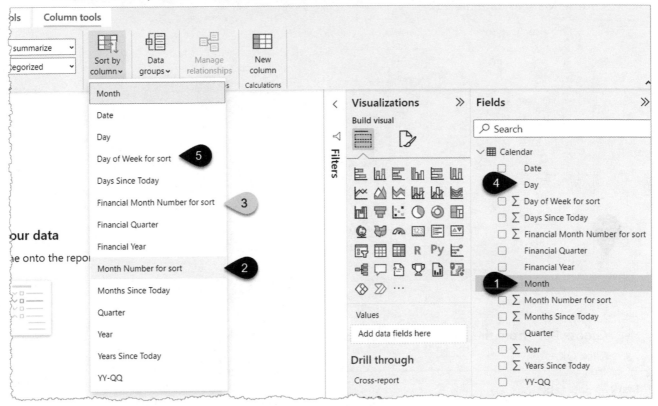

Remember that the Financial Month order and Day order are controlled by your initial inputs in the Power Query Calendar Applied Steps.

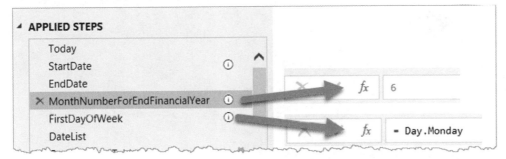

Referring back to the chapter on DAX and the TOTALYTD function, if you are needing to calculate total YTD for a financial year such as July to June rather than January December, then you must sort your Months by "Financial Month Number for sort" and add the optional year-end to your formula: *Don't do this now*

```
= TOTALYTD( [Actual Sales $], 'Calendar[Date], "30/06" )
```

You must also then use the Financial Year field rather than Year in any slicer or visual.

💡 If you need to display some visuals in Calendar month order and others in Financial Month order in the same report then you will need to create two separate Month columns. You can duplicate the month column via a right-click in Power Query. Name one column Month Calendar and the other Month Financial or something along those lines. Then sort them accordingly using the Sort by column button.

Marking as Date Table

One final step you should do is to "Mark as date table".

- Right-click on the Calendar Table (1)
- Choose Mark as date table (2)

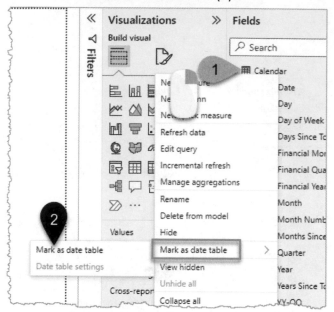

- Choose Date from the Date column drop down (1)
- Click OK

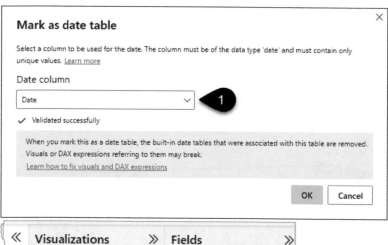

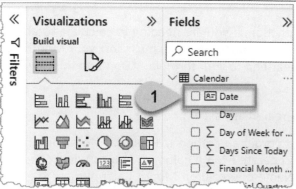

You will then see that a small card icon appears next to the Date column in your fields panel (see the yellow 1 in the image above) indicating this is now the key column.

While your report will likely work fine without doing this it's safer to do so for a couple of reasons:

1. Certain existing and future functionality may rely on marking your date table. For example, "Quick Measures" that incorporate date-based functions may not work if you don't do this. Quick Measures are not covered in this book.

2. If the column you use to connect your Calendar to your Fact table is **not a date column** then functions like TOTALYTD will not work. For example, if your fact table has a "date key" column in the format 20220321 and you add a similar column to your Calendar table and connect them via those columns, the date functions do not work properly unless you've "Marked as Date Table"

☕ For a full explanation of the reasons and causes, Alberto Ferrari has a 5 minute video here url. pbi.guide/MarkDate

Save but don't close this file yet

Chapter 9 - Creating a Template File

This is a very short chapter but could be the most time saving one of the whole book. Creating a template file that contains your Calendar table, a measures table and your preferred colour scheme and settings can save you a huge amount of time in the long run. You can set up a template file for your department or company, include logos and images, and share it with others so that your reports have a consistent structure and look.

Setting Your Default Theme Fonts and Colours

If you closed your Calendar file from the previous example then open it up

- Save your calendar file with the new name "Temp" via File → Save As
- Create your theme via View (1) → drop-down (2) → Customize current theme (3)

After you create your theme, you can save it as a separate .json file if you wish (4) and then share it with someone who can import it using Browse for themes (5).

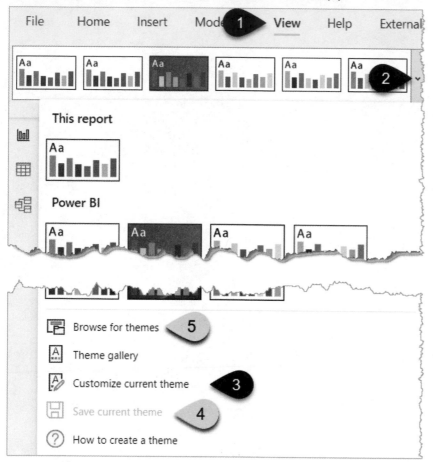

💡 There is also the option to view the Theme gallery that members of the public have contributed to and if you see one you like you can download it for your use.

- Click Customize current theme option as per item 3 above (if you haven't already)
- Give your theme a name (1) such as "Finance Department Theme"
- Selecting the drop-down for a colour (2) gives you the option to manually drag the colour selector or enter the #Hex code or the RGB codes to get the exact colours you need
- You can also change the default fonts and sizes via Text (3)

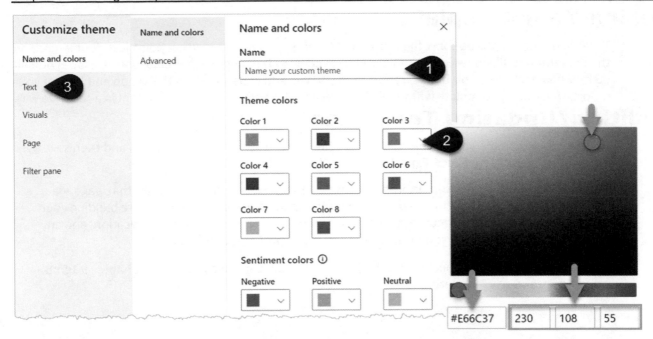

💡 In addition to the general font and size you can change the default Title font and the Cards font. I normally reduce the Cards font to 30 from the default of 45.

Using organisation colours can be a great way to brand your reports and helps to engage the report consumers.

If you change the theme colours on an existing report then those visuals that use the default fonts will change, but any visuals that had the colours adjusted slightly will remain the same.

☕ I'm a fan of Adobe Color Wheel url.pbi.guide/wheel for providing me with a good palette of complementary colours and the #Hex codes I need. It also has a clever Extract Gradient feature where you can upload images or company logos and automatically extract the #Hex codes for the key colours.

Adding a Measures Table

Now that you have your theme set up and your Calendar table in place it's time to add a MyMeasures table to this Temp file.

- Add a MyMeasures table by clicking the Enter Data button on the Home tab → rename as MyMeasures → Load
- Add one measure by right-clicking on the MyMeasures table in the fields list and choose New measure

  ```
  Measure = 1
  ```

- Press Enter
- Right-click on Column1 and Delete from model

Currently your Temp file is a .pbix file. If you open this file to start a new project you will need to remember to immediately do a "Save as" to avoid adding content to this template. A better option is to save your file as a .pbit file because opening it creates a new "Untitled" .pbix copy of your file for you to work on without the danger of overwriting your template.

- File → Export → Power BI Template

You will be prompted to add a description, but you can just click OK unless there is something special about this template that you want to highlight.

- Navigate via the file browser to a place you can easily access the file and name it as MyTemplate
- Close your Temp file, no need to save when prompted

Using Your Template

- To launch a new untitled .pbix file using the MyTemplate file as a starting point just double-click on the MyTemplate file in whichever folder you saved it. By building this template you will save yourself 30 minutes each time you build a report, and you will add consistency to the set up and look of your reports. Sharing the template within a team of people also helps to brand the content in a cohesive way.

Editing/Updating Templates

- To edit a template file you double-click on the file to open it, make your changes, and then save over the existing version via File→ Export→ Power BI Template.

💡 An extra suggestion is to add an instructions page to your template and hide that page via a right-click on the page name. Put a few Text boxes on this page, and then when you are building your reports add some high-level documentation here around data sources, workspace location, and any other information that you or someone inheriting your report would find useful.

You can find both my Temp.pbix file and the MyTemplate.pbit saved as Solutions\Chapter 9 Temp.pbix and Chapter 9 MyTemplate.pbit

Chapter 10 - Intermission for Excel Fans

In the previous chapters, you saw a quick glimpse that Power Query and the Data Model also exist in Excel.

A Little History of Power BI

Power Pivot

For me, the story of today's Power BI begins with an add-in for Excel 2010 called PowerPivot. Power Pivot was originally code-named as Project Gemini internally by Microsoft. It was in October 2009 that they announced this feature as "PowerPivot". Notice the lack of a space in the name, that space was added in a later version.

Excel 2010

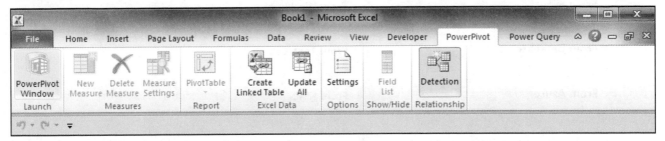

Excel 365

These days Power Pivot is built into Excel and is hidden away under the green "Manage Data Model Button" on the Data Ribbon.

Clicking the Data tab (1) and the Manage Data Model button (2) prompts you to enable the Power Pivot add-in, which then displays as a new tab (3) and opens the Power Pivot window.

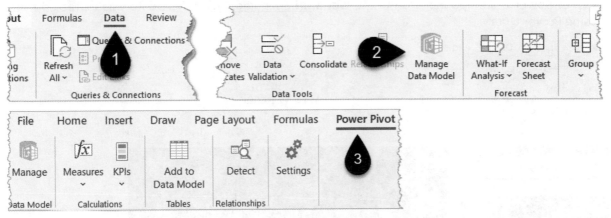

Power Pivot continued to develop and improve up until around 2019. It is still amazingly powerful, and I still use it regularly, but it has not kept up with the Power BI developments of the last few years.

Power Query

Two years after Power Pivot hit the scene a tool called "Data Explorer" was beginning to be demonstrated at conferences. This was the pre-cursor to Power Query. Check out this October 2011 blog post by Chris Webb url.pbi.guide/MDX1.

Excel 2010/2013

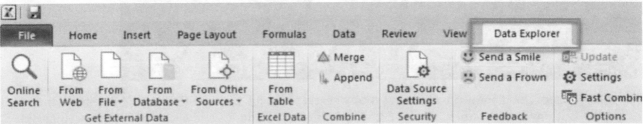

In mid-2013 Satya Nadella announced Power BI for Office 365 (this was when Satya was president of the Server and Tools division). Data Explorer was officially re-branded as Power Query and was an add-in for Excel. It was then built into Excel 2016 and subsequent versions. News story: url.pbi.guide/zNews

Excel 365

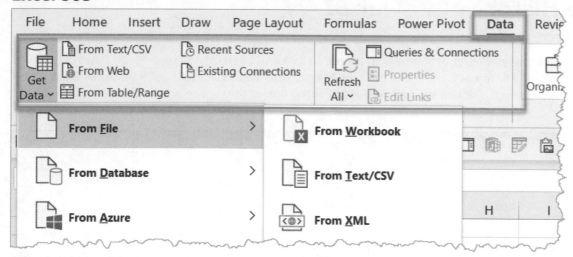

Power Query in Excel continues to develop and keep pace with Power BI, although is a little behind even if you are on the monthly update channel of Office 365.

Power Maps

Power Maps was another part of the group and it's still built into Excel under 3D Map. It's great fun to play with and plot geographic data, add a play axis and even create a video. My first ever video on YouTube was of a 3D map of Power BI companies around the world url.pbi.guide/1stVid. The data was extracted from LinkedIn using Power Query.

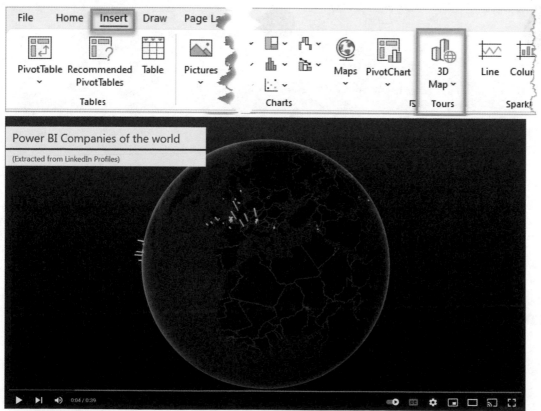

💡 If 3D Maps don't show up on your version of Excel try going to File → Options → Add-ins → then at the bottom of that screen change Excel Add-ins to COM Add-ins and click Go. Hopefully you will see an option for Power Maps that you can tick to enable it.

Power View

The Excel-based suite also incorporated Power View, an interactive visual layer that is now deprecated. This had huge promise with the ability to make visuals interact with each other in a similar way to today's Power BI canvas. Unfortunately, it never worked well and often caused Excel to crash. While all the data processing was done in Excel the sharing of these reports was done via SharePoint online.

Power BI Designer

The Power View and SharePoint online part of the story was never that compelling and the speed of development required to catch up with and overtake the competition meant a decision was taken to strip out the core elements of this "Power" suite and build them into a new tool.

So Power Query, Power Pivot, Power View, and Power Maps were built into a new tool called Power BI Designer – a preview of this was announced in December 2014 by the then relatively unknown Adam "Guy in a Cube" Saxton url.pbi.guide/designer.

> ☕ I'd highly recommend the "Guy in a Cube" YouTube channel url.pbi.guide/GIAC that Adam set up in 2014. It's by far the most highly subscribed Power BI channel around today.

Power BI as we Know it

In May 2015 James Philips (Corporate Vice President Microsoft Business Intelligence Products Group) announced the release of the new Power BI online service and Power BI desktop which are the familiar yet very early versions of what we call Power BI today.

Enough history, time to see it in action...

A Demonstration of Excel's "Power" Features

- Open the Excel Calendar file you created in Chapter 8 and Save As Reporting Demo

> 💡 If you didn't create or save the file then open a pre-saved version found here Exercises\Solution Files\Chapter 8 Excel Calendar.xlsx and immediately use Save As to save it as "Reporting Demo".

If a yellow warning bar appears with an "Enable Content" button, then click it.

The demonstration will be very similar to the process you've already gone through with Power BI, as the features are largely the same. It will involve connecting to the Coffee Sales data using Power Query, joining the tables in the Data Model, creating some DAX measures, and displaying the results in a chart and matrix (Pivot Table) connected to slicers.

Power Query in Excel

- Click Data (1) → Get Data (2) → From File →From Excel Workbook (3)

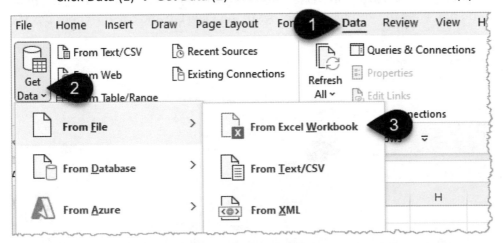

> 💡 These screenshots are from Excel 365 but should be very similar for Excel 2019 and Excel 2021. Excel 2016 will have a slightly different look with a New Queries button instead of Get Data. I would not recommend trying to use Excel 2013 or Excel 2010 for this.

- Navigate to Exercises\Data Sources\Coffee Sales\Coffee Sales Data.xlsx and double-click on the file
- Right-click (1) on Sheet1 and choose Transform Data (2)

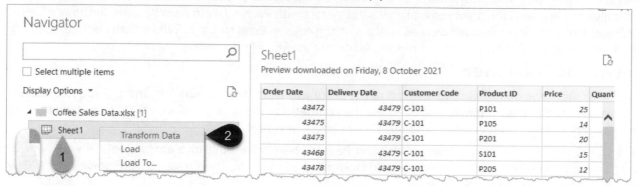

- Change the Data Type for Order Date (1) and Delivery Date (2) to "Date" (3) and choose Replace Current when prompted

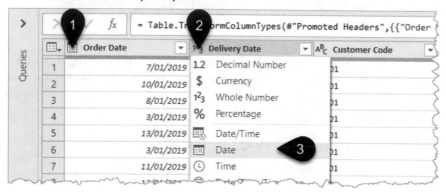

- In the left-hand Queries panel double-click on Sheet1 and rename it as SalesData

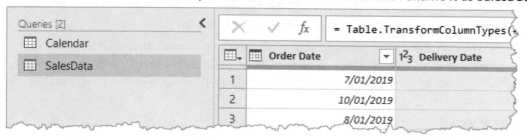

- Click on the Calendar query (1) and go to the StartDate step (2) and in the formula bar change the date to 01/01/2019 (3). If you don't see the formula bar then go to the View tab and tick the check box (4)

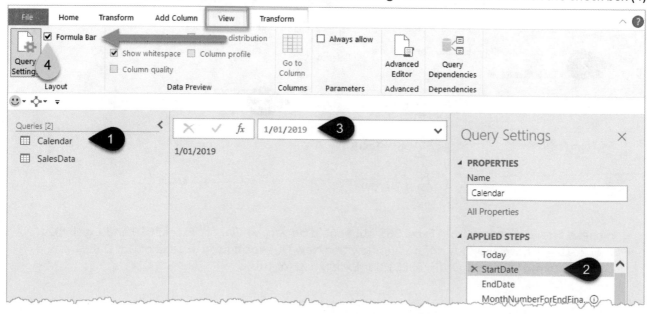

- Click on the EndDate step and type in 31 Dec 2021 and press Enter, it should convert to 31/12/2021 or a version of this depending on your Windows Regional Settings.
- You could now load these 2 tables into the Excel data model, but you will also need the Product Table and Customer Table. Rather than loading these tables and then coming back into Power Query, you can connect to these extra tables while remaining in this Power Query screen.
- On the top right of the Home tab Click New Source (1) → File → Excel (2)

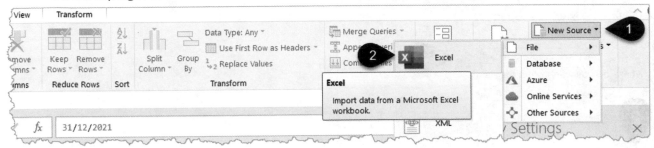

- Navigate to Exercises → Data Sources → Coffee Sales → Lookup (Dimension) Tables.xlsx and double-click on the file
- Tick the box "Select multiple items" (1) and choose tblCustomer and tblProduct (2) then click OK (3)

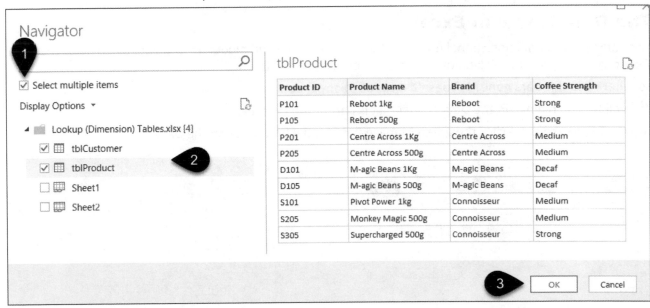

- Double-click on each of the new queries in the left-hand panel and rename them as CustomerTable (1) and ProductTable (2)
- Click the bottom of the Close & Load drop-down (3), then Close & Load To... (4)

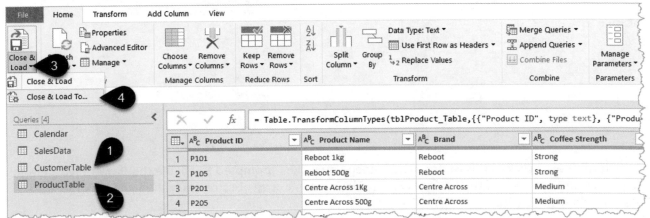

- Select Only Create Connection (1) as you don't need to load these tables into a sheet in Excel
- Ensure there is a tick in the box for Add this data to the Data Model (2) and click OK

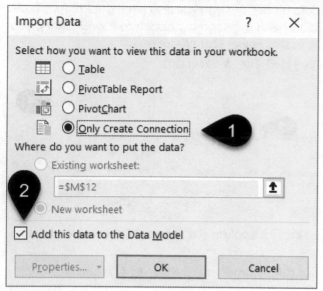

The Data Model in Excel

The Queries & Connections panel appears. This can be shown and hidden at any time by going to the Data Tab on your Ribbon and clicking the Queries & Connections button.

So where has this data gone? It doesn't show up in any sheet.

You will find it "hiding" in the Data Model that is part of the Excel file.

- To see the data, click the green Manage Data Model button (1) on the Data tab

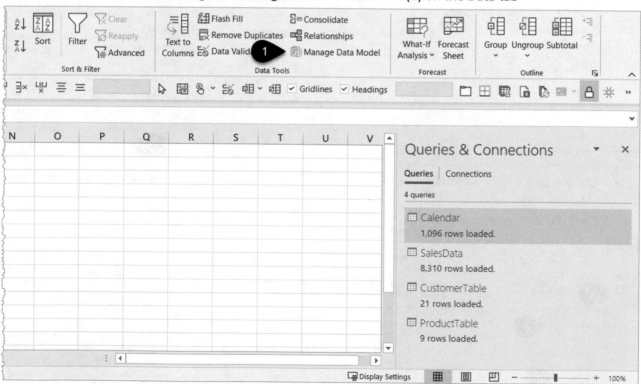

If you haven't ever clicked this button before then you will be prompted to enable the Power Pivot Add-in. Accept this and continue. If the Power Pivot Window doesn't open automatically then just click the Manage Data Model button again.

You should see the Data View with 4 tabs across the bottom of the screen and the Calendar being displayed.

While in the Calendar view you can ensure the months display in the correct order when you build your Pivot Tables and Pivot Charts.

- Click on the Month Column (1)
- Click the Sort by Column button (2) on the Home Tab

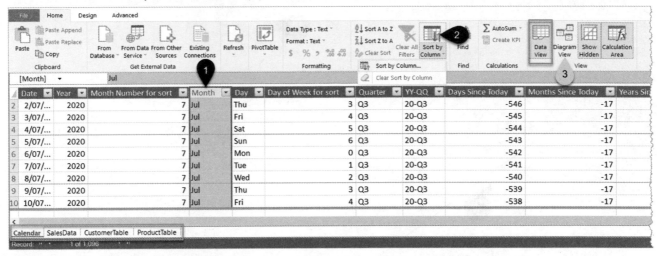

A box will appear for you to pick which column you wish to sort by.

- Click the drop-down (1) and choose Month Number for sort followed by OK

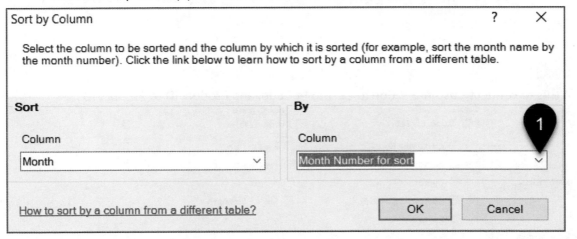

- Repeat this for Day: Click on the Day Column → Sort by Column → Day of Week for Sort

- Now click the Diagram View button (1) in the image below. Does this look familiar? It should do, it's a very similar experience to the Power BI Desktop model view.
- Move Sales data to the bottom of your screen and then drag Order date up to the Date field in the Calendar table (2)

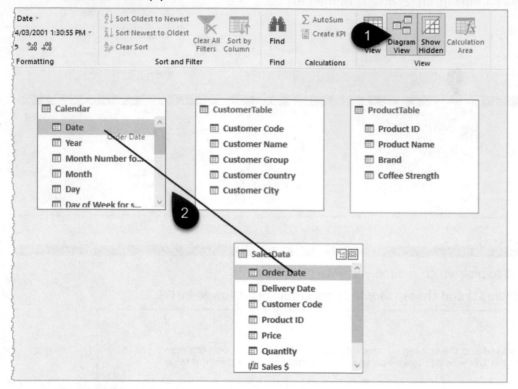

- Repeat this to connect Customer Code to Customer Code, and Product ID to Product ID

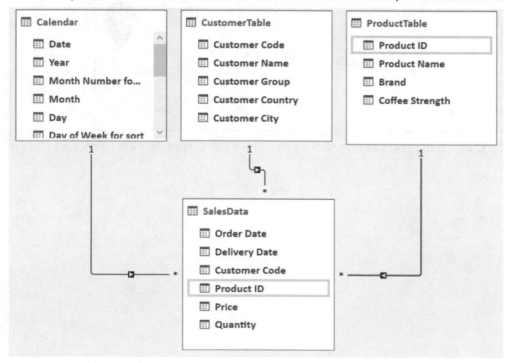

💡 Always hover over the lines after creating a connection to ensure you connected the correct fields. You can also double-click on a line to show and change the connection.

- Close the Power Pivot window by clicking the cross in the top right corner then Save your file
- Click in any cell and go to the Insert tab (1) and click PivotTable (2) and From Data Model (3)

💡 For older versions of Excel just click the PivotTable icon and then click OK. The default option will be a radio button checked against "Use this workbook's Data Model".

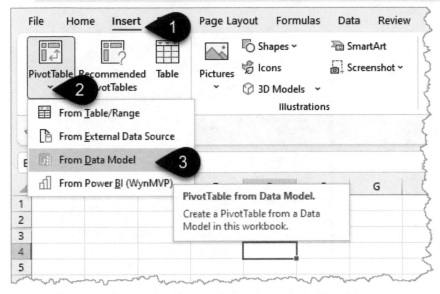

The Pivot Table Fields panel should appear to the right giving you access to all the Data Model Tables and fields just like the right-hand panel in Power BI.

My preference for arranging the Fields section is to click the cog icon (1) and choose the Side-By-Side option (2). This may already be your default setting.

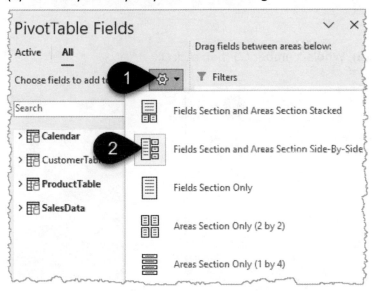

Writing DAX in Excel

- Click the Power Pivot Tab (1)
- Click Measures → New Measure (2)

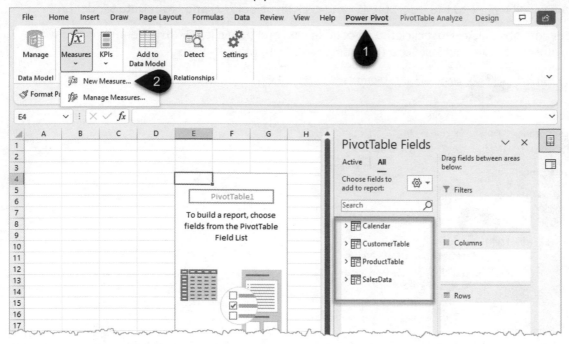

- Click the drop-down for Table name (1) and choose SalesData. This is just the table where the measure will be stored. It's the equivalent of the Home Table option in Power BI and can be changed at any point
- Name the measure Sales Quantity (2)
- Type the following (3)

```
=SUM( SalesData[Quantity] )
```

- Click the Check formula button (4)
- Format as Number (5), 1000 separator (6), Whole Number (7) then click OK

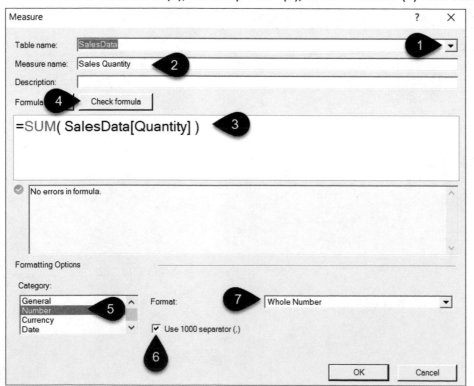

💡 You can make the formula easier to read by increasing the display size in the formula editing window (3 per image above) by holding Ctrl and rolling the Mouse Wheel forwards.

- If Sales Quantity doesn't automatically appear in the PivotTable, then click inside the PivotTable area and then tick fx Sales Quantity measure. The measure is found by expanding the SalesData table in the fields list (see image below)
- Drag Product Name into the rows box

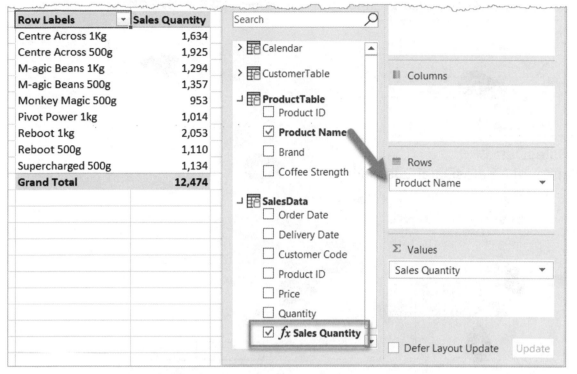

- Drag Month from Calendar into the columns (1)
- Right-click on Year (2) and Add as Slicer (3)

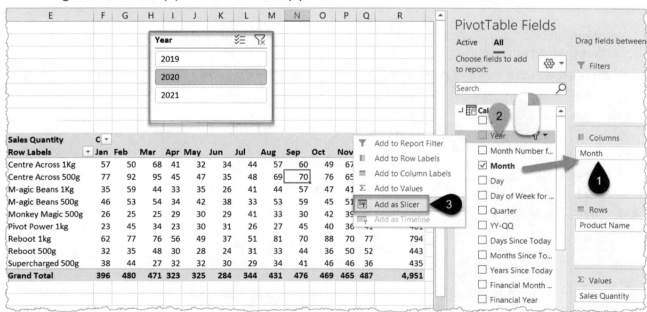

Power Query, Power Pivot, DAX, Pivot Tables, and Slicers were all elements in Excel before being adopted into Power BI Desktop and hopefully, you see the similarities with this example. This book isn't about building Power Pivot reports, but let's build one more measure and a chart to finish off.

- Click on any cell outside of your PivotTable before creating a new measure, otherwise it will automatically be added to that PivotTable

- Go to the Power Pivot tab and choose Measures → New measure
- Choose the SalesData table from the drop-down (1)
- Name it Sales $ (2)
- Type in this formula

  =SUMX(SalesData, SalesData[Price] * SalesData[Quantity])

- Format as Number (4), Use 1000 separator (5) and 0 decimals (6) then click OK

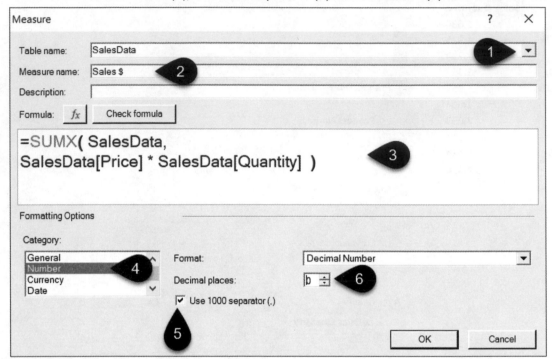

This is a repeat of the measure you wrote towards the end of Chapter 7 on DAX. This SUMX measure is an "iterator" measure that runs down each row of the SalesData table multiplying Price x Quantity and at the end SUMs the results.

⚠ Remember to always put the Table name in front of a column name i.e. SalesData[Quantity] rather than just [Quantity].

As a side note, you can also add measures (2) by right-clicking on the table name (1) in the PivotTable list.

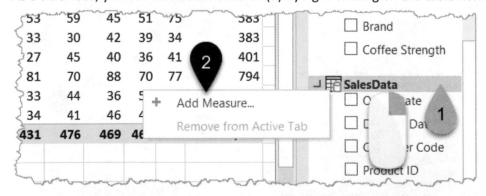

👆 The input box appears to be the same as the one that is accessed via the New measure button. However, it is different and not as useful. At the time of writing, the Tab key jumps you out of the formula and removes any zoomed-in level, and the DAX syntax is not colour coded.

You can also edit a measure (2) by right-clicking on it in the fields list (1) or by going to the Power Pivot tab and choosing Manage Measures. The same issue applies if you use the right-click technique in that the input box is not as useful compared to the Manage Measures approach.

...end of side note ☺.

Create an Interactive Pivot Chart

- Add a new sheet and click in any cell then choose Insert → PivotTable → From Data Model. For older versions of Excel just click on the Pivot Table icon and click OK
- Tick the Sales $ measure from the Sales Data Table then tick Customer Name (1) from the Customer Table
- Create a Bar Chart via the Insert menu (2) and clicking on PivotChart (3)

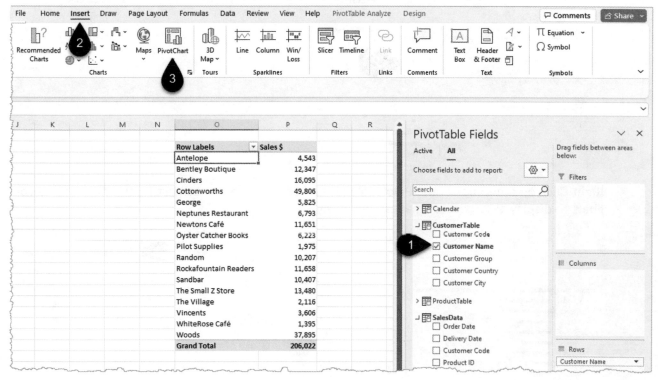

- Choose a Clustered Bar Chart and click OK

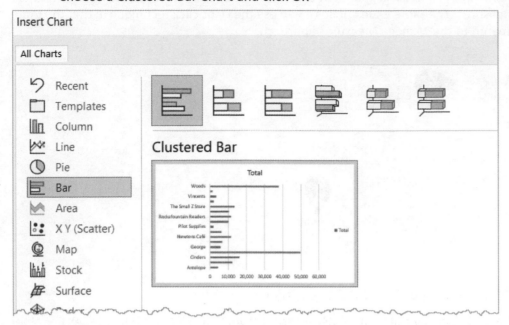

- Right-click on one of the grey chart buttons (1) and choose Hide All Field Buttons on Chart (2)

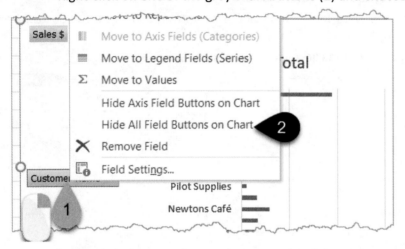

- Right Click on a number in the PivotTable (1) and Sort Smallest to Largest (2) which will force your chart to display as largest to smallest, obviously!

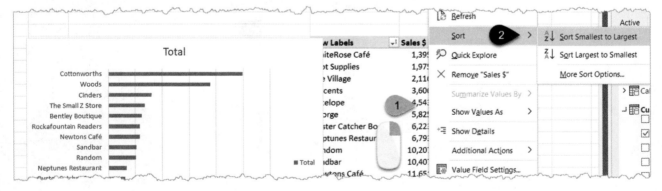

- Right-click on Customer Group (1) and Add as Slicer (2)

You now have an interactive Power Pivot chart. With a bit of extra formatting, you can make it look like the image below.

Formatting a Slicer

The first change to the layout below is the presentation of Slicers as a horizontal band. To do this:

- Click on the slicer (1) and then click the Slicer tab (2)
- Change the number of columns to 6 (3) then drag the slicer wider
- To turn off the borders of the slicer right-click on a slicer style of your choice (4) and duplicate it (5). Then modify this new layout to have no borders via the steps below this image

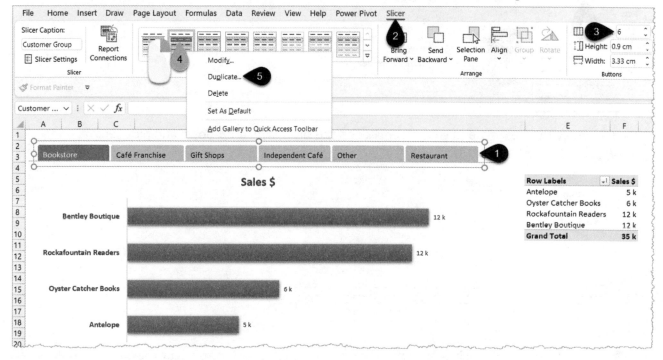

- Give your new Slicer style a name (1)
- Click Whole Slicer (2)
- Click Format (3)

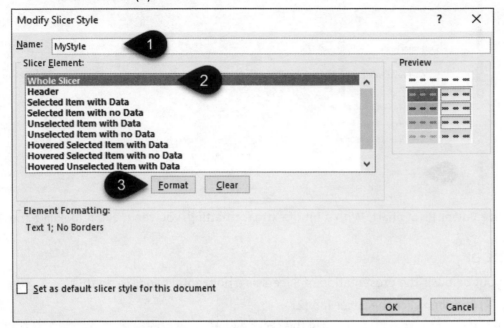

- Choose Border (1) → None (2) and click OK

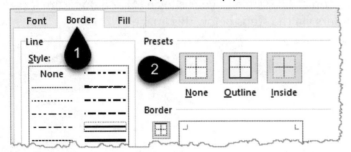

- To apply this new style to your slicer click on the slicer style drop-down and pick your new style

💡 My final trick with the slicer is to make it look more like page tabs by right-clicking on the slicer → Slicer Settings → Uncheck Display Header. Then drag the bottom bar of the slicer up to make it a little narrower so the bottom slicer line disappears.

Formatting Your Chart

Add a few finishing touches to your chart

- Click on you chart then click Design (1)
- Pick a chart style of your choosing. I have selected Style 5, the style numbers appear when you hover over the styles.

- Change the title from Total to Sales $ (3)
- Delete the legend (4) by clicking on it and pressing the Delete key
- Repeat this delete action for the grid lines (5) and the X-Axis (6)
- Add Data Labels to the bars by right-clicking on one (7) and choosing Add data labels

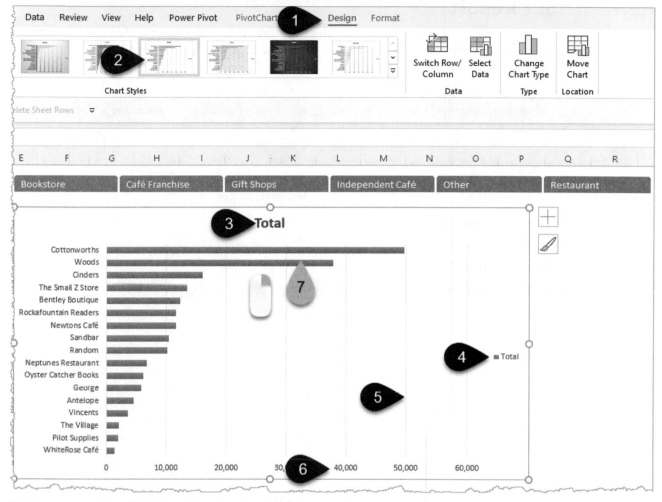

To format your data labels to show in thousands

- Right-click on a data label (1)and choose Format Data Labels (2)
- Click on Number (3) followed by Custom (4)
- If you don't' have the #,##0, "k" format then type it in (5) and click Add

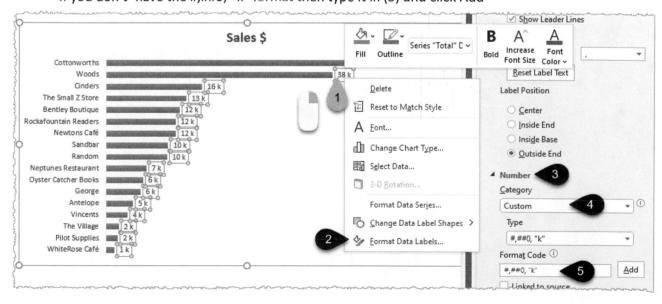

☕ For more information on custom number formatting Jon Peltier has an excellent blog post here url.pbi.guide/charty. There are many resources on charting and dashboard design. I'd recommend you check out the YouTube video on "Interactive Excel Dashboards" by Mynda Treacy url.pbi. guide/mynda.

Refresh Your Report

To refresh the report, click the Refresh All button on the Data Tab. The Power Query steps will run and pull in all the data from the source files. If your source files have new data then your PivotTables and charts will all update to reflect that. This is fantastic!

☕ Learning Power BI is not about replacing Excel, as you can see, many of the techniques taught in this book also add to your Excel skill set. Whether to use Power BI or Excel for a particular report is a grey area. As a starting point I default to Power BI if the report is to be shared with a wide audience or where interactivity in the report is very useful. There are so many factors that influence the decision I hesitate to try and list them. There are things Excel can do that Power BI can't and vice versa so there's an easy decision in those cases, but there's also a huge overlap. It's fantastic to have the choice but this makes the decision harder.

- Close and Save your Excel file

That's it for Excel in this book, but hopefully you get a sense that many of the skills you learn in Power BI can also be applied to your Excel work.

To see my file at this stage open Solutions\Chapter 10 Reporting Demo.xlsx

Chapter 11 - Enrich Your Power BI Report

This section of the book aims to help you take your basic report to the next level by adding engaging user-friendly features that assist the consumers of your report to get the information they need.

You'll start with simple conditional formatting tips and then move on to more advanced capabilities such as Tooltips, drill-through pages, buttons, and bookmarks. Finally, you'll see different visualisation options including a brief step into the world of custom visuals.

Conditional Formatting

Return to your Power BI Coffee House Report file.

- Create a new Page called Conditional Formatting
- Drag Year (1) into the Filters Panel section labelled "Filters on this page"
- Pick Basic filtering (2) then tick 2021 (3)
- Add the Matrix visual (4) and tick Customer Name (5) from the CustomerTable
- Tick Actual Sales $ (6) and Variance Sales $ (7) from the MyMeasures table to give the matrix per below

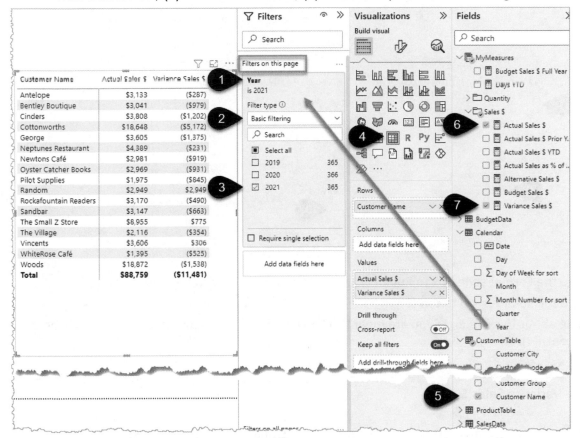

- Click the Format Icon choose Style presets → Minimal
- Display the Actual Sales $ in descending order by clicking the heading Actual Sales $ in the Matrix visual to sort by that value

You will now add 2 elements of conditional formatting to make negative Variance Sales $ numbers display as red and then data bars will be added to Actual Sales $.

Format Negatives as Red

To set or edit conditional formats you click on the small v next to the element you want to add the formatting to:

- Select the Build visual icon (1) so you can see the Rows, Columns, and Values boxes.

- Click the drop-down "v" icon next to Variance Sales $ (1)
- Choose Conditional formatting (2) → Font color (3)

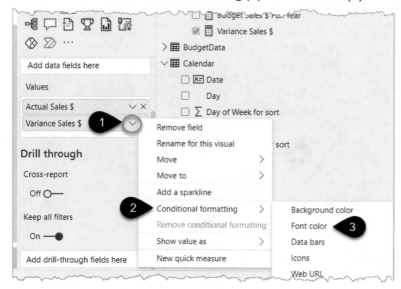

- Change the Format style box to Rules (1) and change "Apply to" to Values and totals (2)
- Change the color for < 0 to red (3)

The crazy thing about this screen is you are meant to know that you ignore the 0 from the >= box because it's set to Percent! (4).

- Click OK

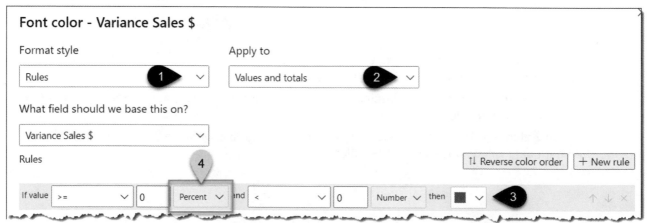

💡 To edit a conditional format, follow the same clicks you used to get to the screen above.

Add Data Bars

To add Data Bars to the Actual $

- Click the "v" next to Actual Sales $ (1) → Conditional formatting (2) → Data bars (3)
- Choose a light blue for the Positive bar (4) and a light red for any negative (5), not that there should ever be negative sales
- Click OK

The matrix visual should now look something like the image below. Adding colour coding and data bars can help consumers of reports understand the information quicker than just presenting numbers alone.

The part of the screenshot that you won't have yet is the "Sales for 2021" heading. That comes next.

Sales for 2021

Customer Name	Actual Sales $ ▾	Variance Sales $
Woods	$18,872	($1,538)
Cottonworths	$18,648	($5,172)
The Small Z Store	$8,955	$775
Neptunes Restaurant	$4,389	($231)
Cinders	$3,808	($1,202)
Vincents	$3,606	$306
George	$3,605	($1,375)
Rockafountain Readers	$3,170	($490)
Sandbar	$3,147	($663)

Dynamic "Measure-based" Headings

The heading of **Sales for 2021** isn't simply typed in, that would be risky given you or someone else may change the year in the Filter Panel and the heading would then not reflect the correct year.

Instead, you can create a measure that "captures" the selected Year, and then you put that measure into the heading.

- Right-click on the MyMeasures table and choose New measure then type this formula and then press enter:

```
Sales Year Heading = "Sales for "& SELECTEDVALUE ( 'Calendar'[Year] ) //
used as heading for Sales Analysis by customer matrix
```

💡 Make sure you also type the 2 slashes and the comment as above. It's a good idea to document your measures using this // technique, especially ones that are used for specific scenarios or are very complex.

- Put this measure into your Matrix title by clicking on your Matrix visual (1) → Format Icon (2) → General→ Title → On(3)
- Click the fx (4) and choose Sales Year Heading from the "Based on field" drop-down (5)
- Click OK

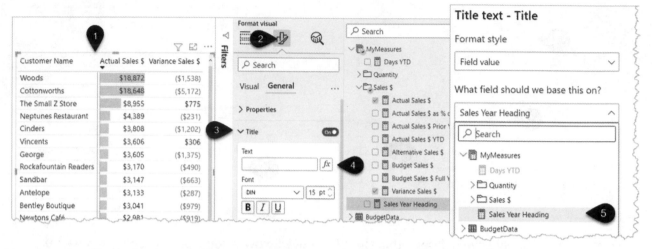

Your Matrix will now have a title that will change if the year is changed in the Filter panel (1).

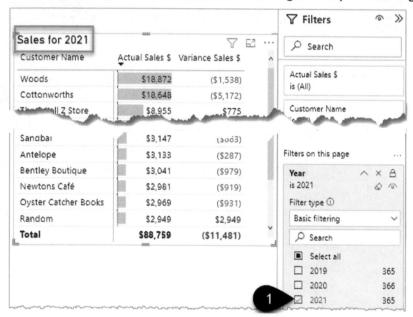

💡 Your formula bar may be covering the heading, so click on some white space on your canvas to hide the formula bar if that's the case.

The measure uses a function called SELECTEDVALUE that returns the value from a column only if that column has been filtered down to one unique value, else it returns a blank. Therefore, because you are filtering for just one year (2021) then it returns 2021. If you picked 2 years in the filter panel it would return blank. You could change the blank to return something else by adding an optional element at the end of your measure as follows:

- Amend the measure by adding "Multiple Years" to the end

```
="Sales for "& SELECTEDVALUE( 'Calendar'[Year], "Multiple Years" )
```

💡 SELECTEDVALUE is not available in Excel, unfortunately you have to use a more complicated construct =IF(HASONEVALUE(VALUES('Calendar'[Year])), VALUES('Calendar'[Year]) ,"Multiple Years")

Before moving on there is a little bit of "housekeeping" to be done.

- Go to the Model view and drag your new measure into the Sales $ folder (1)
- Add a longer description against your measure by clicking on it in the right-hand panel and then typing it into the Description box in the Properties panel (2). The good thing about these descriptions is that they show up (3) when hovering over an item in the right-hand panel.

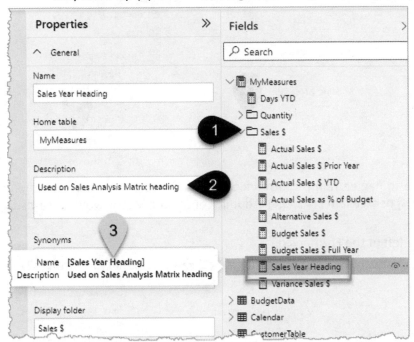

💡 Descriptions can, and should, be added to tables and even columns. Consider including the data source of your tables in the description or some additional information about calculated columns.

Adding Icons

"Traffic Lights" can be a quick, eye-catching, way to flag numbers of interest. Return to the Report view and the Conditional formatting page. You will create this visual:

Customer Group	Actual Sales $ as % of Budget	
Bookstore	🚩	82%
Café Franchise	▭	85%
Gift Shops	🚩	83%
Independent Café	▭	88%
Restaurant	◉	89%
Total		**89%**

- Add a table visual
- Tick Customer Group (1) and the measure "Actual Sales $ as % of Budget" (2) and Minimal Style (3)

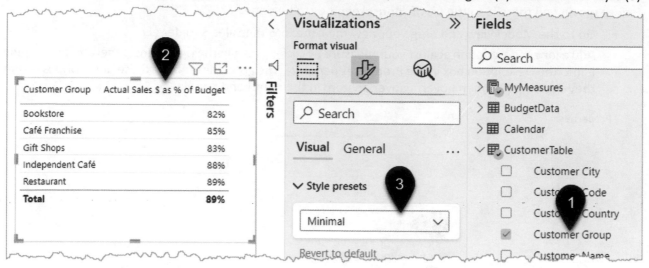

Imagine a business decision was made to flag certain performances against budget as either concerning (<84%), acceptable (<88%), good (<100%) or excellent (>=100%). Adding icons to the Matrix would be a visual way to reflect this.

- Click the Build visual icon to the left of the Format icon
- Click the "v" drop-down next to "Actual Sales $ as % of Budget" (1) → Conditional formatting (2) → Icons (3)

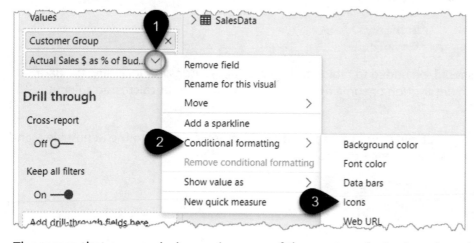

The screen that appears is, in my view, one of the most confusing interfaces in Power BI desktop.

Set it up as per the image below and make sure you change **all** the "percent" drop-downs (1) to be "Number". You will also need to click the +New rule button (2) to add one more rule.

The Max (3) and Min (4) are achieved by deleting the contents after changing the drop-down to "Number".

Note the options to position the Icons to the Left of data (5), you can change this to the right or just show the icon.

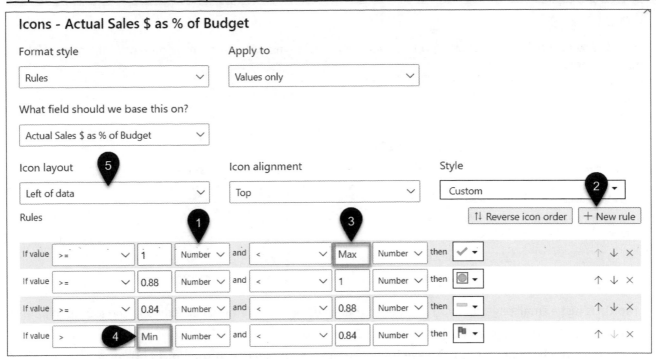

- Click OK once you are done
- If you change the selected year from the Filter Panel (1) you will see the icons change

- After trying this out switch back to the 2021 filter

To see my file at this stage open Solutions\Chapter 11 Coffee House Report Stage 1

Tooltips

Tooltips are fantastic. They allow you to hover over a value in a visual and provide more information about that element.

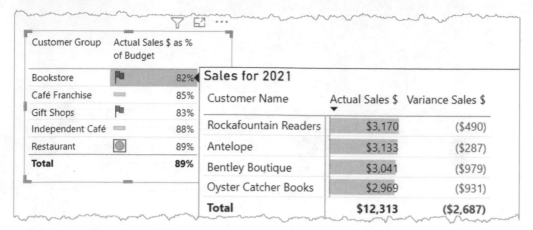

A tooltip is just a small page that you create and then specify what element will "trigger" the tooltip to appear.

- Create a new page and call it Customer Detail Tooltip
- Click the Format Icon (1) → Page information (2) → Allow use as tooltip On (3)
- Canvas settings → Type → Tooltip. The Page then changes to the suggested tooltip size but you can change this to whatever suits your scenario via the Custom type option
- Change the Page size Type to Custom (4) and choose 540 Height and 420 Width
- Copy and paste the Sales by Customer Name Matrix visual from the Conditional Formatting page into this new tooltip page (5)

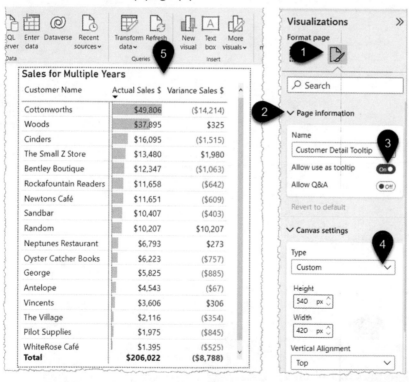

💡 Don't worry if your matrix heading has a blank or "Multiple Years", there is no year filter on this tooltip page. The year filter will be applied when you hover over a customer group back on the conditional formatting page.

- Click on some white space outside the dotted area

- Drag Customer Group into the Tooltip fields box (1). This is the "trigger" to make the tooltip pop up as mentioned earlier

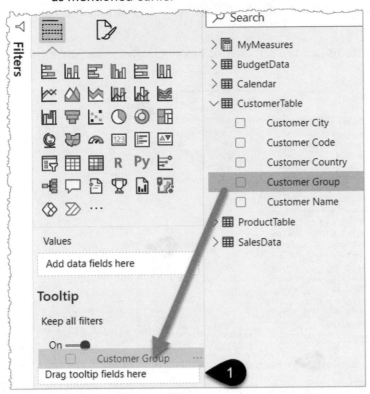

Return to the Conditional Formatting page and hover your mouse over any Customer Group name in your table containing the Icons. Nothing will happen! This is because table and matrix visuals don't show tooltips by default whereas charts will display tooltips automatically.

- Click on the table visual (1) then click the Format Icon (2) → General (3) → Tooltips On (4)
- Hover over any word in the Customer Group (5) and the tooltip should appear (6). The tooltip will be filtered by Customer Group and by Year. By default, all the filters affecting the item you hover over will flow through to the tooltip

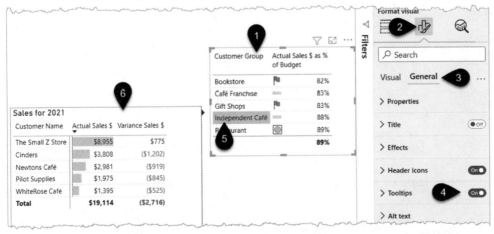

💡 Under the Tooltip drop-down (4 above) there is the option to pick a specific tooltip. This is useful if you have more than one tooltip that is triggered by Customer Group.

As a final step, it makes sense to hide the tooltip page from the report consumer, as they only need to see it when hovering over a visual rather than as a page of its own.

- Right-click on the tab name "Customer Detail Tooltip" and choose Hide

When the report is published the report consumer won't see this page but the tooltip will still work for them.

Drill-through Page

A drill-through page can be very useful to allow you to delve into the details behind a number in a visual.

- Add a new page and name it Sales Details (1)
- Add a Table visual (2) and then tick the items per the screenshot below (3). Note that Date comes from the Calendar table

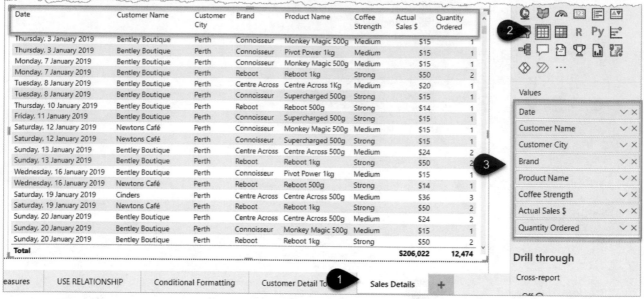

- Click the heading of the Date column in your table visual to sort the table in ascending date order

You can change the displayed date format by going to the Fields panel on the right-hand side, clicking on the word Date in the Calendar table (1) and then going to the Column tools formatting section (2) and picking a date of your choice or even typing in **yyyy mm dd** or a similar combination.

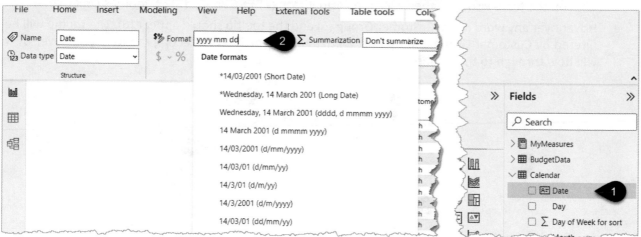

- Click on some white space outside of your table and then drag Customer Name into the Drill through fields box (1)

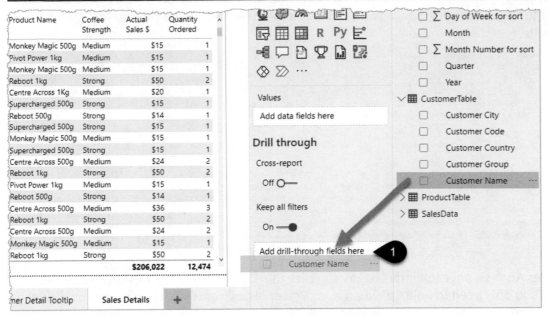

Notice that a "Back" button automatically appears in the top left corner (1). This allows the consumer to jump back to wherever they "drilled through" from.

- Hide this page by right-clicking on the Sales Details tab name and choosing Hide Page (2)

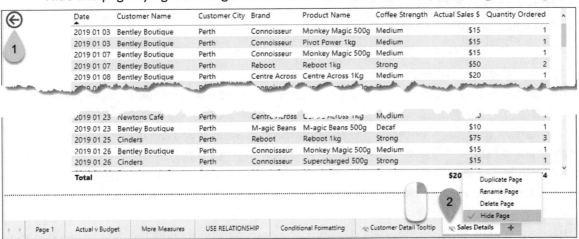

- Go to the Conditional Formatting Page, make sure the page is filtered for the year 2021
- Right-click on Neptunes Restaurant in the Sales for 2021 visual (1) → Drill through → Sales Details (2)

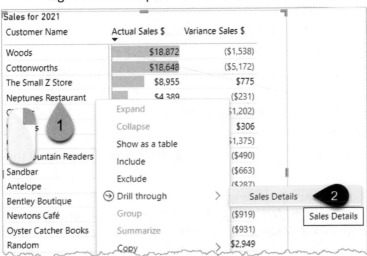

You will now jump to the drill through page you created and see that the table is filtered for 2021 sales to Neptunes restaurant.

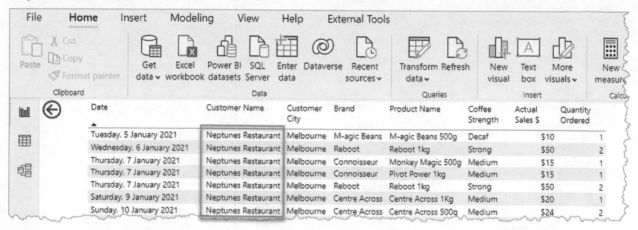

To return to the Sales Analysis page hold the Ctrl key and click the Back button in the top left. As mentioned earlier in the book, you only need to hold Ctrl when using Power BI desktop. Once the report is published to PowerBI.com the report consumer does not need to hold Ctrl.

To see my file at this stage open Solutions\Chapter 11 Coffee House Report Stage 2

Report Design Tips

Here are a few tips when designing a report:

1. Ask yourself or the report consumer what action are you trying to influence with this information?

2. Communicate the key elements as simply as possible

3. Lead the reader of your report through a logical path by setting the scene with the key elements in the top left

4. Don't overcrowd your page. With tooltips and drill-through options you can enhance the story without cramming all the details onto page 1. The first page of your report shouldn't overwhelm new report consumers. 5 visuals is a sensible number.

5. Remove "clutter" from your visuals. Add data labels where possible and then remove unnecessary axis labels

6. Use the right visuals for the right data. Column and line charts are good for date series or trend comparison. For "things" such as Products, Customer Names, etc use a Bar Chart or Table / Matrix instead. Only use Pie charts when comparing 2 items. A 3-segment pie chart should normally be a bar chart instead

7. Keep your number of colours to a minimum. Aim for 3. More colours lead to more "cognitive load" and it's harder to decipher a report when you first look at it

8. Keep colours consistent on a page. If Sales $ is blue on one chart, then use the same blue for Sales $ on a different chart

9. Use lines and white space to group or separate your visuals into sections

10. Spend time to align your visuals vertically and horizontally

11. Do the "squint test". Squint at your report and ask yourself if the thing that stands out is really the most important thing on the page

💡To explore more about data visualisation I'd recommend checking out Microsoft's series of modules called "Design effective reports in Power BI" url.pbi.guide/MDdesign. There's also a popular ongoing series of data visualisation challenges called Workout Wednesday, and you can find the challenges here url.pbi.guide/wow.

Simple Design Features

- Duplicate the Conditional Formatting page by right-clicking on the tab name and choosing duplicate. Rename it as "Design Tips"
- Set up the report page to look like the image below. There are guidance notes underneath the image

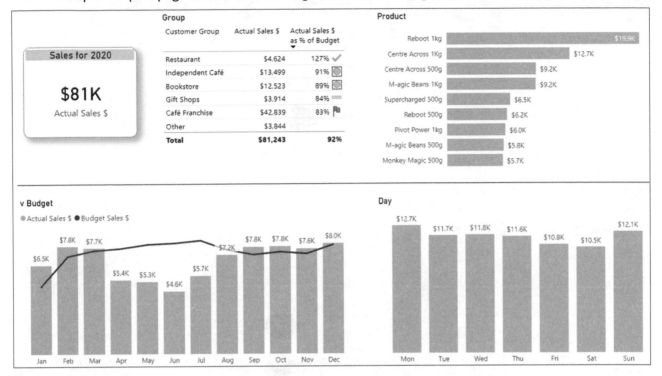

The Card Visual

- Before starting with the Card, change the Year in the Filter Panel to 2020 (1)
- Delete the table showing the Sales $ and Variance Sales $ by customer name
- Add a Card visual (2) with Actual Sales $ measure in it (3)
- Add a title to the card containing the Sales Year Heading measure via the fx option (4)

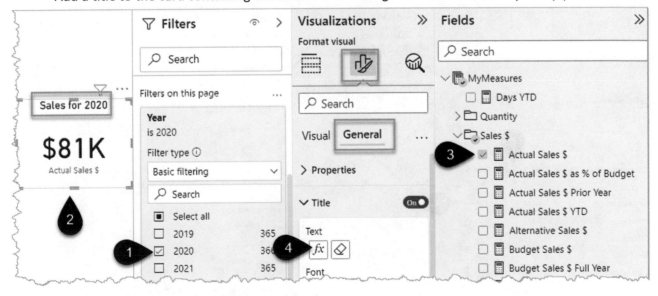

- While in the General section choose Effects and make the visual border rounded 20px and turn the shadow on.
- Change the size of the displayed value via Visual → Callout value → Font reduced to 30

The Table Visual

- Select the Customer Group table visual and increase Row Padding to 5 via Grid (1) → Options (2)
- Increase font size to 11 in the same Options section (3)

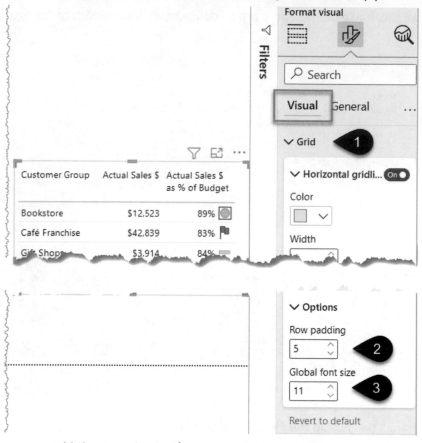

- Add the Actual Sales $ Measure (4) to the table
- Move the conditional formatting icon on the Actual Sales $ as % of Budget values to display to the right of the value via the Conditional Formatting option (5) and selecting Icon Layout → Right of data

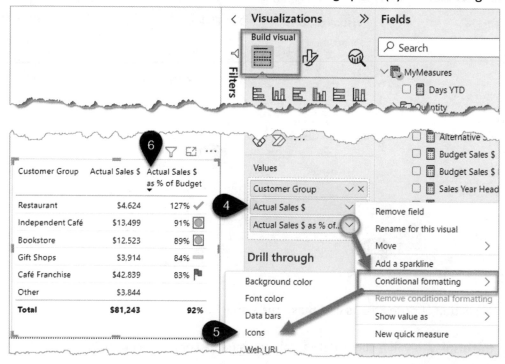

- Sort the visual by % of budget by clicking on that column (6 above)
- Add a Title of "Group" to the visual via Format Icon → General → Title

The Bar Chart

- Add a Clustered Bar Chart (1) with Product Name in the Y-axis (2) and Actual Sales $ measure in the X-axis (3)

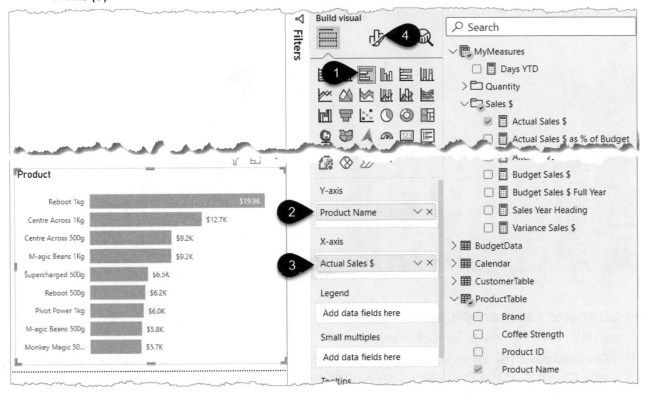

Format the bar chart above with the following steps:

- Format Icon (4 above) → Visual→
- Y-Axis → Title Off
- X-Axis → Title Off
- X-Axis → Off
- Data labels → On
- Bars → pick a lighter blue but not the very lightest shade
- Format Icon → General → Title → type in "Product"

The Column Chart

Now let's create a column chart to show sales by day:

- Copy and paste the chart you just created (Ctrl+C Ctrl+V) and change the chart to a clustered column chart (1)
- Swap the item in the axis from Product Name to Day (2). Note that Day comes from the Calendar table
- Change the title of the visual to "Day" via the format icon and Title

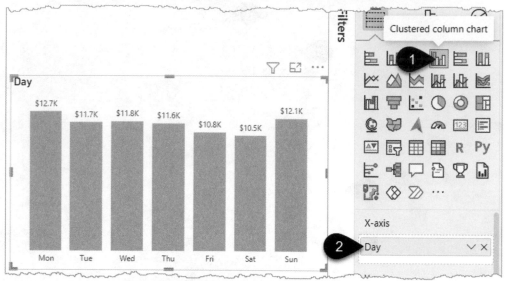

The Line and Clustered Column Chart

And now let's build one final chart for this page:

- Copy and paste the column chart and change the new one to a Line and clustered column chart (hover over the icons on the 2nd row of charts to work out which one that is)
- Change the X-axis to Month
- Add Budget Sales $ to the Line y-axis box
- Turn off the data labels for the budget line via the Format icon → Data labels (1) → Budget Sales $ (2) → Show data labels → Off (3)
- Change the title to "v Budget"

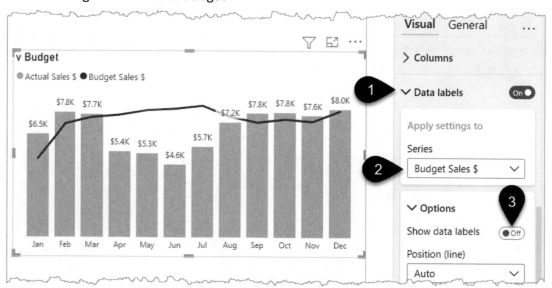

To finish off the layout ensure all fonts are the same and take time to line up visuals. You may find the Format Tab on the ribbon useful as that has various Align options.

You could also give a background colour to the Card Visual title that matches the charts (1) via the Format Icon → General → Title → Background.

Adding a line (2) via Insert→ Shapes → Line helps to break up the page into sections for the user to focus on separately.

💡 Don't forget to minimize the area that your line visual takes up. You should avoid having it overlap and interfere with other visuals.

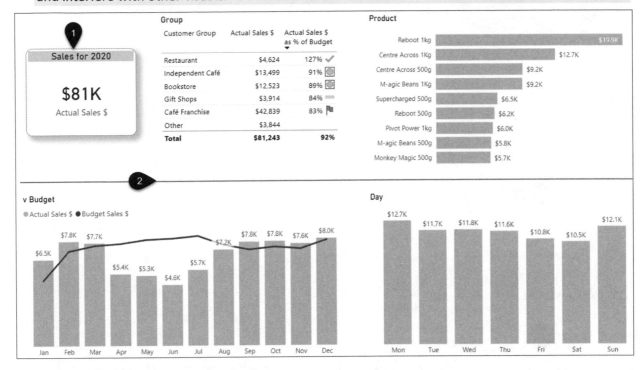

💡 Don't underestimate the power of lines and white space to help make your report easier to consume. At the time of writing this book the way to draw a vertical line is to go to Insert → Shapes → Click the line icon and then change the rotation to 90°. I hope that a vertical line icon is added soon. To suggest or vote for any feature you'd like added you should check out ideas.powerbi.com

Cross Filter vs Cross Highlighting

If you click on the word Gift Shops in the table visual (1), you see it impacts the other visuals. The 3 charts however still show the outline of the original amount in a lighter colour, and the comparisons by product and by month are very small values. It is also difficult to see trends.

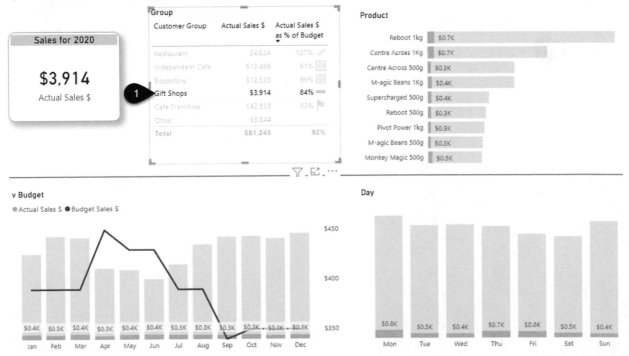

You can change this so that the chart just shows the values of the filtered selection.

- Go to File → Options and Settings → Options
- Scroll down to the very bottom of the left-hand panel to Current File → Report settings (1)
- Tick "Change default visual interaction from cross highlighting to cross filtering" (2)
- Click OK

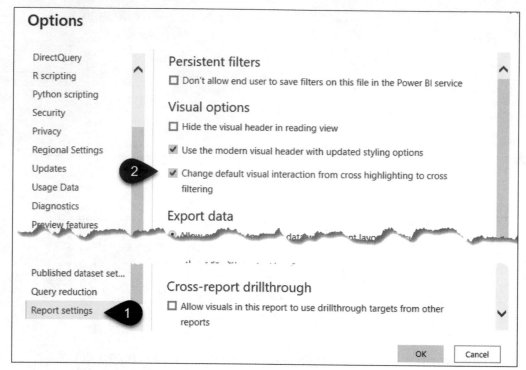

- Click on Gift Shops (1) or one of the other Customer Groups and see what happens

You will see that the original lighter shade outline has gone and now the charts just show the results for the selected value.

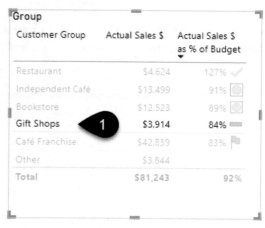

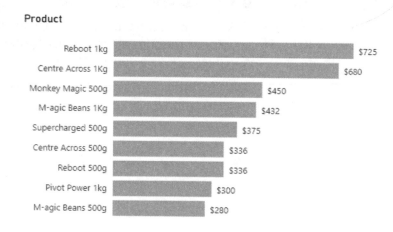

The Budget data you pulled into the file was only at a monthly customer level. Since there is no budget at a Product or Day level it would make sense to prevent the by Product and by Day charts from impacting the Customer Group visual and the "Actual v Budget" chart.

- Click on the Product chart (1)
- In the ribbon click on Format (2) → Edit interactions (3)
- Click on the "Do not filter" icon on the Group table (4)
- Click on the "Do not filter" icon on the v Budget chart (5)
- Click on the Day chart (6) and repeat clicks 4 and 5

After doing this you will see that clicking on a bar in the Product or Day chart has no effect on the Group table or Budget chart.

- Note that the highlight icon (yellow 7) is available if you'd like to override the default interaction and set a visual to cross highlight another visual rather than cross filter
- Click on the Edit interactions button again (3), this hides the icons

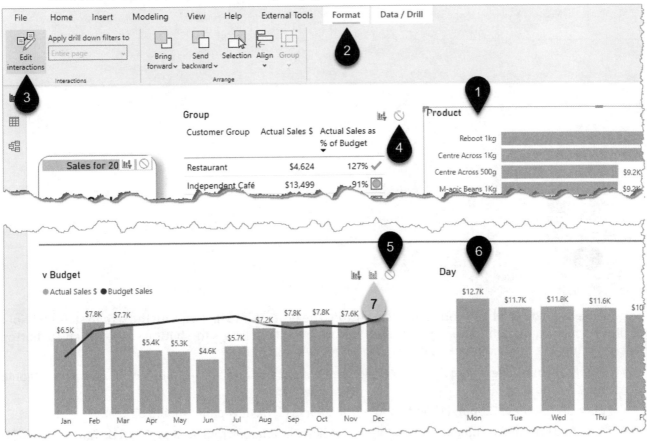

To see my file at this stage open Solutions\Chapter 11 Coffee House Report Stage 3

Bookmarks and Buttons

Bookmarks and buttons are fantastic features for making your report easier to use and more engaging for the report consumer.

For example, if you click on Bookstore (1) and then hold Ctrl and click on the column for March (2) the Card visual should change to $1,060. But there's no obvious "Reset" option to clear the filters that have been applied. You can click on the March column to clear the filter, but this isn't obvious for new users and it doesn't fix the situation if drill downs, filters and slicers have been used.

The good news is you can build your own reset button. The process is to first capture the screen status without any filters applied and then "bookmark" it. Then you assign that bookmark to a button so that when the button is clicked it triggers the bookmark to display the screen without filters.

- Firstly, if your page is showing $1,060 click on Bookstore to remove any filters. Your card visual should now be showing $81K
- Click on the View Ribbon (1) and choose Bookmarks (2). A new panel should appear
- Click Add (3) and then double-click on the new bookmark name and rename it as "Reset Design Tips Page" (4)

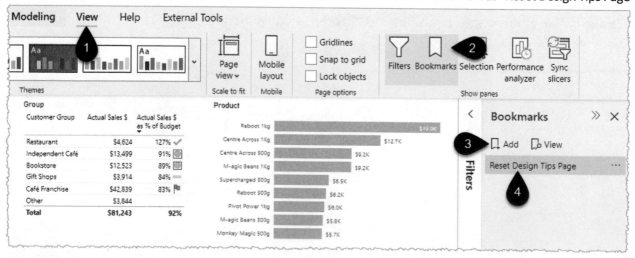

- Test it out by Ctrl-clicking on a few items in your report and then click on the bookmark name (4 above) to "trigger" it and reset your filters

⚠ Remember that earlier on we used the Filter Panel to set this page to be filtered by the year 2020. This filter status would have been captured when you created the bookmark. Therefore, if you go to the Filter Panel, change the year to 2021, and then click the bookmark it would reset to 2020

To set a different year in the filter panel and update the bookmark then:

Set the filter to 2021 (1)

Click the … (2) next to the bookmark name, or right-click on the name, and click Update (3)

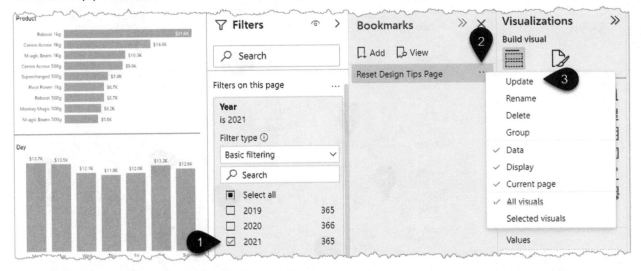

☕ This book is only scratching the surface on many of the topics covered and bookmarks is one you can really delve into. You can even control the visibility of different visuals on a page by combining bookmarks with the Selection panel.
I'd recommend looking up content from Reid Havens url.pbi.guide/ahoy, the Power BI Tips site url.pbi.guide/brew, and Microsoft Docs url.pbi.guide/MDbookmarks to find out more.

- To close the bookmark side panel, click on the Bookmarks button in the View Tab

Now that you have created a bookmark, the simplest way to allow the report consumer to trigger that is via a button.

- On the Ribbon click Insert (1) → Buttons (2) → Blank button (3) and it will appear in the top left corner

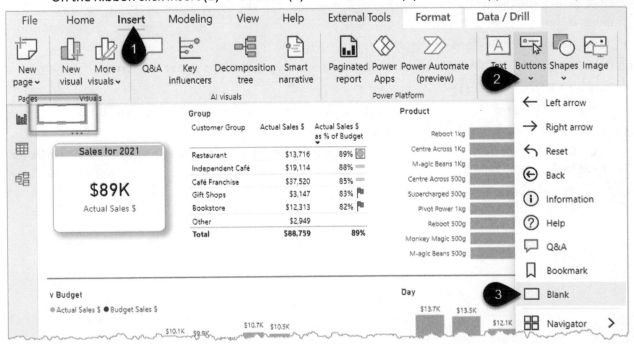

A Format button panel will appear on the right-hand side as per the screenshots below.

- Add an Action to the button by turning Action on (1) → Bookmark (2) → Rest Design Tips Page (3)
- Add the text "Reset" to the button via Style (4) → Text on (5) → Type "Reset" (6) and increase font to 13 (7)
- Reduce the Border (8) to width of 1

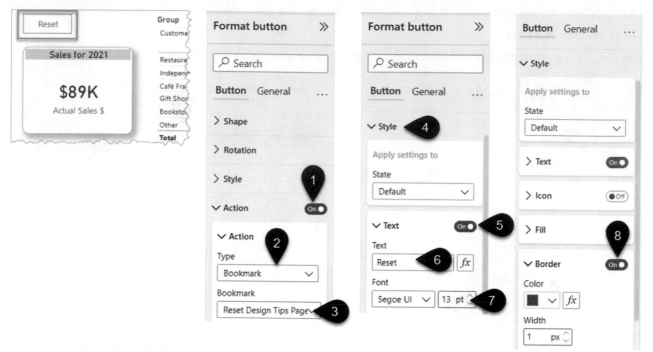

Test it out by clicking on any month in your chart then clicking the Reset button. Did you remember to hold Ctrl when clicking the button? The report consumers will not need to hold Ctrl when they are interacting with a published report.

Page Navigation Buttons

A great use of buttons is to assist with navigating around multiple pages.

- Add a new Page and name it "Contents" then drag the page to the beginning of your report

> 💡 If you have a lot of pages then dragging to the beginning can be a pain as you must do it in several stages. Here's the tip, while dragging the page, press the Tab key a few times until you see the first page and then you can drop it there.

- Click on Insert → Buttons → Blank Button

In the right-hand side "Format Button" panel choose the following settings as per the screenshots below:

- Style → Border → Off (1)
- Action → On (2) → Type→ Page navigation (3) → Destination → "Actual v Budget" (4)
- Style (5) → Text → On (6) → Type "Actual v Budget" (7)
- Icon On (8) → Custom (9) → Browse... (10) → find the Chart Icon image from the Exercises\Other Files folder

Now for a bit of showing off...

- Change the Style → State to On hover (1)
- Change Text (2) → Font color white
- Icon → Delete the existing image and then add a Right Arrow image from the Exercises\Other Files\ folder (3)
- Turn Fill on (4) → Blue (5)

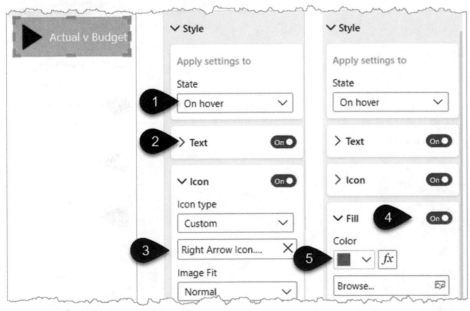

- See what happens when you hover over your button!
- Hold Ctrl and click your button. It should take you to your Actual v Budget page
- Return to the Contents page and copy-paste your button using Ctrl+C Ctrl+V

- Change the text to say Design Tips. Do this via the Format Button → Style → Text
- Change which page the button points to via Action → Page Navigation → Design Tips
- Add a heading to your contents page by inserting a Text box (1) and type in the word Contents → Font size 16
- Insert a line (2) via Insert → Shapes and change its colour via Style → Border

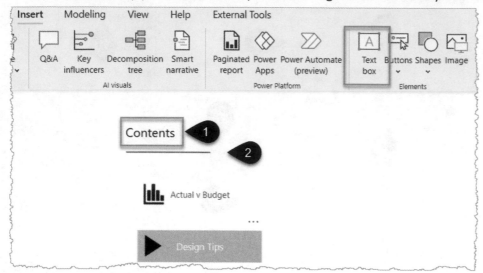

While these formatting steps may seem a bit unnecessary, the art of making your report look and feel engaging for the report consumer is an important one. They never know how much time you've spent developing your Power Query, DAX, and data model, so take a little time to add a polished finish to your report.

To make your cover page look even more inviting you can add a page background image and make it 70% transparent.

- Click on any white space on the page
- Format Icon (1) → Canvas background (2)
- Add Image→ Choose Cover Page Background (3) from Exercises\Other Files
- Transparency 70% (4)

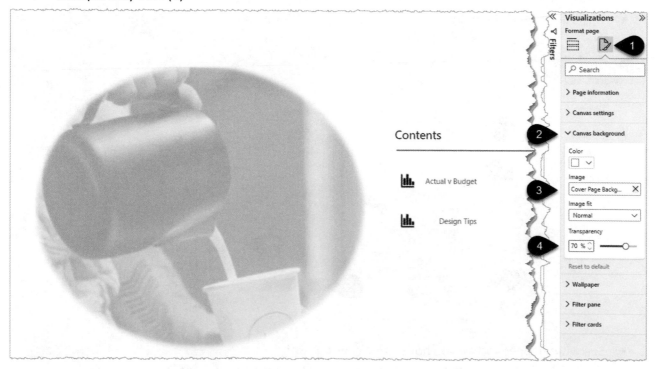

⚠ One thing to realise is that, at the time of writing, the image defaults to 100% transparent tricking you into thinking the image upload hasn't worked.

You may want to turn off the backgrounds of your text box and buttons.

- Select both buttons by holding Shift while clicking on them, or "lasso" them with the mouse
- Style → Apply settings to State → Default → Fill on→ Transparency 100%
- Style → Apply settings to State → On hover → Fill → Transparency 0%
- Go to the General section → Effects → and turn the Background Off

To see my file at this stage open Solutions\Chapter 11 Coffee House Report Stage 4

An alternative quick way to add page navigation buttons is to use the Page Navigator option.

- Click the insert menu and choose Buttons (1) → Navigator → Page navigator (2)
- The Sales Details page is a hidden drill through page and you don't want that to be included. In the right-hand panel change the Show hidden pages option to off (3)

☕ I think hidden pages should be set to off by default and this may be fixed by the time you read this book.

In the image below the following Formatting options have then been selected:

- Shape (4) is set to Pill, the Style (5) → Border is turned off and the Shadow is turned on

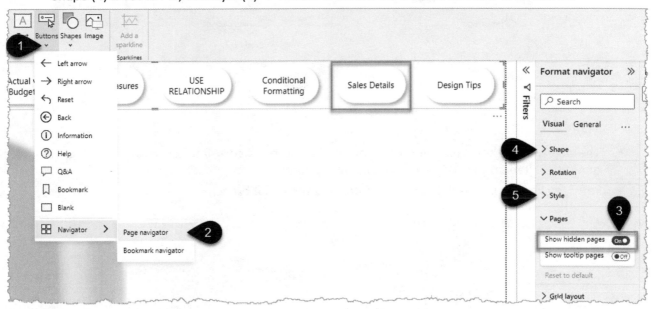

The buttons are dynamically linked to the page names so if you change a page name or add a new page the name in the navigator will also change.

☕ I personally prefer the control of creating individual buttons, so I have deleted this navigator bar for the remaining exercises.

Making Analysis Easier

Decomposition Tree

One of my favourite visuals for assisting with analysing data is the Decomposition tree.

- Create a new page and name it "Analysis", then click on the Decomposition tree visual (1)
- Tick Quantity Ordered (2), followed by Brand and Coffee Strength from the Product table and Customer City and Customer Group from the Customer Table (3)
- Click the + next to Quantity Ordered (4) and choose High value (5)

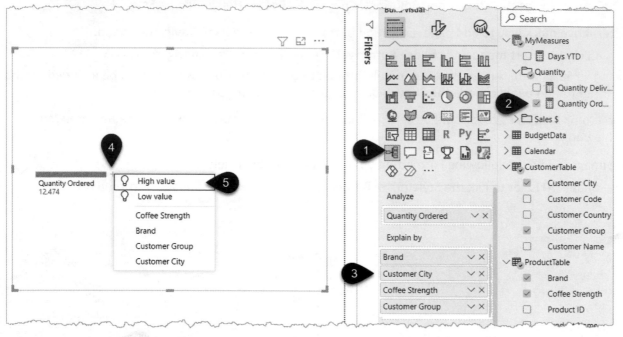

- The algorithms then take over and work out what items correlate to driving your highest order quantities. Repeat this for each branch that is created
- You can click the x in each heading section to remove that branch

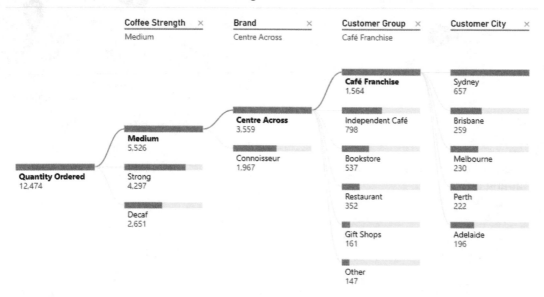

Small Multiples

I've often seen data presented as stacked column charts. Let's build one now.

- Create a new page and name it Small Multiples
- Add this stacked column chart (1) by looking at the screenshot below and adding the items in the X-axis, Y-axis, and Legend boxes

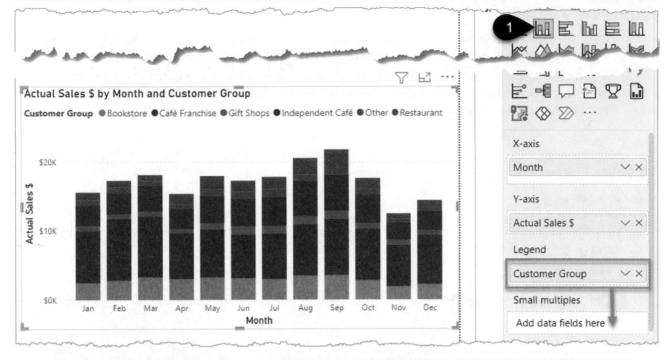

👆 I find stacked column charts very difficult to interpret for just 2 different items let alone the 6 Customer Groups shown above. Let's try something different.

- Drag Customer Group out of the Legend and into the small multiples box as shown in the previous image.
- Click the … (1) in the top right corner → Sort small multiples by Actual Sales $ (2)
- Change the grid to 3 x 2 via Format Icon (3) → Small multiple grid → Columns 3 (4)

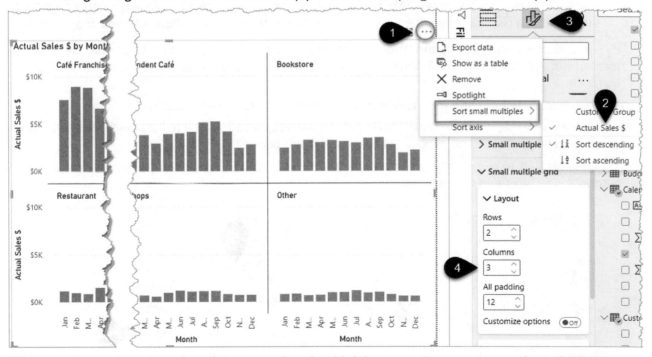

While the visual takes up more screen space, that shouldn't be your primary concern. If you think this layout helps communicate the information more easily then you should use this approach.

Custom Visuals

- Click on the 3 dots in the Visualizations panel (1), followed by Get more visuals (2). This gives you access to hundreds more visuals created by Microsoft and Microsoft partners
- If you click on a visual, you'll see more information about the visual and a button to "Add". Many visuals also have a Download Sample option. The visuals with a blue tick (3) mean that the Power BI team has tested and approved certain code requirements. There's also more information under Learn More (4)

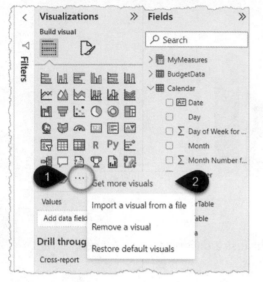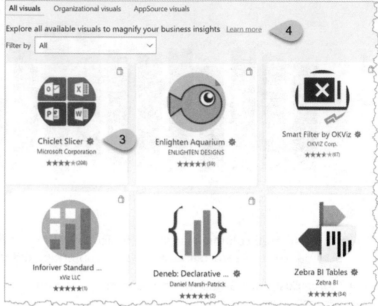

- Scroll through the list, many visuals are free, some are paid, and some have paid features. It can be cost-effective to pay for a visual if it would otherwise require you and future developers to spend days developing your own complex DAX, data modelling, formatting, etc. to achieve something similar. Or the visual you require may not even be possible to create manually in Power BI desktop

⚠ Some visuals may result in importing data from or sending data to, third party or other services located outside of your Power BI tenant's geographic area, compliance boundary, or national cloud instance.

- Search for Enlighten and then click on the Enlighten Aquarium and choose Add

After adding a visual it appears under the main list of visuals (1). If you want it to be available for your future reports then right-click on it and choose Pin to visualizations pane (2).

Don't do this yet, but to remove the visual completely click the 3 dots (3) and choose Remove a visual (4). If you pinned it, you will need to unpin it first.

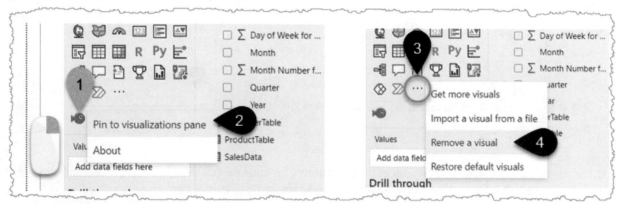

- Create a new page called Custom Visuals
- Click on the Fish (1)
- Add Customer Group (2) and Variance Sales $ (3)
- Use the Format icon → Series → Sharks!

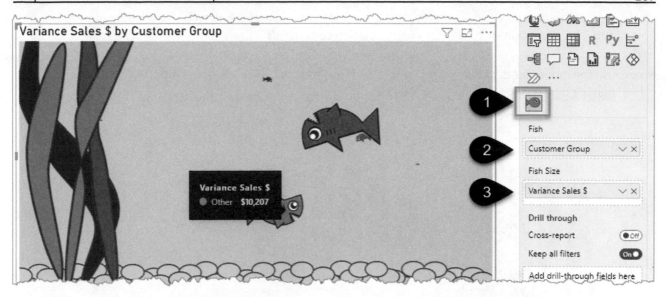

☕ The size of fish/shark is relative to the size of the Variance Sales $. Negative numbers result in the icons flipping upside down and floating to the surface! OK, so maybe this isn't the most practical of charts, but it's fun and illustrates that there really is no limit as to what can be displayed in a custom visual. To see my file at this stage open Solutions\Chapter 11 Coffee House Report Stage 5

Natural Language Queries and AI-Driven Insights

The robots are coming! Seriously though, this next feature is very impressive.

- Start a new page and name it Q&A
- Double-click on any white space (1) avoiding the middle of the page, and a special Q&A visual should appear. If it doesn't appear then try clicking the Q&A button on the Insert tab (A). If that doesn't work then save and restart Power BI Desktop and try again
- Type the following text into the visual "actual sales $ by month for 2020 year" (2)
- Click the small icon (3) to convert it into a standard chart that you can now edit as normal

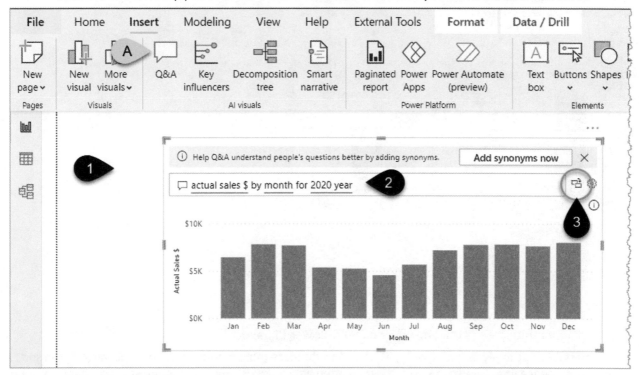

If you expand out the Filter panel you should see that there is a filter for 2020 being applied.

Wow...

This feature is called Q&A and is amazing! I'm guessing it won't be long before we're creating our entire reports in a cloud-based version of Power BI using just voice commands.

If the above doesn't impress you then surely the next thing will! If you ever had to produce a waterfall chart in Excel to explain the movements between two figures, then you'll know it's less than straightforward, but check this out...

- Right-click on the bar for April (1) and choose Analyze → Explain the decrease (2)

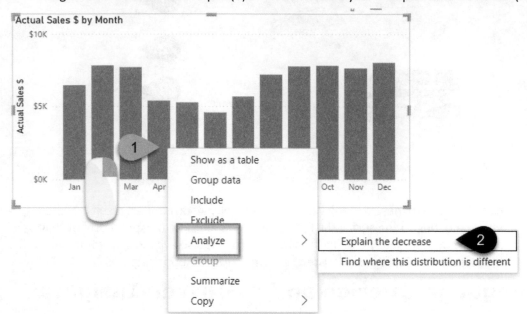

This then creates a scrollable list of waterfall charts to help explain the main drivers of the decrease. Click the thumbs up or down to help inform the algorithms of the type of analysis you prefer for the future and then click the + to add the visual to the page. There are 4 different types of visuals you can choose between at the bottom of each waterfall chart.

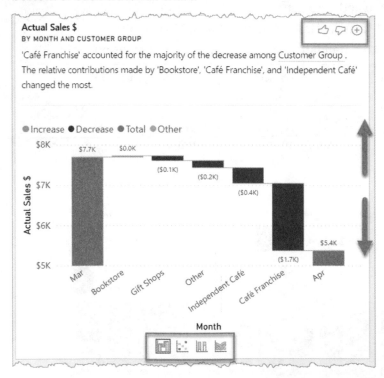

💡 To dismiss this screen click anywhere on your Power BI page

Our jobs are still safe as analysts, for now, ☺, as "the why" for these movements still needs explaining. These sorts of features may appear a little "gimmicky", but they can often help to focus your analysis and save you significant time.

To see my file at this stage open Solutions\Chapter 11 Coffee House Report Stage 6

Chapter 12 - Sharing Your Reports via Apps

In Chapter 3 - Publishing your report, you saw the simplest way of sharing a report which was to publish it to a workspace and then click the share button to get a link or enter a specific user's email address.

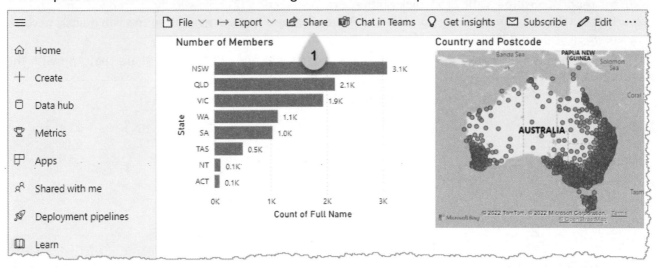

While this is simple it is not my preferred method of sharing. I'd recommend you start sharing reports via the "Apps" experience. This is the topic of this chapter.

Publish Your Report to the Workspace

- Click on the Contents page of your Power BI desktop report and then on the Home tab click Publish. You will be prompted to Save which you should do
- Select the Workspace you created back in Chapter 3. In that exercise I named the workspace PBI XL Demo, you may have named yours zTempTraining – *Your Name*
- Confirm you wish to replace the file
- Click the blue link (1) to open Coffee House Report.pbix in the Power BI service

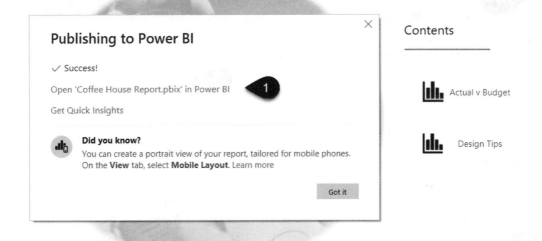

Create an App from Your Workspace

In Chapter 3, you saw how to share a report via the Share button (1). While it is simple to share individual reports this way it can become painful to manage when sharing multiple reports.

Also, for report consumers they can click on the "Browse" section (2) followed by Shared with me and the experience is fine for one or two reports, but as Power BI grows in the organisation this can quickly become overcrowded and confusing.

A better method is to package up your workspace reports into an "App" (3) and share that App with the report consumers.

- Click on the name of your workspace at the bottom of the left-hand panel (4)

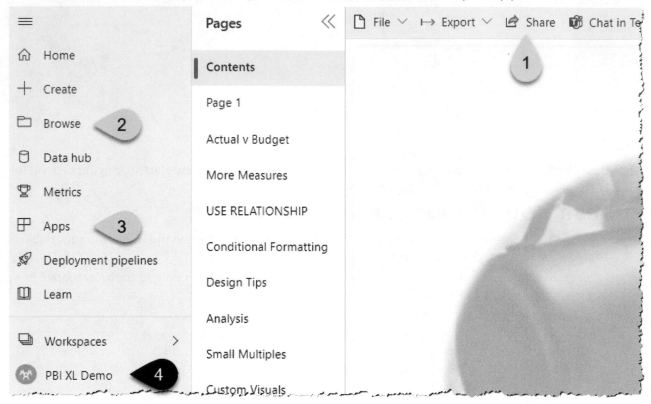

- Click on Create app (1)

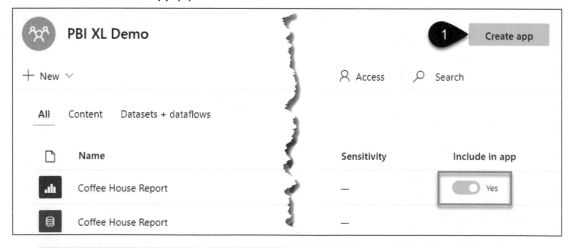

💡 There is a toggle against each report as to whether to include it in the app or not. This is so you can add a report to a workspace, review it online / consult with a colleague about whether it's ready for others to see, and then add it to the App.

On the next screen, you could change the App name (1), but I generally leave it the same as the workspace to avoid confusion. You must add a short description (2). I'd recommend changing the App theme color (3) to light grey otherwise the default colour, such as the dark blue displayed below, can clash horribly with your reports.

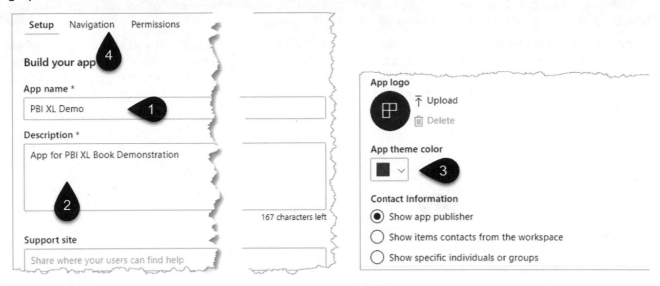

Under the Navigation screen (4 above) you can change the order in which multiple reports would display within the app (1). You can hide reports from the consumer (2). You can also add section breaks and links to external elements such as web pages, SharePoint sites or feedback forms, etc. (3)

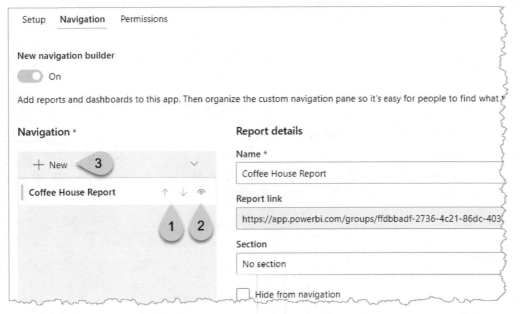

Sharing the App

The Permissions section is where you enter report consumers' email addresses (1). If sharing with a wide audience, it's best if you can use Active Directory user groups or even the name of a Team from Microsoft Teams. Maintaining individual email addresses can be cumbersome.

I would recommend turning off the 2 default yellow ticks (2) unless you are sure you want these options selected. I'd also recommend being cautious about selecting "install this app automatically" (3) as while it is great that it just shows up automatically for the report consumer, they also can't remove it if they don't want it.

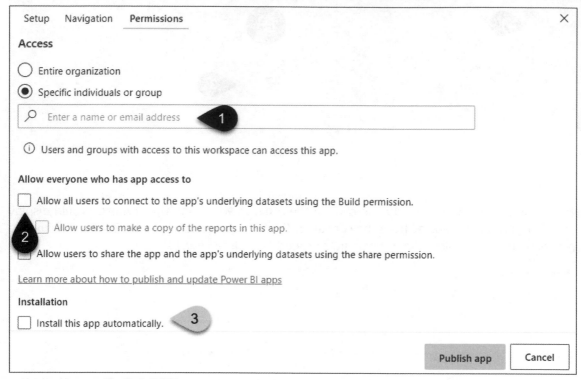

- You can leave the email address field blank for now (1 above)
- Click the Publish app button

You could now copy and send this link to the intended App user. Don't click the Go to app button just yet, it's useful to instead see how the report consumer would discover the app.

- Click Close

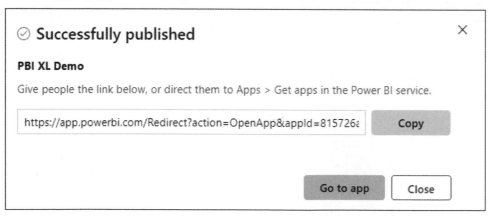

- If you don't share a link with the report consumer, or they lose it, they can follow these steps:
- Click on Apps in the left-hand panel (1)
- Click the Get apps button (2)

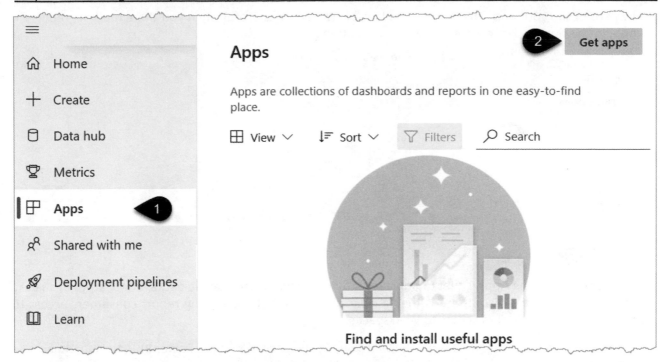

Find and install useful apps

- Click Organizational apps (1)
- If a large number of apps appear then you may need to search for the name of the App you just created
- Hover over the tile for the App you created, and you'll see the description you added (2)
- Click anywhere on the tile to Get it now (3)

Power BI apps

Install apps that provide actionable insights and drive business results

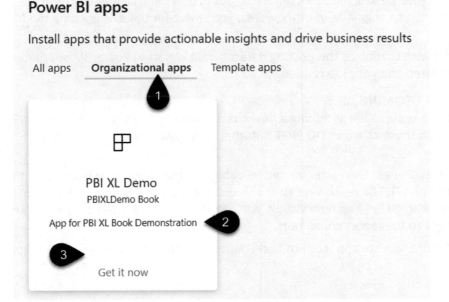

👆 Under the All apps section you will see a large number of applications that have been built by Microsoft Partners. Some of these are free, others have paid features.

.You will then see your app. The Report is collapsible (1), which is useful when you share multiple reports in an App. In the bottom left corner is the Go back option (2)

The real upside of using Apps is that multiple reports from a workspace can be packaged together in an easy to consume "wrapper". Also, there is then a clear distinction between giving report consumers access to Apps, and report developers access to Workspaces.

> ☕ At the time of writing, one App is linked to one Workspace. It's on the Power BI Team's roadmap to allow workspace reports and other elements to be shared in a more nuanced manner with different elements being hidden or shown to different audiences. This functionality may be live by the time you are reading this.

Updating a Report and an App

To update the report, you simply go to your Desktop file, click refresh to pull in new data, click Publish and then select the same workspace you published to originally. In other words, you save over the existing data model and report.

You will be prompted to confirm you wish to replace the existing dataset. Your report in PowerBI.com that is being shared with others will be updated and your job is done.

⚠ IMPORTANT WARNING ABOUT UPDATING APPS
If you make a **physical change** to a report such as adding a new chart, changing the size of the font, changing the colour of a bar then those changes **DO NOT** automatically flow through to the App version of the report.

To make the App show a new **physical** change, then after you've re-published the report you need to go to the workspace (1) and click Update app (2). The reason for this is that the workspace is now like a staging area for review, so if you're making changes/adding new visuals you can double-check what they look like online before releasing those changes to the report consumers.

You will then be prompted to click 2 more "update app" confirmation buttons before the changes flow through to the App consumer.

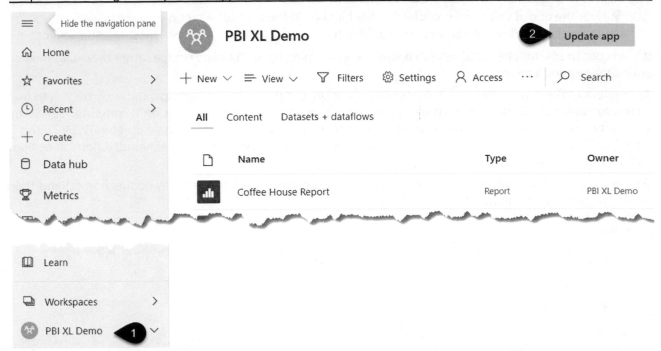

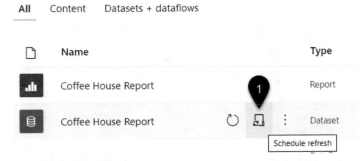

Scheduling a Refresh where a Gateway is Required

Rather than manually refreshing and re-publishing each time you can set up a scheduled refresh.

- Go to your workspace and then hover over the orange Dataset and click on the Schedule refresh icon (1)

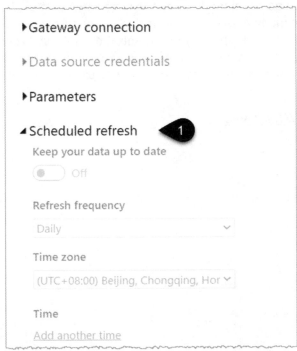

There you will see this tempting Scheduled refresh section but when you expand it (1) you find it's all greyed out.

💡 Near the end of Chapter 4 you saw that a Scheduled Refresh could be set up easily because the data source was an online data source. In that chapter you connected to a file on OneDrive/SharePoint.

It's simpler to set up scheduled refresh if your data is coming from an online source rather than data held on your organisation's network.

To connect to files on your network someone in your organisation needs to set up a Gateway for you to use. Gateways are outside the scope of this book. It's a piece of software that runs on a computer/server on your network. It allows the Power BI service (PowerBI.com) to connect to files on your network. Once this is established and your data source file paths are added to the Gateway then the Scheduled Refresh options will become available.

Gateways are not difficult to set up and you can click the drop down for Gateway connection (1) and then there is a link to Learn more (2).

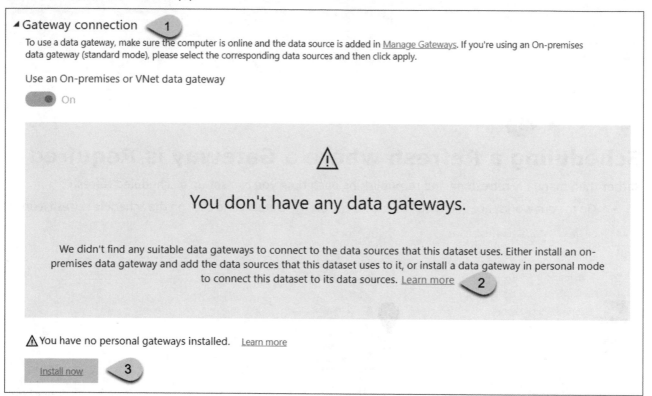

A gateway can be installed on your own laptop or desktop in personal mode using the Install now button (3), but this is **not recommended for real-world use**. There are many reasons for this including the fact that the machine needs to be always on for the refresh to work and other people in your organisation will also likely need to use a gateway and they won't be able to use yours. Centrally managing Gateways on a computer server with sufficient processing power to handle all the queries thrown at it is critical. Take the time to read up on it.

☕ For more information from Microsoft Docs:
What is an on-premises data gateway: url.pbi.guide/MDgateway
Data refresh in Power BI: url.pbi.guide/MDrefresh

Chapter 13 - Additional Important Features

Row-Level Security

A fantastic feature that will make Excel users jealous is the ability to have your report automatically filter down to the data that specific users are allowed to see. For example, in your Coffee House Report, you can add a setting that only allows the person in charge of Bookstore sales to see Bookstore data.

Set Up a Role

- Go to your Power BI Desktop Coffee House report
- Click Modeling (1) →Manage roles (2)

- Click Create (1) and type Bookstore Manager (2)
- Select CustomerTable... → Add filter → Customer Group (3)
- Type over the word "Value" with "Bookstore" (4)

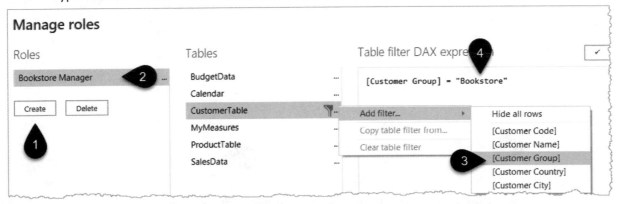

This is telling Power BI to filter the data down to the Customer Group = Bookstore.

It's also useful to add a role where certain report users can see all the data:

- Click Create again and name the role "See Everything". Don't apply any filters
- Click Save in the bottom right corner
- Click the "View as" icon (1) and tick Bookstore Manager (2) to test it out

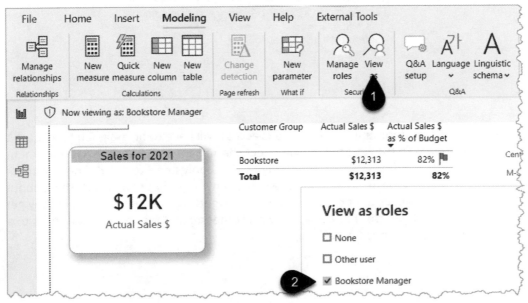

Look at the different pages, the screenshot above is from the Design Tips page.

You will see every page is filtered by the Bookstore Customer Group.

- Click the Stop Viewing button on the yellow bar
- Click on the Contents Page and then on the Home tab → Publish (click Save when prompted)
- Double-click on the workspace you created and choose to replace when prompted
- Click on the blue hyperlink to Open Coffee House Report

Add Report Consumers to Roles

You've just set up 2 roles, and it is now time to add people into those roles.

- Click on your workspace name (1)
- Click the 3 dots next to the Dataset (2) and choose Security (3)

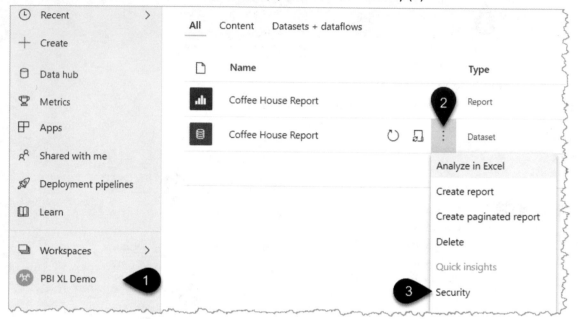

It's in this screen that you then assign users to roles via their email address.

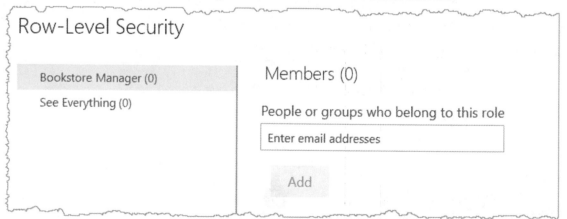

Once you set up row-level security in a report anyone who needs access will have to be assigned to at least 1 role. This is **in addition to** giving access to the report itself via direct sharing or via the app. This requirement to put everyone in a role confused me at first as I thought surely I should only need to put the people that I want to see a filtered view into roles, everyone else should see everything, right? But when you think about it that is not very safe. You could easily share a report with someone forgetting to assign a role and they get to see everything! With this method, if you do share a report with someone and forget to assign them to a role they just see an error warning like the one below.

🖐 There are more advanced ways of setting up and managing row-level security that are outside the scope of this book.
Microsoft Docs RLS guidance: url.pbi.guide/MDrls
RLS with AD Security Groups by Gilbert at Fourmoo: url.pbi.guide/MOOrls
RLS with Org Hierarchies by Reza Rad: url.pbi.guide/RADrls
To see my file at this stage open Solutions\Chapter 13 Coffee House Report

⚠ Row Level Security does not apply to anyone that has any of the following workspace access levels: Admin, Member, or Contributor. People with these permissions will see all the data ignoring any Row Level Security you set. This is another good reason to avoid granting report consumers access to workspaces. While you can set workspace permission to viewer, I'd suggest that having the clear distinction between App access for report consumers and workspace access for report builders is the best way to get started.

Dataflows

One of the most powerful features of Power BI and Excel is Power Query. As you saw in earlier chapters, Power Query is amazing at transforming messy data into clean tables that assist in building useful models for our reports.

Dataflows is the online version of Power Query and allows you to create centralised clean tables of data that can be used by you or others in multiple reports.

You may come across scenarios where you need to use the same clean table in multiple reports and therefore you find yourself repeating the same Power Query steps in multiple files. This is one of the scenarios when you should consider using Dataflows.

Creating centralised tables for your reports rather than re-creating the Power Query steps in each file leads to more consistency in your reports. It can also be used to reduce the number of queries hitting your source systems. For example, the dataflow pulls in the data you need overnight and then your Power BI reports feed off the dataflow tables instead of hitting the source system over and over again as reports are developed and refreshed.

Create a Dataflow

- Go to PowerBI.com and the workspace that you created (1)
- Choose New (2) → Dataflow (3)

- Click Add new tables (1)

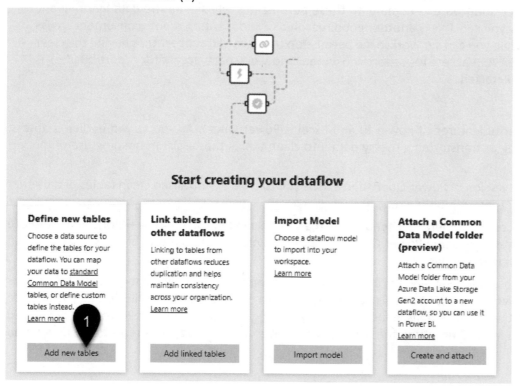

⚠ Note that you cannot create a dataflow in "MyWorkspace".

You then see a list of the data sources you can connect to. This list is growing every month.

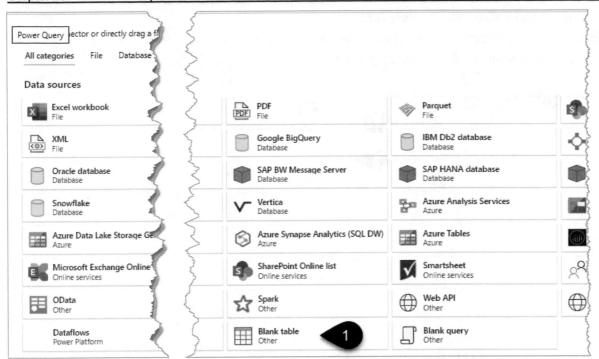

To keep things simple at this late stage in the book this section will just look at creating a blank table. In reality, there's a whole world of connectors you could use to build your centralised table of data.

- Click Blank Table (1 above)
- Type in the information per the screenshot including the heading and click Next

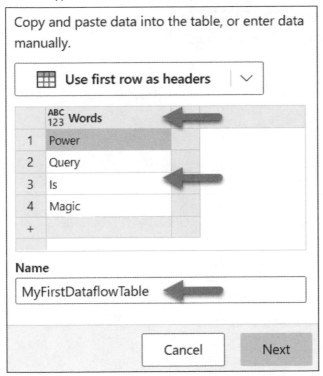

- You will see a familiar Power Query editor screen
- To try out a few buttons you can classify the words as "Long" or "Short" using 2 steps
- Firstly, Add column (1) → Extract (2) → Length (3)

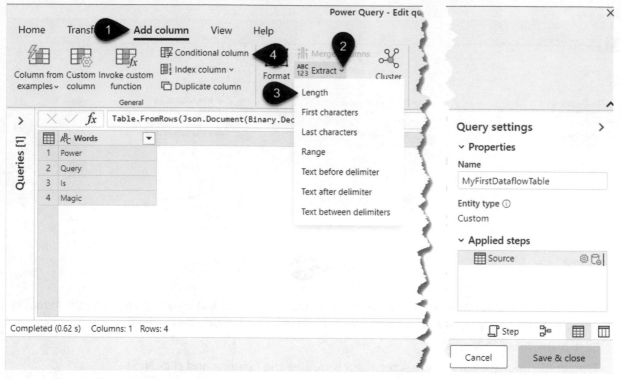

- Then set up the Conditional column (4 above) as per the image below

💡 You will need to click the Add clause button to add the second condition.

- Click OK

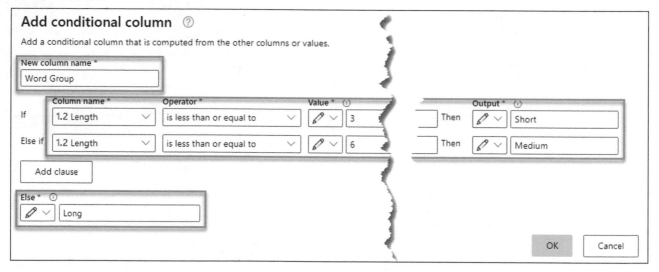

- Change the ABC123 of the new Word Group column to a Text datatype (1)

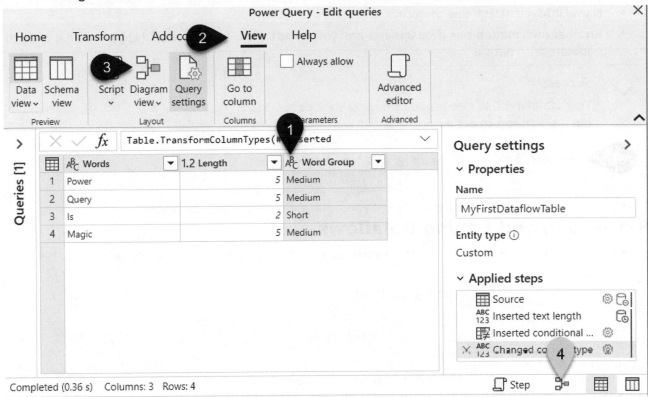

One clever feature of Dataflows that doesn't exist in Power BI Desktop or Excel at the time of writing is the Diagram View.

- Click View (2 above) → Diagram view (3 above) or alternatively just click on the shortcut icon (4 above)
- The Diagram view is very useful for more complex queries, especially where one query feeds into another as you can easily see the interaction and main data sources of each query. There are useful buttons to fit to screen, show a mini-map or go full screen (1). Clicking on the icons in the image (2) is the same as clicking on the applied steps in the right-hand panel and you will see your code and resulting table change as you do so
- Click Save & Close in the bottom right corner

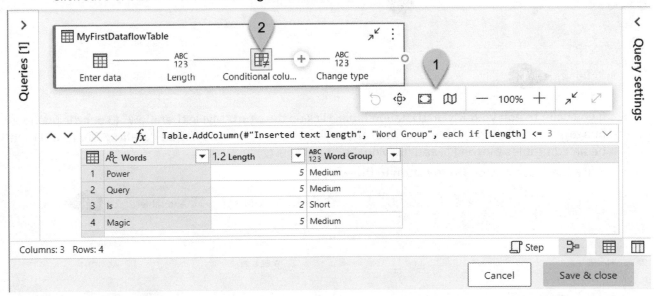

You will then be prompted to name your Dataflow. Think of a dataflow as a folder of Power Query tables.

- Name it MyFirstDataFlow then click Save
- Another information box then appears and you **must** click "Refresh now" (1) to force the table to populate with data

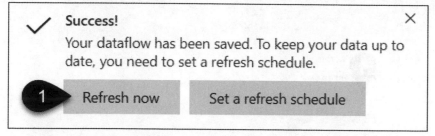

- Click on your workspace name (1) and you will see your new dataflow is listed

Refreshing and Editing Dataflows

- You can refresh a dataflow or set up a scheduled refresh (2) just like with a dataset

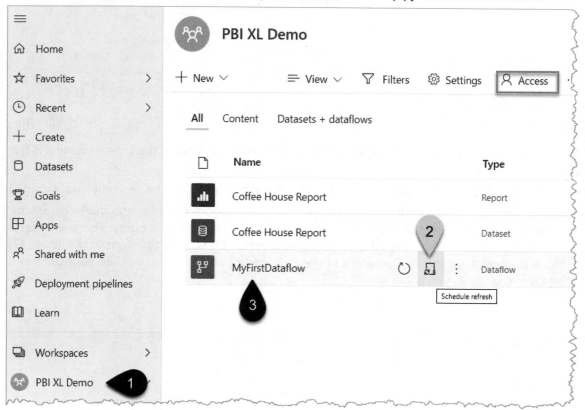

- If you want to edit your MyFirstDataflowTable, click on the word "MyFirstDataflow" (3 per the previous image). This will then show you a list of any tables you have created in that dataflow. There will then be an Edit tables button (1) and individual edit buttons (2)
- Click the Close button (3) to return to the workspace

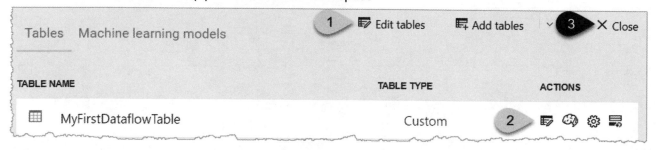

☕ A single dataflow can be thought of as a folder for one or more queries. Refreshing a dataflow, therefore, refreshes all the queries within that dataflow. You can't schedule different refresh times for different queries. If you need that functionality then you need to set up a dataflow for each different schedule.

Refreshing a dataflow does not "push" data into any connected datasets/reports. Those datasets must be refreshed after the dataflow refreshes. This could be automated using Power Automate, which is outside the scope of this book.

Connecting to a Dataflow

- Go to your Power BI desktop file and choose Get data from Power BI dataflows (1)

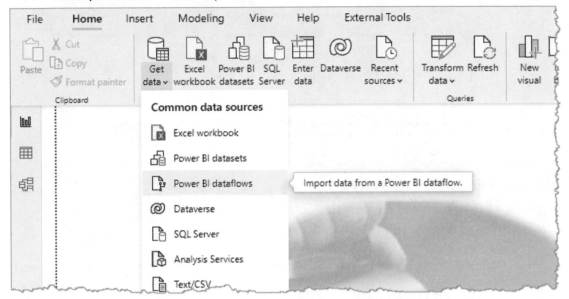

You may then be prompted to sign in. Once you have done that click Connect.

- Navigate to MyFirstDataflowTable via your workspace and your dataflow
- Click Transform Data just as if it was any other data source

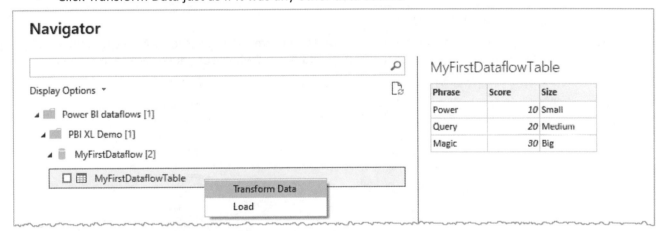

The Power Query editor screen should now appear allowing you to add additional data transformations if needed.

One complaint I have about the dataflows connection in Power Query is that the Navigation step groups together the dataflow name and the query name into one generic step.

- Click the Advanced Editor on the Home tab and you will see some very confusing steps

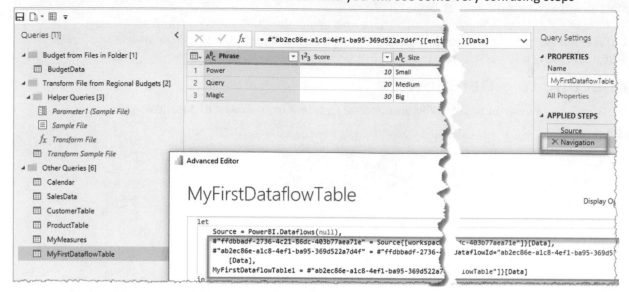

To split out the names and simplify the steps do the following:

- Look at the image below then add the new step SourceSplit = Source,
- Change the next step to refer to SourceSplit rather than Source
- Click Done

```
let
    Source = PowerBI.Dataflows(null),
    SourceSplit = Source,
    #"ffdbbadf-2736-4c21-86dc-403b77aea71e" = SourceSplit[[workspaceId="ffdbbadf-2736-4c21-86dc-403b77aea71e"]][Data],
    #"ab2ec86e-a1c8-4ef1-ba95-369d522a7d4f" = #"ffdbbadf-2736-4c21-86dc-403b77aea71e"{[dataflowId="ab2ec86e-a1c8-4ef1-ba95-369d522a7d4f"]}
        [Data],
    MyFirstDataflowTable1 = #"ab2ec86e-a1c8-4ef1-ba95-369d522a7d4f"{[entity="MyFirstDataflowTable"]}[Data]
in
    MyFirstDataflowTable1
```

- This will split out the Applied Steps
- Rename the Applied steps as per the screenshot. I have named the 3rd step as Workspace PBIXLDEMO as that was the name of my workspace. You should type in whatever your workspace name is

- Click Close and Apply on the Home tab and then save your file. We won't be building any visuals in this exercise. Save your file.

💡 Only those people with access to the Workspace will be able to connect to the dataflow in their Power BI Desktop report. Viewer access is sufficient and needs to be considered in relation to the fact that they will also be able to see all the reports in that workspace. If this is an issue create a dedicated workspace for the dataflow. Workspace access was covered in Chapter 3.

👆 Since connecting to a dataflow is very specific to your own workspace, I can't include a demo file for this section.

Copying and Pasting Existing Queries into a Dataflow

If you have created a Power Query table in a Power BI Desktop or Excel file you can copy that query and simply paste it into a new or existing dataflow.

For example, if you'd like to copy the Calendar table from your Power BI Desktop report to your Dataflow:

- In PowerBI.com go to the workspace you created and click on MyFirstDataflow
- Click Edit Tables (1)

- In PowerBI Desktop go to your Coffee House Report and click the Transform button to go to the Power Query editor window where your existing Calendar query currently sits.
- In the left-hand panel right-click on the Calendar query (1) and copy (2)
- Go to your dataflow Power Query editor screen and right-click in the left-hand panel (3) and choose Paste (4). You'll then be prompted that you need to use Ctrl+V instead, so do that and your Calendar will now appear

If you have the Diagram View still enabled the dataflow should now look like this:

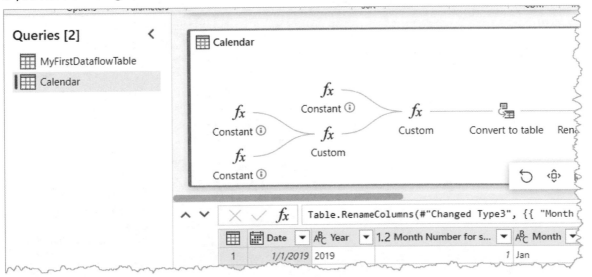

- Click Save and then when prompted click "Refresh Now" and you now have 2 power query tables in your dataflow

☕ The functionality within dataflows is evolving rapidly. More information is available here from Microsoft Docs url.pbi.guide/MDdataflow. I have a video introducing dataflows here url.pbi.guide/DFInfo. Microsoft's intention is to make the Dataflow User Interface the standard across Power BI and Excel and other products.

Connecting to a Dataset via Power BI Desktop

Creating dataflows allows you to build re-usable tables, but you can also connect to a complete dataset that contains your data, relationships, and measures.

You can connect to your Coffee Report dataset using Power BI Desktop, Excel desktop, Excel for Web, or even in Power BI.com. Even though you **can** build reports in Power BI.com I would recommend always building new reports in Power BI Desktop, it's a more complete experience.

In Chapter 3 you saw the method to connect using Analyze Excel or via Excel's Get Data option. A similar method exists in Power BI Desktop.

Creating a "parent" dataset that you or others then build reports off can be one step towards the elusive "single source of truth":

- Open a new empty Power BI desktop file (via File New)
- Click on Power BI datasets (1)
- Double-click on Coffee House Report (2)

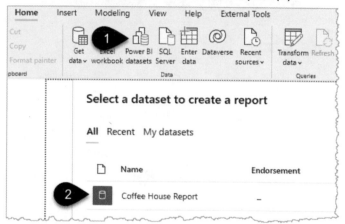

You will then have a new Power BI report containing the tables, relationships, and measures. The obvious difference from the normal view is that the Get data options are greyed out (at the time of writing) and the Data View icon is missing from the left-hand panel.

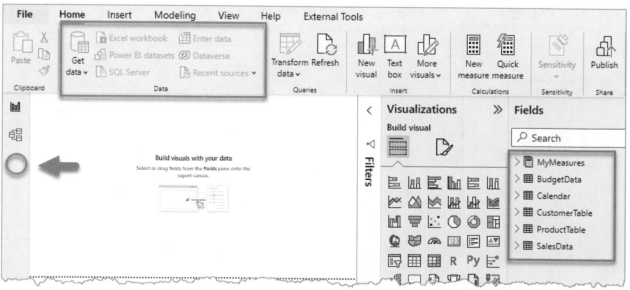

You can build visuals and publish this report to any workspace allowing you to share different reports with different pages and visuals to different audiences.

> 💡 At the time of writing, there is a preview feature available to allow you to add extra data sources to this connected file. File →Options and Settings →Options →Preview Features → DirectQuery for PBI datasets and AS.

When the source dataset is refreshed then these connected reports you have published will also refresh.

> ⚠ Connect to reports cautiously and document the process thoroughly. Anyone who has lived through the nightmare of inter-linked Excel workbooks knows the pain of trying to maintain and manage that process. It starts so innocently and eventually becomes a web of confusion.

The Lineage View (1) in your workspace can assist tracking linked reports in the current and other workspaces (2).

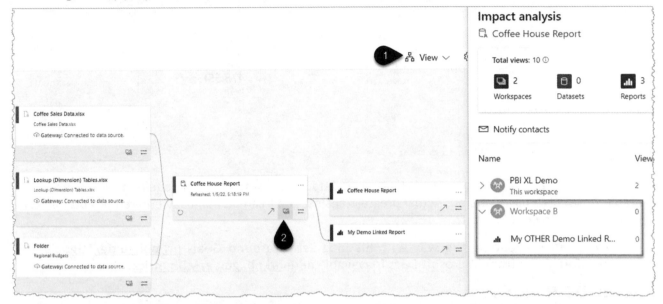

> ☕ Matt Allington has an excellent overview of setting up a parent "Golden Dataset" in his blog post here url.pbi.guide/gds1

Chapter 14 - Where Do We Go from Here?

This final short section is an opportunity to briefly touch on elements that there simply wasn't space to cover without making this book overly long. These features, in my view, are suited to the later stages of your Power BI journey. Power BI is a huge topic and there are also many more features than just the additional few I've highlighted here.

Some Topics We Didn't Cover...

Power BI Metrics (previously called Goals)

Sales Sample Sample scorecard to track sales metrics	15 Metrics	1 Overdue	3 Behind	1 At risk	7 On track	0 Not started	3 Completed

	Name	Owners	Status	Value	Progress	Due date
∨	Achieve a monthly revenue of $500,000	⚐ PBIXLDemo Book	On track	**478.55K**/500.00K ↑ 4% MoM		Dec 31, 2023
	Launch all promised products this year	⚐ PBIXLDemo Book	On track			Dec 31, 2023
	Reduce the number of sales cycle days to 20	⚐ PBIXLDemo Book	Completed	**19**/20 ↓ 14% MoM		Dec 31, 2023

Metrics enable organisations to set target values and track against them. They require a Pro licence and it is simple to set up a basic version. Actual progress against goals can be manually entered or automatically pulled in from a Power BI report.

> ☕ Treb Gatte is leading the way with his blog series around Goals url.pbi.guide/TGgoals. More information from Microsoft Docs is available here url.pbi.guide/MDmetrics.

Power BI Premium

Power BI Premium is a licence that provides several enhanced features. The most notable being that report consumers don't require a licence to view reports that have been shared from a workspace that has been "marked as premium". Once an organisation has a Premium licence then the Power BI Administrator can control who can set Premium workspaces. If you have permission, then in your workspace go to the settings cog, and under the Premium menu change the workspace to Premium. Premium comes with significant extra features that you should read about here url.pbi.guide/MDpremium

Datamarts

Those users with access to Premium Capacity or Premium Per User can create datamarts in their workspaces. Datamarts were only just announced before this book was completed so I don't have much to add about them. They are not a major change in functionality for beginners to Power BI but could be a pre-cursor to a complete cloud-based Dataflow → Dataset → Measure creation experience. There is also the added benefit of datamarts being supported by an Azure SQL database in the background. I'm sure this will evolve rapidly url.pbi.guide/datamart.

DirectQuery

When connecting to a SQL Database and a few other data sources you are prompted to choose Import or Direct Query. Your first choice should always be import mode unless you absolutely must have live data. Direct Query allows you to connect "live" to the data source and therefore your report visuals always show the very latest information. However, the report consumer experience and the developer experience are much better with import mode when the data is stored in the Power BI dataset.

> ☕ Microsoft Docs DirectQuery pages are here url.pbi.guide/MDdq and a useful list of data sources that support DirectQuery are here url.pbi.guide/MDdqs

Paginated Reports

While printing off a page in Power BI is simple, if you want to print multiple-page printouts for visuals that need to be scrolled through or different filters applied before printing each page then you will want to explore Paginated reports. This requires downloading and learning about a completely different piece of software called Report Builder.

> ☕ Microsoft Docs information is available here url.pbi.guide/MDpag

Administration

Being a Power BI Administrator is a job in itself for larger organisations. If you are the person pushing for your organisation to implement Power BI then make sure the role of administrator has been assigned to someone.

> ☕ Microsoft Docs information is available here url.pbi.guide/MDadmin

3rd Party Tools

As you progress in your Power BI journey it is very likely that you will eventually need to use 3rd party tools to enhance your Power BI development experience.

For beginners wanting to review Power BI models and identify where the model is consuming memory and therefore making it slow then take a look at https://bravo.bi/. A more complete/advanced experience for analysing your model is provided by https://daxstudio.org/.

As you become more advanced with your DAX then I highly recommend you buy a copy of Tabular Editor 3 https://tabulareditor.com/. This allows you to write and debug DAX in a much more efficient way than using Power BI desktop on its own.

Finally, I would be letting you down if I didn't insist that you check out Imke Feldmann's Power BI Cleaner tool. Imke is a legend of the Power Query world and has developed a free tool to help you work out what measures and columns are not being used in your report so that you can then remove them and simplify/speed up your model url.pbi.guide/imke.

Next Steps in Your Power BI Journey

Thanks for reading all the way to the end! I hope you got a lot out of the book. It was a challenge to write but has given me a great sense of satisfaction and I hope it was worthwhile. I want to give people a solid grounding in the core elements of Power BI and now it's up to you to practice and keep learning.

This is the beginning, not the end.

The links I provided throughout the book are from many of the people I follow on social media and know personally. If I list them all here at the end I will forget someone and feel bad so my advice is to connect with me on Twitter and LinkedIn and see who I follow and interact with.

Keep an eye on PBI.guide as I will post updates as Power BI evolves and adds/changes features that are relevant to this book.

I will also keep up-to-date links at url.pbi.guide/Wyn where you can find my YouTube channels, upcoming events, training courses, podcasts, and other such joyously geeky ventures.

Diolch

(Thank you in Welsh)

Wyn

Index

Notes

Notes

Wyn Hopkins on YouTube
https://www.youtube.com/c/AccessanalyticAus/

Access Analytic
22.7K subscribers

SUBSCRIBED

HOME   VIDEOS   PLAYLISTS   COMMUNITY   CHANNEL >

Uploads   SORT BY

Dynamic Arrays and Lookup Tables

3.1K views • 9 days ago

Power Query Columns and Text - The Survey Challenge

2K views • 2 weeks ago

Power BI Export Table Feature and a warning

1.4K views • 3 weeks ago

Excel for Web Update as of Jun 2022 including Power...

2.2K views • 1 month ago

Power Query Tips including Excel dataflows

4K views • 1 month ago

Power BI Live Embedding in PowerPoint

2.1K views • 1 month ago

Power BI Guide

Guiding Your Learning Journey

Visit www.pbi.guide for:

- Blog for articles about new features that impact the book
- Download all exercises and solutions from the book
- A list of recommended books
- Recommended video content
- Links to other excellent sites, blogs, and podcasts

Other Titles from Holy Macro! Books